The Leo Frank Case

The Leo Frank Case

LEONARD DINNERSTEIN

BROWN THRASHER BOOKS

The University of Georgia Press

ATHENS AND LONDON

© 1966, 1987 by Leonard Dinnerstein
Published by the University of Georgia Press
Athens, Georgia 30602
All rights reserved

The paper in this book meets the guidelines for
permanence and durability of the Committee on
Production Guidelines for Book Longevity of the
Council on Library Resources.

Printed in the United States of America

97 96 95 94 93   7 6 5 4 3

Library of Congress Cataloging in Publication Data

Dinnerstein, Leonard.
    The Leo Frank case.

    "Brown thrasher books."
    Bibliography: p.
    Includes index.
    1. Frank, Leo, 1884–1915—Trials, litigation, etc.
2. Trials (Murder)—Georgia—Atlanta. I. Title.
KF224.F7D56   1987   345.73'02523   87-10925
                        347.3052523
ISBN 0-8203-0965-6 (alk. paper)

British Library Cataloging in Publication Data
available.

The Leo Frank Case was originally published in 1968
by Columbia University Press.

To Myra

Contents

Preface to Brown Thrasher Edition

THE LEO FRANK CASE is probably the most widely written about and discussed episode in twentieth-century Georgian jurisprudence. It has been approached from the angles of evidence, appeals, political influence, autobiographical and biographical reminiscences, and the use of the pardoning power. It has appealed to novelists like Richard Kluger and Julie Ellis, who wrote fictionalized versions in 1977 and 1980, respectively, and to students, journalists, and historians, the most recent ones being Clark Freshman, who wrote a senior thesis at Harvard on Frank and the pardoning power, and Steve Oney, who wrote an article on Frank and who is currently writing a book about him.[1] The story will soon reach television audiences as well; NBC has announced plans to air a miniseries, "The Ballad of Mary Phagan," based on the Frank case. The nature of the case is simply too powerful and entrenched a tale to erase from one's mind.

I discovered the Frank case in 1964 when I was looking for a dissertation topic on civil rights. Frank, a Jew who had come down from the North to work in Atlanta, had become the central figure in a murder case through no fault of his own. Thousands of documents existed about his plight which led me to

---

1. Kluger, *Members of the Tribe* (Garden City, New York: Doubleday, 1977); Ellis, *The Hampton Women* (New York: Simon and Schuster, 1980); Freshman, "Beyond Pontius Pilate and Judge Lynch: The Pardoning Power in Theory and Practice As Illustrated In the Leo Frank Case" (undergraduate thesis, Harvard College, March, 1986); Oney, "The Lynching of Leo Frank," *Esquire* 104 (September, 1985).

conclude that new insights might be garnered about this al-most nondescript man who for a two year period—from 1913 to 1915—captured headlines in Georgia and then the nation.

On the surface, Frank was arrested and convicted for a mur-der that he could not possibly have committed but which most Georgians firmly believed he had. But on a more profound level Frank and those who supported his claim of innocence evoked the strongest opposition from Georgians who felt hos-tile to outsiders, to industrialism and the changes that it wrought in the region, and who were defensive about the Southern way of life. Moreover, and quite naturally, they be-lieved that justice dictated that there be one law for rich and poor alike—a sentiment cherished as well by Frank's support-ers. On one count, however, many of Frank's Jewish defenders stood alone. They viewed him as an American counterpart to Captain Alfred Dreyfus of France, who in the 1890s stood trial as a Jewish scapegoat for a variety of evils endemic in contemporary society.

After Frank's death each side held firmly to its views for several generations. The Leo Frank case took on a life of its own, capturing the imagination of Georgians who had not even been alive during the height of his notoriety. The sym-bolism of Frank and his purported crime endured with an emotional intensity that I still cannot explain fully.

In 1982, when eighty-two-year-old Alonzo Mann, former office boy in the firm that Frank supervised, came forth with an affidavit stating that he had additional evidence which tended to exonerate Frank of the murder, there was renewed national interest. The Nashville *Tennessean* published a special Sunday supplement on Leo Frank on March 7 that year, and newspapers all over the country picked up the story. Mann claimed to have seen Jim Conley, the state's main witness against Frank at the trial, carrying a girl's body at about the time Mary Phagan had been murdered, and that Conley warned him, "If you ever mention this, I'll kill you." Only thirteen years old at the time, Alonzo stated that he returned home, told his mother what had happened, and was advised by her not to tell anyone what he had seen.[2]

Mann's statement failed to convince those who believed that Frank had been guilty and reinforced the views of those who thought him innocent. By itself, Mann's assertion that he witnessed someone else carrying the dead person's body added only another detail to corroborate Frank's claim of innocence. Those who considered him guilty dismissed it. Nevertheless, in a society more attuned to the nuances of civil rights and civil liberties than in the period of Frank's trial, Mann's assertion gave impetus to reexamining his cause. Jewish organizations in Atlanta, led by the Anti-Defamation League of B'nai B'rith, used Mann's account to spearhead a movement for a posthumous pardon which the Georgia Board of Pardons first rejected and then approved in 1985.

The recent and reinvigorated interest in Frank, and the successful effort to obtain the posthumous pardon, suggested that this might be an appropriate time to reissue my earlier study of Leo Frank. Nothing that has occurred since its original publication has altered any of my opinions or conclusions about his innocence or about what actually happened and who the probable killer was. Thus, on the following pages, the narrative evolves as it first appeared twenty years ago. I hope it will interest a new audience desirous of knowing why the image and memory of Leo Frank evoked so many conflicting emotions for Georgians and others throughout this century.

I would like to thank Samuel McSeveney, of Vanderbilt University, for clipping and passing along to me the many newspaper items about Leo Frank that came across his desk in recent years.

LEONARD DINNERSTEIN

Tucson, Arizona
January 21, 1987

2. *The Tennessean* (Nashville), Special News Section, March 7, 1982.

Preface to First Edition

ONE OF the most infamous outbursts of anti-Semitic feeling in the United States occurred in Georgia in the years 1913, 1914, and 1915. Leo Frank, a Northern Jewish industrialist, was convicted of murdering a thirteen-year-old working girl. The crime channeled the fears and frustrations of the people in Atlanta, themselves the victims of the Southern industrial transformation, and Frank emerged as the focal point for the resentments engendered by a fledgling industrial society. The Frank case, which eventually developed into one of the most talked-about injustices of the Progressive Era, served also to highlight the dilemmas and difficulties facing the American South during that period.

Although the United States, by the beginning of the twentieth century, was changing from an agrarian to an industrial society, the pace and effects of this transformation varied from region to region. The South, distinctive in its attachment to tradition, its relative isolation from the stream of late nineteenth-century immigration, and its esteem for rural values, proved more resistant to industrialism than did other sections of the country. But the old Whigs and their descendants—the Bourbons of the New South—desired to make the South industrially potent. They encouraged Northern industrialists to invest in the region and promised them an abundance of cheap and willing labor.

The introduction of the factory below the Mason-Dixon

line marked the intrusion of an alien culture which threatened cherished traditions. Many Southerners responded to the threat by clinging all the more tightly to their agrarian past. Always proud of their Anglo-Saxon blood, they became toward the end of the nineteenth century violently xenophobic. Long critical of urban ways, they now saw the city as the embodiment of every evil in society. Always fervent in their religious faith, they clung to the Bible as the revealed word of God, to be ignored at one's peril.

Traditionalists tried hard to preserve their old ways, but they failed to stem the tide of change. In the 1880s and 1890s poverty forced many Southern farmers from their rural moorings and into the cities where work might be found. The factory ultimately promised to alleviate poverty, but its immediate effects—slums and sweatshops—brought suffering and frustration. Bewildered Southerners, unable to understand or to control the new forces dominating their lives, attempted unsuccessfully to find security in dreams of a golden past. These people yearned for a bulwark against an incomprehensible new world. In the cities an alien culture threatened to overwhelm rural morality and Protestant fundamentalism. Although the foreign born constituted less than 1 per cent of the total Southern population in 1900, the few immigrants who chose to live in the region seemed a much greater threat than their numbers might indicate.

The "invasion" of strangers, with their peculiar customs, eventually stimulated organized opposition to all non-Protestant, non-Southern, non-American ways and people. But before the banding together of the Fundamentalists and the Ku Klux Klan in the 1920s, antagonisms exploded in isolated incidents. From the Populist Era until the beginning of the first World War increased numbers of Negro lynchings, race riots, and assaults upon foreigners publicized Southern frustrations. None of these outbursts, however, provided more than temporary relief from the perplexities of urban living. In 1913 the people of Atlanta, many of whom had been coaxed from the countryside with the promise of a better life, rose up and attacked a symbol of the new industrial culture which had reneged on its promise. Leo Frank was chosen to stand trial for the tribulations of a changing society.

LEONARD DINNERSTEIN

Fairleigh Dickinson University
Teaneck, New Jersey
December, 1967

Acknowledgments

DURING the course of my research I have benefited from the advice and counsel of a great number of people. It is a pleasure to acknowledge their contributions.

Professor William E. Leuchtenburg of Columbia University directed this book as a dissertation. I am indebted to him for his insightful commentary as well as for his warm support, guidance, and concern during the years that I have known him. Professor Walter Metzger read the manuscript with care and improved the essay immeasurably. Professor Richard Hofstadter made some crucial suggestions.

Yonathan Shapiro suggested the topic and encouraged me in the earliest stages. Fred Israel read several drafts and indicated many areas which needed improvement. Michael Weinberg made astute comments on all the chapters. Murray and Debby Friedman gave the entire manuscript a careful reading and suggested necessary alterations. Philip Hollman provided valuable assistance in the treatment of legal material.

Dr. Stanley Chyet of the American Jewish Archives was extremely generous with his time and counsel. He and his staff have been consistently helpful. The late Mrs. Mary Givens Bryan of the Georgia State Archives was gracious and helpful. Harry J. Alderman of the American Jewish Committee and the late Louis Schreiber of Brandeis University also extended many courtesies.

Personal interviews were granted by Alexander Brin, Harold Davis, and McLellan Smith. Telephone interviews were given by Mrs. Charles Samuels, Mrs. Oscar Cohen, Franklin Garrett, and Wilbur Kurtz.

Access to the Julius Rosenwald papers was granted by the University of Chicago; to the Baltimore *Sun* Library by Clement G. Vitek; to the Anti-Defamation League files in New York City by Nathan Belth; to the newspaper morgue of the Boston *Herald-Traveler* by John J. McMahon; to the Leo Frank papers in the law offices of Nuter, McClennon & Fish in Boston by Benjamin A. Trustman and in Brandeis University by Mr. and Mrs. Harold Marcus. James Marshall and the Marshall family permitted me to quote from the Louis Marshall papers located at the American Jewish Archives in Cincinnati. Kenneth S. Goldstein of the American Folklore Society approved the inclusion of "The Ballad of Mary Phagan" in the appendix. Permission to use pictures was granted by Dr. Chyet and William I. Ray of Atlanta.

The staff at the Information Desk in Butler Library, Columbia University, was always very helpful. My father, Abraham Dinnerstein, translated the section on Leo Frank for me from Abraham Cahan's autobiography, *Blätter Von Mein Leben.* Mrs. Shirley Lerman and Mrs. Sarah Hope, two women with a keen understanding of a historian's needs, typed the manuscript skillfully. Mrs. Gladys T. Hartman, of the CCNY History Department, did supplementary typing and also provided cheerful and efficient secretarial assistance. Edith Cohen helped proofread the galleys. The National Foundation for Jewish Culture provided some financial aid in gathering materials.

Others who have made positive contributions via conversations, correspondence, criticism, clerical assistance, or research include Rose Dinnerstein, Harry Golden, Nancy Hollander, the late Mark de Wolfe Howe, Alton DuMar Jones, Pearl Kluger, Charlotte LaRue, DeWitt H. Roberts, Paul Rosenblum, Alden Todd, and Sydney S. Weinberg.

Finally, I would like to give my special thanks for the infinite patience and judicious counseling of two other people. Fred Jaher read the manuscript more frequently than any other person; his sustained interest and detailed criticism went far beyond the dictates of friendship. My wife, Myra, edited several versions of each chapter. Her assistance has been invaluable.

I am responsible for all errors of fact and judgment which remain.

L.D.

The Leo Frank Case

CHAPTER I

The Murder of Mary Phagan

THE MURDER of a thirteen-year-old girl in Atlanta, Georgia, on Confederate Memorial Day, 1913, served as a catalyst for one of the most lurid displays of intolerance in the Progressive Era. The girl's disfigured body had been found in a condition which provided grist for the sensation-seeking press of the city. The newspapers then exploited the crime for commercial purposes, thereby rousing a taut and horrified populace. When the police apprehended, as one of the prime suspects, the superintendent and part-owner of the factory where the girl had been employed and her body had been discovered, the authorities could barely contain community hysteria. Resentment toward the new industrial society had already become intense in Atlanta, and the arrest of the industrialist provided a focus for the people's rage. Because the superintendent was Jewish, his arraignment complicated the emotional reaction and eventually led to one of the *causes célèbres* of the century.

I

Newt Lee, the nightwatchman of the National Pencil Factory, found the body at about 3 A.M., on Sunday, April 27, 1913. He had gone down to use the Negro toilet in the factory basement. As he started up again a ray of light from his lantern fell upon something that looked like a human form. At first he thought someone must be playing a joke on him, but when he approached the prostrate figure he saw that it was no ruse. He then hastened up the ladder and telephoned the police, who arrived within ten minutes.

The condition of the corpse made the men shudder. Sawdust and shavings covered the girl's body and dry blood caked her skull. Both eyes were bruised and her cheeks had been slashed. A strip of her underdrawers, as well as a piece of jute rope, encircled her neck. (An autopsy would later reveal that the girl had been choked and that her head had been dented with a blunt instrument.) A closer look revealed fingers out of joint and torn clothing. So covered was the corpse with grime that the men had to look beneath her stocking to see that she was white. The girl's purse had disappeared, and there were no means of identification.[1] A sister-in-law of one of the policemen worked in the pencil factory, and she was summoned to identify the dead girl. "Oh my God!" the woman exclaimed, "that's Mary Phagan."[2]

When the police questioned Newt Lee, his "wild and excited manner" aroused their suspicion. Lee claimed that he had arrived for work at 4 P.M., two hours earlier than his normal starting time, on Saturday, April 26. Because it was Confederate Memorial Day and a holiday for most of the employees, Leo Max Frank, the twenty-nine-year-old factory superintendent, had asked the night watchman to come in at 4 P.M. so that he could get away earlier. When Lee arrived, however, Frank had not yet completed his own work and told the night watchman to go out and return again at his usual starting time, 6 P.M. Lee said he had returned at the regular time, and had made his usual rounds, but it was not until 3 A.M., when he went to the basement to use the toilet, that he had discovered the body.[3]

Since the murdered girl had been discovered in the factory, the pencil plant's superintendent and part owner, Leo Frank, was summoned. The superintendent arrived at the factory visibly shaken. Two police escorts had called for him at his home and had taken him to the morgue before bringing him to the pencil plant. When Frank saw the corpse he recoiled in horror. He did not recognize the girl. Afterwards, in the factory, after he had been given her name, Frank checked his cash book and saw that she had been in his office shortly after noon on the previous day to collect her pay. At the time that Frank revealed this information, neither he nor the police realized that no one would ever testify to having seen Mary Phagan alive after she had left Frank's office.

Between the time that the police arrived on the scene, and the appearance of superintendent Frank four hours later, a search had been made for clues. On the basement floor, near the corpse, lay two notes, scrawled on some scraps of yellowed paper. They read:

Mam that negro hire down here did this   i went to make water and he push me down that hole   a long tall negro black that hoo it wase   long sleam tall negro   i wright while play with me

he said he wood love me land down play like the night witch did it but that long tall black negro did buy his slef.[4]

Eventually these scrawled and yellowed papers, commonly referred to later on as the murder notes, would become the center of a seething controversy. But at first the policeman considered them unimportant and discarded them.[5]

The police then discovered a path through the sawdust between a ladder which connected the basement with the first floor to a spot where the body lay. It appeared that the girl had been dragged along this way. At the bottom of the elevator shaft observers saw a girl's hat and parasol, a ball of twine, and "something that looked like a person's stool." As soon as the elevator (which had been on the second floor of the building and had remained there until Frank arrived and began using it) was lowered to the basement, it crushed everything in the pit of the shaft. The mashing of the human excrement resulted in the spread of a foul odor.[6] Unfortunately no one realized the significance of the excrement.

Having concluded their immediate investigation, the authorities left, taking the night watchman, whom they suspected of concealing evidence, to the police station for further questioning. All those who remained in the building (and by that time Frank had summoned some of his subordinates) appeared extremely uneasy. Policemen on the scene would testify at the trial, however, that to them Frank seemed the most ruffled.[7]

To protect the pencil plant's interests, superintendent Frank engaged the Pinkerton Detective Agency to make an independent investigation. The next day the Pinkerton's, together with the police, combed the factory. Frank, however, was not satisfied with the investigation. He complained to a reporter that he deeply regretted "the carelessness shown by the police department in not making a complete investigation as to finger prints and other evidence before a great throng of people were allowed to enter the place." [8]

Indeed, there was some reason to complain of the policemen's lack of skill. They sawed off the boards of the back door in the basement which were covered with bloody fingerprints, and then lost them before an examination could be made. A reporter found bloody fingerprints on the corpse's jacket and brought it to the attention of the authorities. It was "stated that these prints are clearly outlined and may prove of importance in establishing the identity of the murderer." [9] Yet no report was ever issued as to whose fingerprints were found, if, indeed, any examination was made at all.

After two days of evaluating the available evidence, the police arrested Leo Frank on Tuesday, April 29. Frank had been the last person to see Mary Phagan alive. Whenever the police saw him afterwards he appeared extremely nervous. He had also asked Newt Lee, the night watchman, to report early on the day of the murder and then sent him away again, to return at his normal hour. When Lee came back at 6 P.M., Frank left the building. He telephoned an hour later to see if everything was all right at the factory. The superintendent had never done this before but explained afterwards to the police that, as he left the factory, a former bookkeeper had approached the building and wanted to pick up some old shoes that he had left when he was discharged two weeks earlier. Frank had hesitated at first, then permitted him to go in, but asked Lee to accompany him. Therefore, Frank said, he had phoned Lee to make sure that there had been no incident with the bookkeeper.

The day after the discovery of the corpse, blood stains and hair "identified positively as the dead girl's" were found in a workroom opposite Frank's office.[10] The blood stains allegedly formed a path from a lathe in the metal workroom to the elevator.[11] This new information, coupled with the superintendent's suspicious behavior, led to the arrest of Leo Frank. Reporters seemed surprised at the turn of events and assumed that the police must have more information than they had revealed. But when they queried Chief of Detectives Newport Lanford about Frank's detention, the Chief refused to give out any information and would say only, "The town seems to be very much wrought up over the murder and I think this is the wisest course to take." [12]

2

Leo Max Frank was born in Paris, Texas, on April 17, 1884. His parents, Rudolph and Rae Frank, had moved to Brooklyn, New York, a few months after their son's birth. Frank had a fairly typical middle-class Jewish upbringing, attending the Brooklyn public schools, Pratt Institute, and Cornell University, where he received the degree of Mechanical Engineer in 1906. The B. F. Sturtevant Company, in Hyde Park, Massachusetts, a Boston suburb, gave him his first job.

Frank did not remain long in Massachusetts. He moved back to Brooklyn and worked there for a short time before accepting the invitation of his uncle, Moses Frank, to help establish the National Pencil Factory in Atlanta. The young man had a small financial interest in the business.

In 1910, Frank married Lucille Selig, daughter of a wealthy and established Atlanta family. The newlyweds made their home with the bride's parents. In Atlanta, Frank, achieved some degree of social prominence within the Jewish community; the local B'nai B'rith elected him its president in 1912. He had never attracted any public attention until April 29, 1913, when the police arrested him on suspicion of murder.[13]

At the time of his arrest the *Constitution* described Frank as a "small, wiry man, wearing eyeglasses of high lens power. He is nervous and apparently high-strung. He smokes incessantly and stuffed a pocket with cigars upon leaving for police headquarters. . . . His dress is neat, and he is a fluent talker, polite and suave." [14] A business associate later recalled that upon first meeting Frank he found him uncongenial. "His was the nervous, bilious temperament which at first repels rather than attracts." [15]

The news of Frank's arrest stunned those who knew him. His wife rushed to the police station but was refused permission to see her husband. To a *Georgian* reporter she sobbed, "My husband is absolutely innocent. . . ." [16] Frank's friends expressed their indignation over his detention and declared it to be impossible for him to have had anything to do with the murder. *The Augusta Chronicle* noted that "the Jewish people are also standing by Frank, having every confidence in his innocence and ready to do anything necessary to establish that fact." [17]

Frank had engaged counsel to protect the National Pencil Factory's interests because the murder had occurred in the pencil plant. When the police first brought him to headquarters for questioning on April 28, the day after the murder, attorney Herbert Haas, who represented the firm, and Luther Rosser, who would become chief defense counsel at the trial, joined him there. Although Frank was not formally arrested until the next day, word spread through

Atlanta that he had hired counsel beforehand. This rumor led many to conclude that the superintendent had a guilty conscience.[18]

3

The murder of Mary Phagan, as an isolated event, was shocking. For Atlanta's working classes, however, the crime seemed to climax a series of urban calamities. Most of the city's laborers had emigrated from rural Georgia,[19] where they had learned to expect, and in some measure to cope with, poverty and suffering. In the city, however, many "found it impossible to make a quick and easy adjustment to the system of urban values."[20] The reason for this may have been that, difficult as rural life was, it provided traditional social guide posts. But the city undermined the strong family and community ties which had characterized the past.

Working conditions in Atlanta compared unfavorably with those in other parts of the country. Cotton mills, the city's leading industry, turned out children "sapped of their lifeblood . . . starved, stunted and all but demoralized." Despite a shortage of workers, factory wages were low and hours long. The normal work week lasted sixty-six hours and, except for Saturday, the working day generally extended from 6 A.M. to 6 P.M., with only a half hour for lunch. In 1914 there were children working in Atlanta for as little as 22 cents a week. According to an official of the National Child Labor League, Georgia did not have even the semblance of factory inspection, and employers openly violated existing laws prohibiting employment of minors under ten.[21]

Living conditions in Atlanta compounded the difficulties of its residents and seriously threatened their health. In their squalid factory slums, the laborers, mostly white tenant farmers who had come to the city in an attempt to improve upon their wretched lives on the farm, suffered from hunger and destitution. In 1908, fifty thousand persons, or approximately one-third of Atlanta's population, lived without water mains or sewers and used well water and surface closets. In 1911 more than half of the white school children, and slightly under three-quarters of the Negro school children, suffered from malnutrition, anemia, enlarged glands, and heart disease. The United Textile Workers Union complained in 1914 that far too many Atlanta children fell victim to pellagra—a disease without a known cure at that time. The death rate in the city was appalling. A United States census report for 1905 noted that of three hundred and eighty-eight cities in this country, only twelve had a higher death rate than Atlanta. The requests for welfare, which also reflected the city's poverty, increased sharply between 1910 and 1913. Atlanta's *Journal of Labor* noted that it had received 2,000 calls for help in 1910, 4,000 in 1911, 5,000 in 1912, "and the gloomy forecast presents itself that the winter of 1913–1914 will establish a new record in this respect." A statement of the Atlanta relief warden succinctly summarized the situation: "There are too many people on the ragged edge of poverty and suffering." [22]

The crime rate in Atlanta highlighted the stresses of the new urbanites. In 1906 a demoniac race riot, spurred on by a gubernatorial campaign with strong appeals to prejudice and the reports of sensational newspapers which exaggerated stories of alleged Negro assaults upon white women, attracted national attention.[23] A year before, Atlanta had arrested more children for disturbing the peace than any other city in the country. In 1907 only New York, Chicago, and Baltimore, cities with considerably larger populations, exceeded Atlanta's figure for child arrests. In 1905 the Atlanta police apprehended 17,000 persons out of a total population of 115,000, and the following year 22,000. These figures more than tripled the number in New Orleans, although that city had twice Atlanta's population. More than two-thirds of those detained were guilty of disorderly conduct and drunkenness.[24]

The city police force proved unable to cope with the new

problems thrust upon it. In fact, at times, the policemen went to irrational extremes in attempting to cope with certain difficulties. On one occasion, when Atlanta experienced a labor shortage, the police attempted to rectify the condition by arresting all able-bodied men found on one of the main streets. Employed and unemployed, black and white, were hauled into court, fined, and sentenced to the stockade without being given a chance to defend themselves. One man so punished had been in the city for only three days. Neither relatives nor employers were notified of the round-up or the sentencings. According to one observer, the policemen also acted with brutality. In 1909 they allegedly beat one Negro to death and chained a white girl to the wall until she frothed at the mouth. In 1910 a commission investigating prison conditions in the city uncovered "stories too horrible to be told in print." [25]

The pathological conditions in the city menaced the home, the state, the schools, the churches, and, in the words of a contemporary Southern sociologist, the "wholesome industrial life." [26] The institutions of the city were obviously unfit to handle urban problems. Against this background, the murder of a young girl in 1913 triggered a violent reaction of mass aggression, hysteria, and prejudice.

4

Southern attitudes toward "the sweetest and purest thing on earth—a young girl" [27] also conditioned Atlanta's response to the murder. For generations Southerners had feared assaults upon women. An attack upon a white woman was considered an attack upon the South itself.[28] *The Memphis Commercial Appeal* commented upon the prevailing sentiment editorially:

Today after centuries of progression, we have reached a plane where there are other things dearer than life, and chief among these is female virtue. When this is slain . . . with devilish deliberation and cunning . . . the avenger has the right to go forth in quest of blood-atonement and if he does not do so he is unworthy of the civilization of the day.

There is a higher law . . . and that law readeth "Thou shalt protect female virtue at all hazards." [29]

But the idealization of womanhood which was so important to the South had undergone some rude shocks under the pressure of industrialization. The poverty that sent the farmers into the towns also pushed their women into the factories. Although economic necessity may have forced women into industrial occupations, they undertook such employment with trepidation. Southerners considered factory work for women degrading and contact with male workers corrupting.[30] Husbands and fathers hesitantly violated Southern traditions by sending their wives and daughters to the factory, but they were tormented with guilt. As the owner of a cotton textile mill explained: "It was considered belittling— oh! very bad! It was considered that for a girl to go into a cotton factory was just a step toward the most vulgar things. They used to talk about the girls working in mills up-country as if they were in places of grossest immorality. It was said to be the same as a bawdy house; to let a girl go into a cotton factory was to make a prostitute of her." [31]

With the murder of Mary Phagan, a haunting fear was realized. The murder of the child symbolized all that was evil and most feared about the city. "No girl ever leaves home to go to work in a factory," Atlanta's Judge Arthur Powell wrote in later years, "but that the parents feel an inward fear that one of her bosses will take advantage of his position to mistreat her, especially if she repels his advances." [32] Mary Phagan's mother sobbed to a reporter, "There are so many unscrupulous men in the world. It's so dangerous for young girls working out." [33] Atlanta's *Journal of Labor* expressed the working class sentiment: "Mary Phagan is a martyr to the greed for gain which has grown up in our complex civilization, and which sees in the girls and children merely a source of exploitation in the shape of cheap labor. . . ." [34]

Mary Phagan would have celebrated her fourteenth birthday a few weeks after the murder. A native of Marietta, Georgia, she typified the small-town Southerner who left her home to seek work in the urban factories. When her widowed mother remarried in Atlanta, Mary did not have to remain in the factory any longer. She continued at her job only because she liked her work. But after her death, Mary became a symbol for all the young women who had never been permitted a choice.[35]

Grieving friends and relatives were heartbroken over the slaying. Ten thousand mourners, "the largest crowd that ever viewed a body in Atlanta," came to pay their respects. The funeral attracted more than one thousand persons. As the white coffin "befitting the innocence of the young girl lying within it" was brought into the church, the choir sang, "Nearer My God to Thee," and Mary's mother fainted. At the cemetery in Marietta, Mary's grandfather cried, an aunt let out a "piercing scream," and the child's mother collapsed again. The presiding minister supplicated, "May God bring the man guilty of this terrible crime to justice." [36]

5

The newspapers of Atlanta exploited the sensational nature of Mary Phagan's death and helped to stir up public excitement about it. In 1913 the city had three daily papers: *The Atlanta Constitution*, which monopolized the morning field, and *The Atlanta Journal* and *The Atlanta Georgian*, which competed with each other in the afternoon. Of the three, the *Journal* had the largest circulation and was clearly the most popular, until 1912 when William Randolph Hearst purchased the *Georgian*.[37]

Hearst, who aimed for newspapers that "made the reader recoil in shock," [38] attempted to give Atlantans the show that his audiences in San Francisco, New York, and Chicago had come to expect. He sent Keats Speed, the editor of his New

GIRL SLAIN IN STRANGLING MYSTERY Mary Phagan, 14-year-old daughter of Mrs. J. W. Coleman, 146 Lindsay Street, whose slain body was found in the basement of the National Pencil Factory, 37-39 South Forsyth Street. The girl left her home Saturday morning to go to the factory, where she had been employed, to draw wages due her. She was seen on the streets at midnight Saturday with a strange man. She was not seen alive thereafter.

One of the first published pictures of Mary Phagan. Note the sentence in the caption above the picture: "She was seen on the streets at midnight Saturday with a strange man." This was later proved to be erroneous. She never left the pencil factory after she had entered it shortly after noon on April 26, 1913. But for a number of days so little was known about how she had died that the newspapers resorted to printing unsubstantiated statements.

Courtesy of *The Atlanta Georgian*, April 28, 1913

York *Journal,* to Atlanta to spruce up the new acquisition, and soon banner headlines, photographic layouts, advice to the lovelorn, comic strips, and syndicated features became prominent. Formerly, the last edition of the *Georgian* had gone to press at about 2:30 P.M. Speed added several editions so that news of the latest doings, the ball scores, and any sensational items might reach Atlantans sooner. Editions went "onto the street everytime anything happened that would justify a headline, and frequently when it wouldn't." [39] The populace reacted to the new policy with enthusiasm, and the newspaper's circulation began to rise. [40]

With the murder of Mary Phagan, the *Georgian* developed "the greatest news story in the history of the state, if not of the South. . . ." [41] Screaming streamers and banner headlines appeared on "extra" after "extra" as the factory girl's death received the full Hearst treatment. In only four months, from the end of April through August, 17,686 column inches, or the equivalent of more than 100 pages the size of *The New York Times,* were devoted to the case. By the end of August the *Georgian* had tripled its normal sales of about 40,000 papers a day, and it boasted the largest circulation of any Southern daily paper through 1913. [42] The *Georgian* had inaugurated its dramatic handling of the case with twenty "extras" and five pages of pictures and stories about Mary Phagan and her family. [43] The *Journal* and the *Constitution,* both of whose usual formats featured conservative, one-column headlines, were forced to compete with the Hearst paper by expanding their coverage of the murder. The more space the newspapers devoted to the murder, the larger the headlines, and the more vociferous their editorials, the more intense was the public reaction.

The rural Georgians who flocked to Atlanta at the beginning of the century expected the daily newspaper to provide them with the information that they needed to comprehend their strange new urban environment. They also wanted gossip, entertainment, and drama—items they had customarily received from their small-town weeklies.[44] In addition to helping the immigrants adjust to their new surroundings, the papers also incited popular passions. Characterized by innuendo, misrepresentation, and distortion,[45] the yellow journals' account of Mary Phagan's death aroused an anxious city, and within a few days, a shocked state.

The first reports after the murder suggested that Newt Lee, the night watchman, might have committed the crime. He was arrested the morning that the body was discovered, and the police intimated that he knew more than he had yet revealed. That afternoon the detectives brought Lee back to the factory to help them obtain additional information. A large crowd of spectators had already surrounded the building. As the people spotted Lee, some of them cried, "He ought to be lynched." [46]

It was later proved that Lee's only connection with the crime was the discovery of the corpse, but early newspaper slanders disregarded known facts. The *Journal* claimed to have "proven conclusively" that Newt Lee "mistreated and murdered pretty Mary Phagan" or knew who did. The police also suspected Lee, and they allegedly tortured him mercilessly. For three days they kept the night watchman manacled to a chair and put him "through a searching, grilling 'third degree' that left him weeping and nerveless." No amount of questioning, however, could get the Negro to change his contention that he knew nothing about the murder. Nevertheless, the readers of Atlanta's newspapers were told that the police believed Lee "has the whole story at his tongue's end and that he will eventually clear the mystery." [47]

After three days of grilling Newt Lee without gaining any new information, the police dispatched the Negro to a basement cell and practically forgot about him. But this lack of police interest in him did not prevent the *Georgian* from running a streamer, "LEE'S GUILT PROVED." There seems to have been no evidence or information to support this last contention other than the remark of Atlanta's chief detective, Newport Lanford, that "We Have Evidence in Hand Which Will Clear the Mystery in the Next Few Hours . . . ." [48] The next day, Atlanta's other dailies condemned the *Georgian*'s absurd and inflammatory conclusion.[49]

After four days of newspaper hysteria following the discovery of the body Atlanta's Mayor urged the police to refrain from releasing so much information about the crime. He had received numerous complaints about the sensational newspaper extras with their distortions and exaggerations and had been warned that these newspaper excesses were "calculated to inflame the people and might possibly result in grave damage." [50] The Governor of Georgia also seemed alarmed. He readied ten companies of the state militia to protect the prisoners, Newt Lee and Leo Frank, in case of an attack upon their lives. There had been "persistent rumors" that an attempt would be made to storm the jail and relieve officials of their two celebrated charges.[51] A week after the murder *The Augusta Chronicle*'s Atlanta correspondent summed up the climate in the state capital. "Feeling here is still high, the horror of the deed gripping people fast. The deadline between calm and unbridled rage is narrow, and the fear is strong that if the guilty [one] is caught at last inflamed people will seek to wreak summary punishment." [52]

The newspapers had not only inflamed the public but had challenged the mettle of the police as well. Speaking for an enraged city, the *Constitution* demanded that the girl's slayer be found: "If ever the men who ferret crime and uphold the law in Atlanta are to justify their function it must be in apprehending the assailant and murderer of Mary Phagan." [53] The police had quickly arrested seven suspects,[54] but two weeks passed without any conclusive evidence about the murder being presented to the public. The *Constitution* refused to accept what it considered official incompetence and displayed a scathing cartoon on the front page of its Sunday edition. The cartoon portrayed a woman carrying a scroll called "Mary Phagan Mystery" and pointing at a door marked "Detective Dept." The woman was saying to herself, "I wonder if they're all asleep in there?" [55]

In desperation, or perhaps in an attempt to "scoop" its competitors, the *Constitution* sought to obtain outside aid. The paper started a fund to "Bring Burns Here to Solve Mary Phagan Mystery," and the next day it expressed the opinion that only William J. Burns, "the world's greatest detective," could solve this baffling case.[56] A public subscription raised enough money to lure Burns to Atlanta, and the famed detective dispatched one of his best agents to investigate the situation preparatory to his arrival.[57]

The invitation to the "world's greatest detective" was a direct attack upon the city police. The record of the police provided ample justification for such action. For two years preceding Mary Phagan's death, about eighteen Negro women had been murdered in the city, but none of the assailants had ever been found.[58] Although no violent protests had erupted when the slayers of Negroes escaped, these unsolved murders had left the impression that the police were incompetent. The rapidity of the city's growth not only increased the amount of vice and crime but seemed also to overwhelm those charged with upholding the law. "A force of village constables" suddenly found themselves "face to face with crime conditions of a great city hall," and could not cope with them.[59] The police were frightened. They had repeatedly failed, and this time, with a white victim, inefficiency would not be tolerated. The Mayor reflected public sentiment when he warned the police: "Find this murderer fast, or be fired!" [60]

6

Four days after the murder a Coroner's Jury began an inquest. Leo Frank, the chief witness, related his activities on the day of the murder and repeated information he had already given to the police. Numerous witnesses corroborated

Frank's statements; no one contradicted any of his claims.

The inquiry also provided a forum for those who questioned Frank's moral rectitude. George Epps, a youth who lived near the Phagan family, said he rode into town with Mary on the fatal day. He stated that she confessed that she feared the factory superintendent because he acted in too familiar a fashion and made advances to her.[61] A number of former employees of the pencil factory also testified that Frank flirted and "indulged in familiarities with the women in his employ." The sister of a former employee swore that when she had come one day to collect her sibling's pay Frank had behaved improperly. He had taken a metal box from his drawer. "It had a lot of money in it. He looked at it significantly and then looked at me. When he looked at me he winked. As he winked he said, 'How about it?' I instantly told him that I was a nice girl." [62]

The Coroner's jury ordered both Frank and Lee held for further questioning despite the fact that the two detectives who had been spending the most time on the investigation, Harry Scott of the Pinkerton's and John Black of the city detective force, testified that "they so far had obtained no conclusive evidence or clues in the baffling mystery. . . ." [63]

On May 11, two days after the inquest ended, a special policeman damaged Frank's case further when he revealed that a year earlier he had apprehended the superintendent "and a young girl in a desolate spot of the woods. . . ." At that time the policeman claimed to have obtained a confession from Frank that he had taken his young companion "to the woods for immoral purposes." [64] The policeman later admitted that he had been mistaken about Frank's having been the person he had seen, but this information, unlike the accusation, never reached the front pages of the newspapers.

On May 23, the Atlanta police released an affidavit from Mrs. Nina Formby, the proprietor of a "rooming house" in Atlanta, disclosing that on the day of the murder Frank had telephoned her repeatedly and had attempted to secure a room

for himself and a young girl. Mrs. Formby allegedly informed
him each time that all her rooms were occupied. The city detectives announced that "this is one of the most important bits
of evidence they hold," and indicated strongly that they believed Frank to be the culprit.[65]

7

The crime shocked Atlantans, who not only followed the
hunt for information about the murderer intently but were
also ready to believe any tale circulated, no matter how fantastic. The newspapers needed but to hint at some new item
of discovery or outlandish conclusion, and within hours the
account, greatly embroidered, would circulate throughout
the city.[66] Three days after the killing, the *Constitution*
printed an article beneath the headline, "Every Woman and
Girl Should See Body of Victim and Learn Perils." Most
females did not see her, but rumors had it that the girl had
been drugged and rendered helpless before being slain, that
she was slashed in many places with a knife, and that her
"breasts had been bitten and gnawed." [67]

It would be impossible to enumerate all the rumors that
traveled through Atlanta and the state of Georgia after
Frank's imprisonment, many of them printed in the newspapers. The most prominent concerned sex and religion.
Gossipers authoritatively related that the tenets of the Jewish
faith forbade the violation of Jewish, but not Gentile,
women.[68] Other tales were that Frank's wife was about to
divorce him; that his wife knew he was guilty and therefore
did not visit him in jail; that he had another wife in Brooklyn;
that he had had another wife in Brooklyn whom he had
killed; that he had numerous children out of wedlock; that his
wife knew all the foregoing facts and had already applied for
a divorce; that he was a pervert, and that he went out on
street car lines waiting for young girls, "pulling them off the
cars in spite of their crying and resistance." [69] It was even

said that Frank "was a Mason and the Masons were all for him; that he was a Catholic and they were all for him; that he was a Jew and the Jews were all for him." [70]

The charge of perversion probably did the most damage. The newspapers never clearly explained what was considered perverse about Frank, and the word meant different things to different people. Everyone could agree that murder and rape [71] were perversities. But some would consider the alleged escapades with young girls and the rumored extramarital affairs as indications of sexual abnormality. Later on, in court, the prosecutor would make veiled allusions to Frank and his supposedly delicate relationship with an office boy. This, too, would reinforce the opinions of those who believed that Frank was some type of sexual deviant.

8

The police desperately needed a conviction; the public demanded that Mary Phagan's assailant be found. The Solicitor-General of Atlanta's circuit, Hugh M. Dorsey, who directed and coordinated the state's case, also needed a conviction. He had recently prosecuted two important accused murderers and had failed each time to convict them. *The Savannah Morning News* would later observe, "Another defeat, and in a case where the feeling was so intense, would have been, in all likelihood, the end of Mr. Dorsey as solicitor. . . ." [72] On the other hand, if he successfully prosecuted Mary Phagan's killer, future political success would doubtless be assured. Therefore he was concerned about putting together a case which would hold up in court.

The search for the murderer, however, was handicapped by the fact that various investigators worked alone, rather than in unison. At one point there were four separate groups independently groping with the same facts. The *Constitution* reported that "the detectives of police headquarters, who were first to investigate the slaying, are now working alone, refusing to give information to anyone. The Pinkertons [hired by Frank], who were next retained, are working exclusively. Cooperation, however, is found in the joint investigation being promoted by Solicitor Dorsey and the Burns agent now in the city." [73] The *Constitution* might have made a mistake about the last point because ten days later, when the Burns agent left the case, he told reporters that "open opposition and efforts to frustrate our work" forced the resignation.[74] In addition to the major groups, the *Journal* noted that "practically every private detective in Atlanta, and they are legion, has . . . been quietly lending his efforts to a solution of the mystery." [75]

Friction and competition among groups of detectives made it difficult even to assemble a complete and accurate account of what was an extremely complex case. But as the days passed, it became evident that police, detectives, and the solicitor were focusing their efforts on finding enough material to convict Frank.[76] Harry Scott, the head of the Pinkerton Detective Agency, although originally hired by Frank, later admitted to newspaper reporters that the Pinkerton's had directed their efforts "to obtain evidence supporting the theory that Frank is the slayer." Scott supposedly told one of his subordinates that "unless the Jew is convicted the Pinkerton Detective Agency would have to get out of Atlanta." [77]

The findings and opinions of the various investigators formed the basis of the information which Solicitor Dorsey presented to the Grand Jury when it met on May 23, four weeks after the murder, to consider an indictment of Leo Frank. The Solicitor brought several witnesses along with him who told the jury what the public had been told weeks before. The state's case impressed the Grand Jury, which deliberated less than ten minutes before granting the indictment on May 24.[78]

On the very day that the Grand Jury indicted Frank, the newspapers in Atlanta headlined an admission from Jim Conley, a Negro sweeper at the pencil factory, that he had

written one of the murder notes.[79] Throughout the rest of
the case Conley was to be a central figure, bizarre and puz-
zling, but nevertheless crucial. The police had jailed the
sweeper two days after Frank's arrest because a foreman had
informed them that Conley had been trying to wash blood
from a shirt. Strangely enough, the authorities "were inclined
to attach little importance to his arrest." No one even bothered
to have the city bacteriologist test the blood stains on the
shirt.[80]

The Grand Jury had not been informed of Conley's statement when considering the case against Frank. It is possible
that had the Negro's participation been known, he too might
have been indicted. Moreover, it might have been more difficult to indict Frank after the sweeper's incriminating admission because the earliest assumption—of both police and
public—had been that the author of the murder notes had
probably murdered the little girl also. But the members of the
Grand Jury, like almost everyone else, found out about
Conley's revelations from the newspapers.

According to the newsworthy affidavit, Frank had called
the sweeper to his office on Friday afternoon, April 26, the
day before the murder. He had asked Conley if he could
write, and then, after getting an affirmative answer, handed
him a note pad and dictated the following phrases: "dear
mother," and "a long, tall, black negro did this by hisself
[sic]." Frank allegedly asked him to repeat this "two or three
times," and then supposedly mumbled something which
sounded to Conley like "Why should I hang?" Conley stuck
to this story despite additional questioning. No, he had not
written anything else. No, he had not seen any dead girl. No,
he had not been to the factory on Saturday. And so forth.
The entire truth, Conley maintained on May 24, was in his
affidavit. He claimed to know nothing else about the crime.[81]

Jim Conley, short, stocky, ginger-colored, was the very
opposite of the long, tall, black Negro described in the
murder notes. Twenty-seven years old, he had already served

several jail terms for petty thievery besides having been fined on many occasions for disorderly conduct. On the morning of the murder he had been seen drinking beer and whiskey and may even have been drunk. Some people thought that Conley "always seemed to be kind of nervous or half drunk." [82]

The authorities had not considered Conley a serious suspect until they discovered that he could write. The Negro sweeper had originally denied his ability to read and write, but the news that he could eventually reached Harry Scott of the Pinkertons because of a chance remark made in front of Leo Frank. "I know he can write," Frank said, "I have received many notes from him asking me to loan him money." [83] Scott immediately confronted Conley with this information. Forced to write, the Negro penned a duplicate of the murder notes that appeared almost identical to the originals. [84]

The test took place on May 18, six days before the Grand Jury indictment. But on May 19, a detective announced that "the examination of the handwriting of the negro . . . failed to connect him with the writing of the notes." [85] This statement was not corrected until the release of Conley's first affidavit on May 24. [86]

Conley's sensational revelation failed to impress the editors of the *Georgian*, who considered the Negro's statement "exceedingly peculiar." The paper could not understand why Frank would have muttered "Why should I hang?" or have taken the Negro sweeper into his confidence. It certainly was not like Frank to speak so freely. In fact, the superintendent's silence since his arrest had been such that newspapers labeled him "The Silent Man in the Tower." Therefore Frank's alleged remark appeared "entirely outside the realm of probabilities. . . ." Another improbability was that Frank had called Conley to his office the day *before* the murder and had asked him to write a note. This would indicate that the superintendent had been planning the crime ahead of time. Such an idea had never been entertained by the investigating authorities because they had concluded from the nature of the murder that the killer must have acted without premeditation.[87]

Despite the difficulties involved in believing everything in Conley's affidavit, the police were enthusiastic about it. They considered Conley's sworn statement as the final link in the chain of evidence against Frank, or at least that is what they led the public to believe. Newport Lanford declared himself "perfectly satisfied" that the murder had been solved and assured reporters that "Frank will be convicted. He is the guilty man and we will show it beyond a doubt." Both the Pinkertons and the Burns agent agreed with Lanford. In fact the Burns investigator dropped out of the case at this point because Solicitor Dorsey informed the chief of the detective agency in Atlanta "that the investigation has been so thorough and successful that, really, the Burns men would not be greatly needed any longer." [88]

For public consumption detectives maintained that they "never for a moment" thought that Conley might have been guilty. Only reluctantly, in fact, did they eventually concede that he had written both the notes that were found next to the body.[89] Yet doubts remained, and the newspapers continued to assert that Conley's tale did not ring true. The inconsistencies in the Negro's story would have to be cleared up. Therefore the sweeper underwent further rounds of interrogation. Reporters were told that no prisoner had ever been put through such severe cross-examinations as Conley.[90] Pinkerton Detective Scott later explained to a packed courtroom the procedure he and Atlanta's Chief Detective Lanford used to elicit "the truth" from the Negro. "We pointed out things in his story that were improbable and told him he must do better than that. Anything in his story that looked to be out of place we told him wouldn't do." [91]

The lengthy interrogation proved fruitful. On May 28 Conley made another affidavit in which he added considerably to his first one and acknowledged his presence at the factory on the day of the murder. In his second sworn statement Conley recalled that he had been drinking on the morning of the murder. He had accidentally met Frank in the street, and the superintendent had asked him to come to the factory. When they arrived at the pencil plant, Conley claimed, he had been instructed to wait on the main floor until Frank whistled for him to come up. At about 1 P.M. the whistle sounded, and Conley went up to Frank's office. As soon as he reached the inner office, Frank allegedly remarked that two female employees were coming up the steps and Conley must get into the wardrobe. After the women left Frank supposedly dictated the note that Conley alleged he had written on Friday. The rest of the second affidavit repeated substantially the things said in the original one.[92]

The *Georgian* questioned Conley's new tale. "With his first affidavit repudiated and worthless," the paper noted, "it will be practically impossible to get any court to accept a second one." In fact, the *Georgian* thought the case against Conley stronger than that against Frank. After all, Frank had "answered all the questions" put to him at the Coroner's inquest "in a straightforward, unwavering manner, never once being trapped in a lie or misstatement," whereas Conley had lied continuously. Nevertheless Newport Lanford, the chief of detectives, exuded confidence and beamed happily over Conley's second affidavit, calling it "the final and conclusive piece of evidence . . . against Frank." [93]

But the detectives realized that Conley's second affidavit had some shortcomings also and therefore they decided to put the sweeper through another interrogation "with a view to clearing up the weak points in his statement." [94] During the course of what the *Georgian* described as a "merciless sweating" [95] on May 29, Conley's interrogators "dragged sentence by sentence from the frightened negro" [96] a more plausible explanation. The next morning Atlantans read the results of the previous day's "sweating": "CONLEY SAYS HE HELPED CARRY BODY OF MARY PHAGAN TO PENCIL FACTORY CELLAR." [97]

The latest of the Conley revelations added significantly to his previous affidavits. Conley now alleged that after Frank had called him up to the office, the superintendent had told him that he had let a girl fall against a machine in the metal room and that he wanted Conley to remove her. Conley had gone into the room and had found the girl dead. He had reported this to Frank, but the superintendent had ordered him to carry the body to the elevator anyway. Together they had taken the corpse to the basement and Conley had dumped her in the corner. It was after this that Conley and Frank had returned to the second floor office, and the sweeper had written the notes. The rest of the third affidavit was similar to the previous ones except that this time Frank had supposedly given the Negro $200, and then took the money back with the promise that he would return it again.[98] The *Journal* regarded Conley's latest remarks as "the most sensational development in the Phagan murder case since the arrest of Superintendent Frank," and the detectives considered it "the most import link in their chain of evidence against the factory official." [99]

After his third affidavit, the detectives took Conley back to the pencil factory and had him reenact the events of the murder day. The sweeper, the *Georgian* reported, "went through the grim drama with a realism that convinced all who listened and watched that he at last was telling the whole truth." [100]

Shortly after Conley made the last of his sensational statements he was removed from the police jail, where he had been for a month, and placed in a cell in the Fulton County Tower, where reporters would have free access to him. But within a few days, after Conley had complained that Frank's visitors intimidated him with such remarks as "I could shoot you through the bars of your cell right now" and "Don't you think you ought to be shot?," [101] Solicitor Dorsey petitioned the presiding judge of the Fulton County Criminal Court, Leonard Roan, to take the prisoner back to the police jail.

Dorsey argued that he did not want anyone to tamper with Conley "in any manner which might destroy his value as a witness." [102] Roan acceded to the Solicitor's request. Once the sweeper was back in the police jail, Chief Detective Lanford remarked: "We wanted Conley where we could get to him at any time we thought advisable." [103]

But the transfer had the effect of insulating the prisoner. In the city jail Solicitor Dorsey, or one of his staff members, screened Conley's visitors, a thing they could not do had he been in the county jail. When Pinkerton Detective Scott announced in July that he was reexamining his conclusions as to who murdered Mary Phagan, the police immediately curtailed his access to Jim Conley. Chief Detective Lanford explained the action as follows: "We did not want to embarrass Scott by requesting him to keep silent and did not risk the probability of letting new developments reach Frank's attorneys, therefore we were forced to prevent him from seeing the negro." [104] Until August, when Conley would testify in court, no one who was skeptical of the Negro's innocence or of Frank's guilt was permitted an interview with the sweeper.

Once the authorities were satisfied with Conley's sworn statement, they continued their search for other witnesses who might substantiate their case against Leo Frank. The next affidavit they obtained came after the arrest of Minola McKnight, the Negro cook at Frank's home. Albert McKnight, Minola's husband, reportedly informed his employers that his wife knew something about Frank's actions on the day of the murder. The employers told this to the police, who arrested the cook at the beginning of June and held her, without a warrant, for twenty-four hours. Reporters heard Mrs. McKnight screaming from behind locked doors that she was going to be hanged for a crime that she knew nothing about.[105] When finally released, after being "quizzed to a point of exhaustion," [106] she left an affidavit behind her indicting Leo Frank.

Mrs. McKnight swore that Frank came home for lunch at

about 1:30 P.M. on the day of the murder but left ten minutes later without eating. The cook then claimed that she overheard a conversation the following day between Mrs. Frank and her mother, Mrs. Selig. The younger woman supposedly told her mother that Frank had been drunk the night before, and that he wanted to shoot himself. He allegedly confessed to his wife that he was in trouble and that he did not know why he would want to commit a crime such as he had earlier in the day. Mrs. McKnight swore that her wages had been raised twice since the murder, "but it was not for my work, they didn't tell me what it was for . . . but of course I understood what they meant. . . . I understood it was a tip for me to keep quiet." [107] After being released, Minola McKnight repudiated her entire affidavit, but once again the repudiation did not make front page headlines as did the accusation.[108]

The imprisonment and methods used to obtain a statement from the cook finally broke the silence that the Frank family had maintained since the superintendent's arrest. In a letter to the three Atlanta dailies, Mrs. Frank denounced Solicitor Dorsey and the city police. She castigated the law enforcers for torturing Mrs. McKnight "for four hours with the well-known third degree process," in order to get the confession. Under the circumstances, Mrs. Frank wrote, anyone would have confessed to anything.

Mrs. Frank also used this opportunity to defend her husband and deny the gossip about their relationship. "Every conceivable rumor has been put afloat that would do him and me harm, with the public, in spite of the fact" that they are untrue. "I know my husband is innocent," she concluded, "he is utterly incapable of committing the crime that these detectives and this solicitor are seeking to fasten upon him." [109]

Solicitor Dorsey, who up to this point had also kept his own counsel, now answered Mrs. Frank's accusations: "The wife of a man accused of crime would probably be the last person to learn all of the facts establishing his guilt, and certainly would be the last person to admit his culpability, even though proved by overwhelming evidence to the satisfaction of every impartial citizen beyond the possibility of reasonable doubt." [110]

9

Two weeks after the public exchange between the Solicitor and Mrs. Frank, another significant episode in the Phagan murder case made headlines. In the middle of June the maid at Mrs. Formby's "rooming house" said that the detectives had been pestering her on numerous occasions to make an affidavit supporting Mrs. Formby's contention that Frank had phoned half a dozen times for a room on the evening of the murder. The maid refused because she claimed that there had been no such call that evening, and if there had been she certainly would have answered the phone.[111] One of Dorsey's assistants shortly afterwards announced that the state never attached much importance to Mrs. Formby's affidavit, "except for the first few days," and had no intention of using it at the trial.[112] One of Frank's attorneys denounced the prosecution in these words:

I see the detectives are gradually giving it out that Mrs. Formby will not be called as a witness, although her affidavit has been paraded before the public bearing the unqualified endorsement of the detective department as being perfectly reliable and true. Worse than this, an intimation was published in the newspapers that Frank's friends had persuaded her to leave town. In this and in many other ways our client has been done a very great injustice. The effort seems to have been not to find the criminal but to try by all means to put the crime on Frank.[113]

In July lawyers for the defense "leaked" an affidavit they had in their possession from an insurance agent who tried to sell Conley insurance on the day of the murder. The sweeper had no intention of purchasing any insurance at that time, and feeling annoyed about the solicitation threatened the agent: "I've killed a girl today; I don't want to kill nobody else." According to the affidavit, the insurance agent had gone to the police and also to some factory officials (not including Frank) on April 29 with his tale, but no one seemed interested. In the factory the insurance agent was allegedly told that there were no Negroes at the pencil plant on the day of the murder.[114] The detectives responded quickly to this "leaked" affidavit, and the *Georgian* reported: "CONLEY IN SWEATBOX AGAIN." [115]

Despite the state's conviction that Frank had killed Mary Phagan, the Grand Jury now wanted to indict Jim Conley. The foreman asked Solicitor Dorsey to call the group into session, but he refused to do so.[116] Then the foreman threatened the Solicitor that action would be taken without him. It was "the first time the grand jury [took] up the consideration of a criminal case in this county over the protest of the solicitor general." [117]

When the veniremen met, Dorsey pleaded with them not to indict the Negro sweeper. The Grand Jury finally acceded to his request, but "the solicitor did not win his point without a difficult fight. He went in with a mass of evidence showing why the indictment of the negro would injure the state's case against Frank and stayed with the grand jurors for nearly an hour and a half." [118]

10

A careful reading of the three Atlanta newspapers throughout the pretrial period reveals that there was a difference in their coverage of the case that extended far beyond the quantity of words expended, the size of the banner headlines, or the number of extras put out.[119] Hearst's *Georgian*, despite its sensationalism, and the *Journal*, its competitor in the afternoon, presented a more judicious view of the affair than did the morning *Constitution*, which seemed to assume Frank's guilt.[120] One reason for the *Constitution*'s attitude might have been that it had friends in the police department, and therefore accepted the official version more easily. Whenever the police wished to publicize materials incriminating Frank, the *Constitution* usually got the exclusive story.[121] The *Constitution* also gave greater prominence to the theories of the police. The *Journal*'s methods might have been influenced by the character and integrity of its chief reporter on the case, Harold Ross, who later won fame as the editor of *The New Yorker* magazine. Ross would later write, "Without making the assertion that Frank is innocent, it may be said that his conduct from the outset was that of an innocent man. . . ." [122] There are two possible explanations for the *Georgian's* approach. In the first place, it was primarily concerned with selling newspapers rather than with the guilt or innocence of any of the suspects. Hence there would be no reason to concentrate on building up a case against any single individual. On the other hand, Hearst had sent some of his top reporters to Atlanta after he had purchased the *Georgian*. He sent additional talent after Mary Phagan had been murdered. These people were carefully selected on the basis of their journalistic skills. It is possible that they were perhaps more sophisticated and had learned from their experiences in other cities that the authorities, like everyone else, could make mistakes. And since they were from out of town, they would not have to keep in the good graces of the local authorities to insure tips on future stories. It was a *Georgian* reporter, in fact, who observed that Hugh Dorsey "has never shown any unusual skill as a detective." [123] The *Georgian* questioned the nature of the prosecution's evidence so frequently that other newspapers in the state charged that the Hearst daily had been "bought to defend Frank." [124]

It would be inaccurate to state that material favorable to Frank did not appear in the *Constitution* or that the *Journal* and the *Georgian* constantly showed concern for the prisoner's welfare. But each paper did handle the news differently. Whereas the *Journal* gave a front page headline to the item that "Frank's Treatment of Girls in Factory Described as Unimpeachable by One Young Lady Employee," [125] two weeks later the *Constitution* buried a similar comment at the bottom of an inside page, where its readers might easily overlook it.[126] The *Georgian*, on the other hand, printed a letter from a questioning Atlantan in type large enough to catch the eye: "Is not the case against Leo Frank so far presented against him palpably weak? And does not the far greater weight of evidence now point unmistakably to the negro Conley as the sole perpetrator of the crime?" [127] One would hardly expect the *Constitution* to give prominence to such a comment. Less than two weeks earlier, its readers had been informed that Conley's narrative "is so straight-forward and coincides so perfectly with other phases that have already been brought out that it is said to be indisputable." [128] The greatest contrast in coverage, however, occurred ten days before the trial opened. Harry Scott, the chief Pinkerton detective on the case, changed his mind about the key suspects. The *Journal's* lead read: "PINKERTON'S NOW DECLARE LEO M. FRANK IS INNOCENT," [129] whereas the next morning's *Constitution* headlined: "SCOTT BELIEVES CONLEY INNOCENT, ASSERTS LANFORD," and in smaller type, " 'Open to Conviction' Scott Tells Reporter." [130]

Northern journalists who investigated the affair in Atlanta afterwards wrote that the city's newspapers had assumed Frank's guilt from the time of his arrest.[131] This was not true. The *Constitution*, alone, assumed Frank's guilt, and even that paper severely criticized the police for the way in which it had handled the investigation during its earliest stages.

None of the three dailies commented upon the case editorially until after the trial was over. Both the *Georgian* and the *Journal* would later comment about the public hysteria in Atlanta during the course of the judicial proceedings, and each would suggest the necessity for reexamining the evidence against the defendant.[132] The *Constitution*, on the other hand, remained silent for the rest of Frank's life.

II

Although the newspapers devoted a great deal of space to
the murder they did not sufficiently explain why the police
and the populace could so easily accept the indictment against
Frank. To understand this more fully, an examination of the
social milieu in which the case unfolded is necessary. The
keynote to much of Southern society was a commitment to
tradition and an opposition to change. The Southern heritage,
moreover, had nurtured a strong in-group loyalty which at
times manifested itself in a paranoic suspicion of outsiders.
Leo Frank as a Northerner, an industrialist, and a Jew represented everything alien to the culture.

When rural Southerners flocked to the cities at the end of
the nineteenth century their impressions of the Jew combined
the traditional notion of financial omnipotence with the time-
worn prejudice against strangers.[133] To many, the Jews also
symbolized the city. Since the Jews dealt mainly in trade and
commerce, the lifeblood of the town, many considered them
the urban people, *par excellence*. The public schools tended
to glorify rural virtues and depicted the city as the locus of
evil. Rural dwellers usually held some vague suspicion of urbanites even before their arrival in the big towns; subsequent
experiences tended to confirm the earlier prejudice. For lack
of a more specific target, the unpleasant experiences in the
city could easily be attributed to the mysterious Jew who
controlled finances, practiced strange customs, and personified urban perfidy.[134]

Leo Frank was a Jew. He would not have been condemned
for that fact alone. But "once suspicion had been directed
against him there was a universal effort to prove him guilty,
and every conceivable argument that tended to support the
theory was evoked, including the fact . . . that he was a
Jew." [135] A chronicler of the Frank case put this argument
somewhat differently: "One man, after asserting that there is

no prejudice against Frank, because he is a Jew, grows eloquent and says Mary Phagan is our folks." [136]

A variety of other factors, however, complicated Frank's situation. He had provoked community wrath as an employer of underpaid female labor. "What was uppermost in the minds of those who were indignant," *The Outlook* commented afterwards, "was the fact that the accused represented the employing class, while the victim was an employee." [137] John Higham wrote that many working class people "saw in Frank a symbol of the northern capitalist exploiting southern womanhood." [138] Atlantans were further prejudiced against the factory superintendent because of his alleged escapades with young girls. None of the accusations was ever proved, but each charge had a profound effect upon the public.

Given Southern feelings about the Negro, an attempt must be made to understand why the authorities did not build up a case around Jim Conley, particularly in view of later findings that the proof against Frank was inconclusive. Unfortunately lack of sufficient information makes it impossible to arrive at a wholly satisfactory explanation for the decision, but some clues may be garnered from the statements of Southerners. Tom Watson, the former Populist, would eventually emphasize "the indescribable outrage committed upon 'the factory girl' *in the factory*," [139] thus indicating that at this particular time and in this particular case resentment against a symbol of alien industrialism took precedence over the usual Negro prejudice. And the pastor of the Baptist Church attended by Mary Phagan's family wrote: "My feelings, upon the arrest of the old negro nightwatchman, were to the effect that this one old negro would be poor atonement for the life of this innocent girl. But, when on the next day, the police arrested a Jew, and a Yankee Jew at that, all of the inborn prejudice against Jews rose up in a feeling of satisfaction, that here would be a victim worthy to pay for the crime." [140]

The authorities, of course, might have sincerely believed

Frank guilty. One of Dorsey's assistants maintained that such was the case many years after the trial.[141] Perhaps while examining Conley the police had become convinced that parts of his story, especially the incriminating remarks about Frank, were true.

There is also a possibility that members of the police force had become so deeply committed to the theory of Frank's guilt at an early date that evidence obtained afterwards made it, at best, psychologically difficult for them to change or, at worst, politically inexpedient. The mounting public pressure added to their anxiety. The *Constitution* started a fund to bring one of the world's most prominent sleuths to Atlanta to solve the murder—William J. Burns. The police felt threatened. They were forced to act quickly, and perhaps in their haste they overlooked materials which under other circumstances might have been more soberly considered.

The opinions and activities of the police helped to condition the public's reaction. The police led the people to believe that the strands of hair which had been found on a metal lathe in the workroom opposite Frank's office had been "identified positively" as that of the dead girl. This, in fact, was not true, but it is impossible to discover whether the authorities knew that it was false when they released the information to reporters. Similarly the red spots on the floor near the metal lathe, called "blood stains" by the police, and repeated as such in the newspapers, were proved to be something other than human blood, but this information did not reach the public until 1914.

The behavior of officials other than the police might also have weighed heavily against Frank in the public's mind. In July the members of the Grand Jury wanted to indict Jim Conley, but Solicitor Dorsey convinced them not to do so. Atlantans might have assumed that Dorsey presented the veniremen with arguments compelling enough to dissuade them from their intended course. Perhaps the people recalled the assurance that the *Georgian* had given its readers in May:

"That the authorities have very important evidence that has not yet been disclosed to the public is certain." Even more plausible, however, is that the people of Atlanta had assumed, and quite naturally, that the Solicitor would not have prosecuted a white man, rather than a Negro, "unless the evidence was overwhelming." [142] Two days before the trial began, in fact, Hugh Dorsey proclaimed that "the possibility of a mistake having been made is very remote." [143]

As Leo Frank prepared himself for court, he confidently expected an acquittal.[144] His four weeks in the courtroom, however, would provide him with a series of shocking experiences. He would eventually come to realize that the rumors of his alleged indiscretions, and the alien image that he presented, significantly affected the course of his trial.

CHAPTER II

Prejudice and Perjury

NO TRIAL IN GEORGIA'S history rivaled Leo Frank's for public interest. No Georgian appeared indifferent to the fate of the accused. Even outside Atlanta one could hardly find "a hamlet or wayside, city or township in Georgia that [was] not submerged head over heels, in interest in the Frank case." [1]

For more than four months the newspapers featured the crime above all other subjects, and outside the state the trial made front page headlines in the largest cities of the South. But a reporter for *The Atlanta Constitution* lamented that "because it is not in New York, the papers of that fickle metropolis have not, in all, carried more than a column of the entire case." [2] He also might have mentioned that outside the South few people knew that Leo Frank existed. The situation would soon change, however, and Georgians would not be very happy about it.

I

The trial opened in an atmosphere unfavorable to the defendant. A *Georgian* reporter observed that "the public has not *yet* become convinced—and may never become convinced—that Leo Frank is innocent of the crime for which he has been indicted." Gossip about the murder had been so widespread and the details of the investigation so frequently recalled, that some people in Atlanta doubted whether a jury could be assembled which would "be willing to view the evidence coolly, without prejudice or without bias." [3] In fact, the temper of the crowd surrounding the courthouse was so ugly that twenty officers guarded the courtroom, and someone suggested, as a further precaution, that spectators be searched for dangerous weapons before entering the building.[4]

Leo Frank had engaged two of Georgia's outstanding lawyers to defend him. His main counsel, Luther Z. Rosser, had a reputation for being "the most persuasive and the most domineering lawyer in Atlanta in the art of examining witnesses." Rosser's associate, Reuben R. Arnold, "perhaps the best-known attorney in Georgia," had long been regarded as "one of the ablest criminal lawyers in the South." [5] The brilliant reputations of the defense attorneys would eventually prove disastrous to Frank's cause because they failed to display their forensic talents at the very moment they were most needed. For the prosecution Solicitor Hugh Dorsey added Frank Hooper, another well-known Georgia attorney. The combination of Rosser and Arnold against Dorsey and Hooper guaranteed, according to *The Atlanta Constitution*, the "Greatest Legal Battle in the History of Dixie." [6]

The prosecution began with a repetition of published information. The state sought to establish, through different witnesses, that blood spots on the floor and strands of Mary Phagan's hair on a lathe nearby indicated that the murder had occurred in the second floor workroom, opposite Frank's office, and that the superintendent, the last person known to have seen the girl alive, had the opportunity to kill her. Doctors testified that Mary Phagan's death probably occurred between 12:00 and 12:15 P.M. The state also introduced Monteen Stover, one of the factory employees, who had arrived to collect her pay on the day of the murder at 12:05 P.M., looked into Frank's office, did not see him, waited five minutes, and then left the building. This employee's testimony was especially damaging because at one of his first

THE ATLANTA GEORGIAN

Read for Profit---GEORGIAN WANT ADS---Use for Results

VOL. XI. NO. 250.   ATLANTA, GA., FRIDAY, MAY 23, 1913.   2 CENTS EVERYWHERE PAT NO More

THE GEORGIAN ARTIST'S DIAGRAM OF PENCIL FACTORY USED BEFORE GRAND JURY TO EXPLAIN PHAGAN SLAYING

PLAN OF THE BUILDING WHERE TRAGEDY OCCURRED, SHOWN BY ARTIST WHO STUDIED IT CAREFULLY.

Drawn by Bert Green

KEY TO DIAGRAM.

(A).—Machine room where murder was committed
(B).—Course by stairs taken to elevator.
(D).—The elevator shaft.
(E) and (C).—Route taken with body to cellar.
(F).—Pencil shaving dump.
Cross—Where body was found.
Arrow.—Where lock and staple were pulled from rear door.
(H).—Location of office.

The prosecution and defense postulated opposite theories as to where and how the murder had taken place. The diagrams represent the two views.

Courtesy of *The Atlanta Georgian,* May 23, 1913

THEORY OF PHAGAN MURDER ADVANCED BY DEFENSE

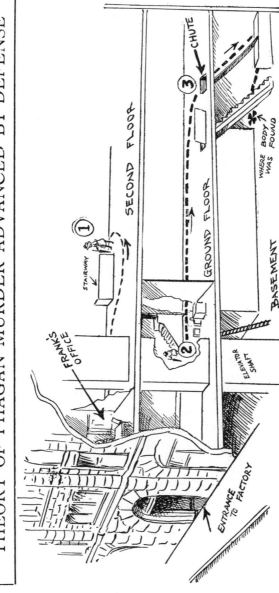

Questions asked witnesses by Attorneys Rosser and Arnold indicate that the defense may attempt to convince the jury that it would have been possible for the little girl to have been killed on the first floor of the factory and her body later disposed of through a chute leading from the first floor to the basement at the rear of the building. According to this theory the girl was met at the foot of the stairs leading from Frank's office, taken toward the back of the building and killed. Her body was then dragged to the trap door leading to the chute and dropped into the basement. Later, according to the theory, it was taken to the spot where it was found by Newt Lee. The accompanying drawing was made from the model of the factory which is being used by the defense at the trial.

interrogations, on April 28, Frank had told Chief Detective
Lanford that Mary Phagan arrived between 12:05 and 12:10
P.M., and that he had not left his office between 12:00 and
12:30 P.M.[7] The state's case appeared clear. The prosecution
would try to prove that Leo Frank murdered Mary Phagan at
the very time Monteen Stover had waited for her pay.

During the first week of the trial, testimony of the state's
witnesses furnished the background for Jim Conley, the
Negro sweeper, whose story would provide the crux of the
prosecution's presentation. Most observers agreed that
Frank's fate rested upon the jurors' willingness to believe the
sweeper's tale.[8]

When Conley finally reached the witness stand, an obvious
transformation had taken place in his appearance. Habitually
he wore dirty clothes and presented a rather shabby if not
downright filthy, appearance. In the courtroom, though, his
face was scrubbed, his hair cut and combed, his clothes clean
and new.

Solicitor Dorsey led Conley through his paces and the
Negro responded with alacrity. In the courtroom, Conley
both added to, and elaborated upon, his earlier affidavits. The
Journal commented afterwards that the sweeper's glibness
had a rehearsed air.[9] Nevertheless, Conley unfolded a tale
filled with painfully vivid detail.

The sweeper explained that he had arrived in the factory
on the day of the murder at 8:30 A.M., as he had on other
Saturdays, and that he spoke with Frank, who instructed him
to go out, take care of some errands, and then return. The
superintendent allegedly mentioned that he was expecting a
young lady who could come to "chat" for awhile. Conley
then told the court that he had "watched out" for Frank on
other occasions when ladies came to "chat" and that when
Frank stamped his foot the sweeper would lock the front
door; then he would wait in the lobby and unlock the door
when Frank whistled.[10]

Conley then related how Mary Phagan arrived and went

upstairs. After that he heard footsteps going back to the metal workroom (where the prosecution contended that Mary had been murdered), a girl scream, and then saw Monteen Stover enter the building and go up to the second floor. "She stayed there a pretty good while," and then left the building. After that Conley heard footsteps tiptoeing to the office and then back to the metal room. At that point the sweeper dozed off. A stamping foot from the second floor awoke him, and he locked the front door. A few moments later the whistle came, and Conley unlocked the same door and went up to the superintendent's office. When he arrived he found that

Mr. Frank was standing up there at the top of the steps and shivering and trembling and rubbing his hands. . . . He had a little rope in his hands—a long wide piece of cord. His eyes were large and they looked right funny. He looked funny out of his eyes. His face was red. Yes, he had a cord in his hands just like this here cord. After I got up to the top of the steps, he asked me, "Did you see that little girl who passed here just a while ago?" and I told him I saw one come along there and she come back again, and then I saw another one come along there and she hasn't come back down, and he says, "Well, that one you say didn't come back down, she came into my office awhile ago and wanted to know something about her work in my office and I went back there to see if the little girl's work had come, and I wanted to be with the little girl, and she refused me, and I struck her and I guess I struck her too hard and she fell and hit her head against something, and I don't know how bad she got hurt. Of course you know I ain't built like other men." The reason he said that was, I had seen him in a position I haven't seen any other man that has got children. I have seen him in the office two or three times before Thanksgiving and a lady was in his office, and she was sitting down in a chair and she had her clothes up to here, and he was down on his knees, and she had her hands on Mr. Frank. I have seen him another time there in the packing room with a young lady lying on the table, she was on the edge of the table when I saw her. He asked me if I wouldn't go back there and bring her up so that he could put her somewhere, and he said to hurry, that there would be money in it for me. When I came back there, I found the lady lying flat of [sic] her back with a rope around her neck. The cloth was also tied around her neck and part of it was under her head like to catch blood. . . . She was dead when I went back there and I came back and told Mr. Frank the girl was dead and he said, "Sh-Sh!" He told me to go back there by the cotton box, get a piece of cloth, put it around her and bring her up.

Conley claimed that he did as he was bid. He rolled the girl up in the cloth, tried to pick her up but could not lift the bundle to his shoulder, let her fall, and called out to his boss, "Mr. Frank, you will have to help me with this girl, she is heavy." The sweeper then related that Frank came and caught her by the feet and helped Conley take the body to the basement, via the elevator, deposited it there, and then took the elevator back to the second floor. Conley then recalled having followed Frank back to his office. As soon as they arrived, the sweeper continued, they heard footsteps coming up the stairs and Frank put Conley in the wardrobe. After the people left, Frank allegedly released the Negro and asked:

"Can you write?" and I said, "Yes, sir, a little bit," and he taken [sic] his pencil to fix up some notes. I was willing to do anything to help Mr. Frank because he was a white man and my superintendent, and he sat down and I sat down at the table and Mr. Frank dictated the notes to me. Whatever it was it didn't seem to suit him, and he told me to turn over and write again, and I turned the paper and wrote again, and when I done that he told me to turn over again and I turned over again and I wrote on the next page there, and he looked at that and kind of liked it and he said that was all right.

Then Frank allegedly gave Conley another piece of paper, dictated another note, approved of what the sweeper wrote, and handed him $200.

After awhile Mr. Frank looked at me and said, "You go down there in the basement and you take a lot of trash and burn that

Hugh Dorsey during his interrogation of Conley. This drawing captures the intense interest of the spectators in the trial.

Courtesy of *The Atlanta Constitution*, August 5, 1913

package that's in front of the furnace," and I told him all right. But I was afraid to go down there by myself, and Mr. Frank wouldn't go down there with me. . . . And I said, "Mr. Frank, you are a white man and you done it, and I am not going down there and burn that myself." He looked at me then kind of frightened and he said, "Let me see that money" and he took the money back and put it back in his pocket, and I said, "Is this the way you do things?" and he said, "You keep your mouth shut, that is all right." And Mr. Frank turned around in his chair and looked at the money and he looked back at me and folded his hands and looked up and said "Why should I hang? I have wealthy people in Brooklyn," and he looked down when he said that, and I looked up at him, and he was looking up at the ceiling, and I said, "Mr. Frank, what about me?" and he said, "That's all right, don't you worry about this thing, you just come back to work Monday like you don't know anything, and keep your mouth shut, if you get caught I will get you out on bond and send you away," and he said, "Can you come back this evening and do it?" and I said "Yes, that I was coming to get my money." He said, "Well, I am going home to get dinner and you come back here in about forty minutes and I will fix the money," and I said, "How will I get in?" and he said, "There will be a place for you to get in all right, but if you are not coming back let me know, and I will take those things and put them down with the body," and I said, "All right, I will be back in about forty minutes."

But Conley recalled that he never did return that day. Instead, he went to a beer saloon, ate and drank, and then went home, where he "laid down across the bed and went to sleep, and [I] didn't get up no more until half past six o'clock that night. . . ." [11]

On the witness stand Conley told his story with such dramatic realism that "every spectator in the crowded courtroom hung on his words." The narrative struck the presiding judge as unfit for innocent ears, and after a few hours barred women and children from the courtroom for the remainder of the sweeper's testimony. The women could not have even the vicarious pleasure of reading Conley's whole story because the newspapers held that "the most startling features of the negro's testimony are unprintable." [12]

Rosser and Arnold cross-examined Conley for sixteen hours on three consecutive days. By the end they had forced the sweeper to admit that he had lied on a number of previous occasions, that he had told only partial truths in previous affidavits, and that his memory was exceedingly poor except for the specific questions which Hugh Dorsey had required him to answer. Yet the defense attorneys, in their attempt to confuse Conley and catch him in a major misstatement, forced him to talk of the other times that he had "watched for" Frank and the witness vividly described other women who had come to "chat" with the superintendent while he had guarded the front door. Most important, however, was the sweeper's admission that he had defecated at the bottom of the elevator shaft on the morning of the murder. It was an extremely significant remark, but its import escaped both reporters and jurors. There is no indication, either, that Frank's attorneys realized its implications.[13]

Conley's revelations shocked the spectators "into almost irresponsible indignation. . . ." After he stepped down from the witness stand one reporter wrote, "If so much as 5 per cent" of the story sticks, it "likely will serve to convict" Frank. The *Journal* questioned whether "this illiterate negro [could] have conceived and fitted together such a set of detailed circumstances without some foundation in fact?" [14]

The weight of Conley's words assumed greater import because the defense attorneys had failed to upset his account. Many Georgians assumed that Conley must have told the truth because Luther Rosser, "the most dreaded cross-examiner at the Georgia bar, and who knows the negro character thoroughly . . . was unable to make a dent in the negro's story." [15] People believed Conley could not be flustered because he told what he had seen and done rather than what he might have been drilled to say. Fifty years after sitting in the courtroom and listening to the sweeper's testimony, McLellan Smith, who had covered the trial as a cub reporter for the *Georgian*, was still certain that Conley had told the truth. "A man of his mental capacity," Smith insisted, "could have been broken if he was lying." [16]

That the defense attorneys permitted Conley to discuss previous occasions on which he had "watched for" Frank while the superintendent entertained women in his office seemed strange to many observers. Why they pursued this line of questioning was never explained, but speculators assumed that Rosser and Arnold felt confident that they could break the sweeper's story. After a day of cross-examination, however, which failed to change any major aspect of the narrative, defense counsel moved to have the testimony referring to Frank's alleged assignations struck from the record. Instantaneously the prosecutors jumped to their feet. One of Dorsey's assistants agreed that the testimony should have been ruled out, but he doubted the right of the defense to ask for this after having examined the witness on these points. Dorsey echoed his assistant's protest: ". . . able attorneys here have sat and let testimony enter the records without making protest, cross-examine him for two days, and twenty-four hours later, decide to complain." [17]

The motion to strike incriminating remarks from the record backfired. "By asking that the testimony be eliminated," the *Constitution* wrote, the defense "virtually admit their failure to break down Conley." Throughout Atlanta the "news spread that the negro had withstood the fire and that Frank's attorneys were seeking to have the evidence expunged from the records." This serious defense miscalculation "made Frank's road to acquittal a thousand times harder to journey." [18]

The presiding judge, Leonard S. Roan, allowed Conley's remarks to remain as recorded. The Judge observed that while the words "may be extracted from the record . . . it is an impossibility to withdraw it from the jury's mind." Roan's ruling electrified the spectators, who "broke out in a wild uproar like a bloodthirsty mob at a bull fight." The Judge immediately pounded the gavel for order and announced that he would tolerate no further demonstration; but courtroom decorum was restored "with some difficulty." The *Constitution* reported the scene in a banner headline: "SPONTANEOUS APPLAUSE GREETS DORSEY'S VICTORY." Reuben Arnold, Frank's attorney, sprang to his feet after the outburst subsided and announced: "If that happens again I shall move for a mistrial." [19]

2

After Jim Conley finished testifying, the prosecution called a few relatively unimportant witnesses and then rested its case. The first Atlanta publication to editorialize upon the state's presentation was *Frost's Magazine*, which to that point had refrained from any commentary upon the murder. The editor of the magazine stated that heretofore comment had been withheld because Dorsey and Lanford had given the public the impression that they possessed evidence which would assure Frank's conviction. After hearing the testimony, the editors of *Frost's Magazine* asserted that Atlanta's Chief Detective and the Solicitor both "misled the public. We cannot conceive that at the close of the prosecution, before the defense has presented one single witness, that it could be possible for any juryman to vote for the conviction of Leo M. Frank." *Frost's Magazine* based its conclusions primarily on Conley's testimony. "He did not adhere to his original story. He was shown by the cross-examination of Attorney Rosser to be absolutely unreliable in veracity and memory. One thing the negro did was to reply that 'he did not remember' to everything that did not tend toward the guilt of Frank, and would always fall back to his invented story." The periodical assumed that the additions Conley injected in the courtroom could have been made up from reading the newspapers

and/or coaching from his attorney or Solicitor Dorsey. Of
the Solicitor, *Frost's Magazine* observed, "It is evident that he
has sought self-aggrandizement in his ruthless effort to make
out a case where he knew beforehand that he had no case." [20]

3

When Rosser and Arnold assumed the burden of presenting their client's defense they attempted to show that Frank
had conducted himself in his usual manner on the day of the
murder and that he would not have been able to do so if he
had performed so heinous a crime. Numerous witnesses testified to Frank's whereabouts on the fatal day to establish that
the superintendent did not have enough time alone to commit
the crime of which Conley had accused him.

The defense attorneys thought they had a convincing case.
Conley had sworn to being with Frank at times when other
persons claimed to have seen the superintendent. None of the
defense witnesses was impeached; all were of good character;
and practically all were white—an important consideration
with a Southern jury.

The problem of time loomed largest in Conley's narrative
and Frank's refutation. According to the sweeper, Mary
Phagan had arrived in the pencil factory to collect her pay
before Monteen Stover. Miss Stover swore that she had been
in Frank's outer office from 12:05 to 12:10 P.M., and then
left. The motorman and conductor of the trolley car on
which Mary Phagan had come to town testified that she left
the trolley at 12:10 P.M. Other witnesses agreed that it took
about two to four minutes to walk from the trolley station to
the factory. Therefore either Monteen Stover or Jim Conley
had made a mistake. Two employees who claimed that they
had arrived at 11:45 A.M. to collect their pay had come after
1:00 P.M. according to the sweeper.

Frank claimed that he had gone home for lunch at 1:00

P.M. The defense introduced witnesses who had seen the superintendent between 1:00 and 1:30 P.M. Another state witness, Albert McKnight, had sworn that he had seen Frank at home at 1:30 P.M. Yet Conley had testified that he and Frank had been in the factory at 1:30 P.M. Furthermore, Frank's attorneys produced witnesses who attested to the superintendent's whereabouts during most of the period that Conley claimed they had been together. According to the sweeper, and others, it would have taken Frank and Conley more than half an hour, if they had worked as quickly as possible, to perform the time-consuming tasks of murdering the girl, bringing the body to the cellar, returning to the superintendent's office on the second floor, hiding in the wardrobe, and writing the murder notes.[21] Yet, with the exception of about eighteen minutes (between approximately 12:02 and 12:20), Frank's time seemed to have been accounted for between 11:30 A.M. and 1:30 P.M. The *Constitution* observed that the "chain of testimony, forged with a number of links, has established a seemingly unbreakable corroboration of Frank's account of his whereabouts. . . ."[22]

Leo Frank climaxed the defense presentation with a four-hour effort to convince the jurors of his innocence. He briefly outlined his life history, his reasons for coming to Atlanta, and his actions on the day of the murder. At times he specifically touched on points that the prosecution had scored against him. He explained that Monteen Stover may not have seen him in his office when she arrived because when he sat at his desk "it is impossible for me to see out into the outer hall when the safe door is open, as it was that morning, and not only is it impossible for me to see out, but it is impossible for people to see in and see me there." On the other hand, he thought he might have been out of his office momentarily because of "a call of nature." The superintendent branded Conley's entire narrative "a tissue of lies," and again denied participating in the crime. A *Georgian* reporter wrote afterwards that "Frank was far and away the very best witness the

Frank on the stand was cool, perfectly poised and at all times the master of himself. He showed no trace of nervousness. He looked the jury squarely in the face. He was at times explicit when explaining the details of his business, argumentative when telling of things that had looked dark for him, eloquent as he concluded.

Leo Frank on the witness stand.

Courtesy of *The Atlanta Constitution*, August 19, 1913

defense has put forward," and the *Constitution* observed that Frank's words "carried the ring of truth in every sentence." [23]

Altogether the defense introduced more than two hundred witnesses, including over one hundred who testified to Frank's good character, and at least a score who insisted that they would never believe Jim Conley under oath or otherwise because of his notorious reputation for lying.[24] When Solicitor Dorsey cross-examined these witnesses he asked them if they knew of Frank's reputation for lascivious behavior? The solicitor also asked witnesses if they had heard of Frank putting his arm around some girls and bouncing others on his lap? [25] Dorsey even asked one man if he had ever heard of Frank "kissing girls and playing with their nipples on their breast . . . ?" [26] It mattered not how the witnesses responded. Conley had already said enough to damage Frank's reputation, and the reiteration of the subject refreshed the jurors' memories. At one point Solicitor Dorsey's questions resulted in an unexpected outburst from the defendant's mother, Mrs. Rae Frank. Dorsey asked a witness if he had ever heard of "Frank taking a little girl to Druid Hills [Park], setting her on his lap and playing with her?" Before the witness could answer Mrs. Frank jumped up and shouted at the prosecutor, "No, nor you either—you dog!" [27]

Dorsey implied that Frank might also be a homosexual. He asked a former office boy if Frank had not made improper advances toward him, and though the boy denied it, the insinuation that Frank indulged himself in this fashion "went from mouth to mouth gaining credence as it went." [28]

After the defense concluded its presentation the state offered rebuttal witnesses. Most of them swore that Frank did have a reputation for lascivious behavior. The state also brought forth George Kendley, a trolley car conductor, who remembered seeing Mary Phagan walking in the direction of the factory at about noon on the day of the murder. The defense rebutted with people who made incriminating remarks about Kendley. One man claimed to have heard the trolley

conductor say that "Frank was nothing but an old Jew and
they ought to take him out and hang him anyhow." Another
recalled that Kendley expressed the sentiment "that Frank
was guilty as a snake, and should be hung. . . ." [29] The remarks attributed to the trolley conductor were less important
for their content than for the attitudes expressed. It was the
first time that any indication of overt anti-Semitism appeared
in the court.

4

The lawyers for both sides finally concluded their cases
after four weeks of testimony. The state received whatever
advantage might accrue from having both the opening and
closing arguments before the jury with Frank's lawyers sand-
wiched in between.

In his summary argument, one of Solicitor Dorsey's assistants suggested that Frank was a Dr. Jekyll and Mr. Hyde,
presenting one facet of his personality to friends and relatives
and another to the girls working in the pencil factory. Arnold
and Rosser accused the prosecutors as well as the city detectives of misrepresentation and duplicity. Arnold suggested
that "if Frank hadn't been a Jew there would never have been
any prosecution against him" and that the entire case was the
"greatest frame-up in the history of the state." Finally, he
likened the scene in Atlanta to the Dreyfus affair in France:
"the savagry and venom is . . . the same." [30]

Though Rosser and Arnold, as well as Hooper, spoke well,
Hugh Dorsey received the most extravagant praise from the
newspapers. In his concluding argument, characterized by the
Constitution as "one of the most wonderful efforts ever made
at the Georgia bar," [31] the Solicitor reviewed the state's evidence and asked the jurors to bear in mind that Rosser and
Arnold, "two of the ablest lawyers in the country" had been
unable to break Jim Conley. "They" introduced the race
question, Dorsey reminded the jurors, "the word Jew never

escaped our lips." The prosecutor spoke kind words of Disraeli, Judah P. Benjamin, and the Strauss brothers, but he also emphasized the activities of such Jewish criminals as Abe Ruef, the former Mayor of San Francisco, Abe Hummell, "the rascally lawyer," and "Schwartz, who killed a little girl in New York. . . . [The Jews] rise to heights sublime, but they also sink to the lowest depths of degradation!" Dorsey dismissed the argument that Frank had a good character. He noted that Judas Iscariot and Benedict Arnold were considered honorable men before they committed their treacherous deeds.[32]

"A perfect case"[33] is what the Solicitor claimed the state had against the accused. He cited, as proof of this, part of a letter the defense had introduced which Frank wrote to his uncle on the day of the murder. The letter read, in part: "It is too short a time since you left for anything startling to have developed down here." Dorsey found this sentence "pregnant with significance, which [bore] the ear-marks of the guilty conscience. . . ." "Too short! Too short! Startling!" Dorsey fulminated before the jury. "But 'Too short a time,' and that itself shows that the dastardly deed was done in an incredibly short time."[34] Dorsey also mentioned in his summation that Mrs. Frank did not visit her husband until two weeks after he was imprisoned because she knew that he was guilty.[35]

Then the Solicitor moved on to the murder notes. He contended that proof that these notes had originated in a white man's mind was supplied by the use of the words "Negro" and "did." If Conley had relied upon his own vocabulary, Dorsey argued, he would have employed the expressions "nigger" and "done" since Negroes never used the other terms. At this point Rosser interrupted the Solicitor and disputed Dorsey on the words that Conley had written. Rosser noted that according to the stenographic report of the trial, Conley had used the word "did" on a number of occasions. Dorsey responded that the court stenographer must have recorded the word incorrectly, but the stenographer then

announced to the court that "the shorthand character for
'did' is very different from 'done' [and] there's no reason for a
reporter confusing the two." Dorsey refused to yield, however, and announced, "Let it go then, I'll trust the jury on
it." [36] He then resumed his summary.

Dramatic incidents in the courtroom punctuated the Solicitor's final talk. On the first day that he spoke, Mary
Phagan's mother "became hysterical and let out several piercing screams. . . ." She was overcome with emotion just at the
moment that Dorsey pointed his finger at Frank and declared
that the child gave her life to defend her honor. Dorsey's
"impassioned reference to the slain girl . . . had many in the
courtroom in tears." [37] Dorsey's performance obviously
pleased the crowd. As he left the courthouse each day the
admiring throng greeted him with thunderous ovations.

The temper of the crowd frightened the editors of all three
Atlanta dailies. They petitioned Judge Roan not to let the
case go to the jury on a Saturday, the second day of Dorsey's
summation, because they feared that if the jurors' verdict
came that night, a riot similar to that of 1906 might occur.[38]
Judge Roan agreed, and that Saturday afternoon he con-
ferred, in the presence of the jury, with Atlanta's Chief of
Police and the Colonel of the Fifth Georgia Regiment as to
how they would handle the crowds after the announcement
of the verdict. Both men were known, by sight, to the jurors,
and the defense later alleged that this indicated to the jury
that a riot would ensue should Frank be declared innocent.[39]
In any case Roan interrupted Dorsey before he concluded his
final argument, thus forcing a recess until the following
Monday.

As Hugh Dorsey entered the courtroom to conclude his
argument, the assembled throng welcomed him with a noisy,
enthusiastic demonstration. The apprehensive judge demanded that the sheriff quell the demonstration and threatened to clear the courtroom if his order was not obeyed.
"Your honor," the Sheriff responded, "that is the only way it

can be stopped." [40] Roan then held a hurried conference with defense counsel and suggested that neither they nor their client be present to hear the jury's verdict. Rosser and Arnold agreed. They neither asked for, nor received, Frank's consent for this action.[41]

The solicitor then proceeded to speak. After three hours, he finally ended "the most remarkable speech which has ever been delivered in the Fulton county courthouse" with the words, "Guilty, guilty, guilty!" The chimes of a nearby Catholic Church tolled the hour of noon as Dorsey finished his oration. The punctuation of the bell before each of the concluding words "cut like a chill to the hearts of many who shivered involuntarily." Judge Roan then charged the jurors, and they retired to make their decision.[42]

The jury—a representative cross-section of Atlanta's residents [43]—needed less than four hours to decide the case. When the men returned to their chairs, the courtroom was empty except for a few officials, newspapermen, and friends of the defendant. "It took no student of human nature to read . . . the verdict. . . . On the face of each juror was the drawn look of men who had been compelled through duty to do an awful thing—to consign a fellow creature to the gallows. There was no mistaking that look. The strongest of the men shook as if some strange ailment had stricken them [sic]." The foreman pronounced the judgment: Guilty! But as Judge Roan attempted to poll the individual members, their responses were drowned by the din which had erupted from the outside as soon as a reporter had thrust his head out of the window and shouted the verdict. Roan requested that the windows be shut. Again he took his poll; each juror responded, "guilty." Prudence, Roan decided, required the sentencing at some other time. He therefore adjourned the court.[44]

Leo Frank awaited the verdict in his prison cell. Surrounded by cheerful friends and relatives, he appeared confident that the jury would acquit him. But at 5:25 P.M. a friend brought the news, which cast a sudden pall over the group. "My God!" Frank exclaimed, "even the jury was influenced by mob law. I am as innocent as I was one year ago." Mrs. Frank sobbed bitterly and then fainted. "The silence was dreadful." [45]

But outside the courtroom "a mob thousands strong . . . went wild with joy. . . ." [46] The next day the *Constitution* reported that trolley car conductors left their stations and joined the rejoicing throngs; women in fashionable social circles clapped hands; the local ballpark posted the news on the scoreboard and fans in the grandstands cheered wildly. Around the courthouse "a veritable honeycomb of humanity" yelled itself hoarse as the

cry of guilty took winged flight from lip to lip. It traveled like the rattle of musketry. Then came a combined shout that rose to the sky. Hats went into the air. Women wept and shouted by turns. As Solicitor Dorsey appeared in the doorway of the courthouse while the crowd yelled its reception of the Frank verdict, there came a mighty roar. . . . The Solicitor reached no further than the sidewalk. While mounted men rode like Cossacks through the human swarm, three muscular men slung Mr. Dorsey on their shoulders and passed him over the heads of the crowd across the street to his office. With hat raised and tears coursing down his cheeks, the victor in Georgia's most noted criminal battle was tumbled over a shrieking throng that wildly proclaimed its admiration. Few will live to see another such demonstration.[47]

Judge Roan and members of the jury were also greeted with applause and huzzahs as they left the courthouse. Mary Phagan's stepfather gratefully shook hands with each of the jurors, in turn, as they posed for newspaper photographers. The minister of Mary Phagan's church later recalled that the jury did exactly as he wished, and at the time, he "applauded the verdict." [48]

Throughout the state Georgians received the news of Frank's guilt "with great enthusiasm." In Greensboro, "a wave of actual jubilation swept over the city," and *The Savannah Morning News* editorialized that "those who viewed the case . . . on the evidence and independently of their sympathies or their wishes are not surprised by the verdict." [49]

The day after Frank had been found guilty, Judge Roan secretly convened the principals in the case and sentenced Frank to hang. The proceedings had been arranged quickly and without fanfare because Roan feared the consequences of having Frank appear in public again. Not even Mrs. Frank was informed of the event. She did hear about it, but by the time she reached the court her husband was just returning to jail. She accompanied him. [50]

In a public statement, after Roan's sentencing, Frank's lawyers characterized the previous weeks in the courtroom as "a farce and not in any way a trial." They condemned the fact that "the temper of the public mind . . . invaded the courtroom and invaded the streets and made itself manifest at every turn the jury made; and it was just as impossible for this jury to escape the effects of this public feeling as if they had been turned loose and had been permitted to mingle with the people." The attorneys then announced their intention to appeal the decision. [51]

5

Frank's lawyers apparently assumed that they were handling a routine murder case. They completely misjudged the nature and extent of the public hostility against Frank, as was evident by their failure to request a change of venue. Furthermore, their trial strategy was not well planned. By cross-examining Jim Conley for sixteen hours—without eliciting anything favorable from him—they merely reinforced in the minds of the jurors the impression that the Negro had been telling the truth. But they also managed to obtain Conley's admission that he had defecated at the bottom of the elevator shaft on the morning of the murder. The next day, however, police noticed formed feces at the bottom of the shaft before the elevator descended and mashed it. Since the elevator always touched the bottom of the shaft when it reached the basement, the question of whose waste was observed should have been pursued. If it was indeed Conley's, then the elevator had not been to the basement since the previous morning. And if the elevator had not been to the basement, how did Mary Phagan's body get there? It is possible that an exploration of this single point could have blown open the state's entire case because the prosecution insisted that the girl had been murdered on the second floor and had been removed to the lower level via the elevator. Abraham Cahan, the famous editor of the Jewish *Forward*, later lamented that "when one reads the long stenographic report of this cross examination [of Conley] one cannot help thinking that in New York or Chicago, you could find dozens of lawyers who would have done a much better job." [52]

Moreover, Frank's lawyers showed little foresight or imagination. On direct examination by the prosecution, the city bacteriologist discussed blood chips allegedly found in the workroom opposite Frank's office where the girl supposedly had been murdered. In cross-examining this witness, the defense attorneys did not inquire about the strands of hair which the prosecution claimed had been pulled from Mary Phagan's head. In 1914 a more zealous investigator would get the bacteriologist to admit that he could find no resemblance between the hair given to him for analysis and the hair found on the dead girl. [53] Also, the defense called Northern friends, Jews, and factory employees—who really could not have said otherwise and retained their positions—to substantiate Frank's good character. The prosecution rebutted this character evidence with testimony of native Southerners who swore that Frank did have a reputation for ungentlemanly behavior. As was to be expected, the jury found the testimony of its neighbors more credible than that of the "alien" strangers. In the early 1950s the Anti-Defamation League in Atlanta commissioned a study of the Frank case. After considerable investigation DeWitt H. Roberts, the author of the work, concluded that "the defense of Leo Frank was one of the most ill-conducted in the history of Georgia jurisprudence." [54]

6

In retrospect it is difficult to see how the outcome of the trial could have been different. As Edmund M. Morgan, co-author of *The Legacy of Sacco and Vanzetti*, observed, "every experienced judge and every experienced lawyer know [that] it is almost impossible to secure a verdict which runs counter to the settled convictions of the community." [55] And in the South, where, according to Ellen Glasgow, the Virginia novelist, the people never developed the habit of independent thought—"there was, indeed, no need for thinking when everybody thought alike, or, rather, when to think differently meant to be ostracized"— [56] dire social and economic consequences awaited those jurors who would forget tradition and ignore their fellow citizens' attitudes toward Leo Frank.

Atlantans had freely expressed their hostile views both before and during the trial. On the day the jury rendered its verdict *The Augusta Chronicle* summarized the existing feeling:

The last day of the criminal trial which has absorbed the city's attention for four weeks was marked by an impatience which was evident in every move of the public. There was a nervous tension apparent in the very atmosphere today. Wherever two or three persons were gathered there was a discussion of the probable outcome, of the time the jury would be out . . . and more than all else—of the possibility of "something happening" in the case of acquittal.

That is the black shadow which has hung over Atlanta for a month—the unspoken fear of "trouble"—of violence. Nobody will admit there was such a danger—but the feeling was there. There was a fear of the same element which brought about the great Atlanta riot of 1907 [sic]—the lower element; the people of the back streets and the alleys; the near-beer saloons and the pool rooms.

That is recognized as the real reason the trial of Leo Frank was abruptly adjourned Saturday and a recess taken until today. The Saturday night crowd in Atlanta, beer-drinking, blind-tiger frequenting, is not an assemblage loving law and order. A verdict which displeased these sansculottes of the Marietta street might well result in trouble should it be published in flaring extras after dark.

The report that state troops have been given some kind of warning to be ready will not down. . . . There was vigorous denial that any steps had been contemplated—but still the rumors persisted, and even yet it still persists.

The Atlanta papers have been wiser than in the days before the riot when the headlines of at least one paper inflamed the mob to action. There has been no word of the fear of violence, no mention of troops or riot; a careful avoidance of stirring up passion except in the printing of the court record, with its inflammatory speeches. Atlanta wants no more trouble of the kind which brought a reign of terror in 1907 [sic].[57]

The antagonism toward Frank expressed itself more clearly than just a "spirit" in the air. The defense attorneys and Judge Roan had received communications during the trial to the effect that they would not leave the courtroom alive if the "damned Jew" were turned loose. There is some indication that the jurors were similarly threatened. Crowds outside the courthouse chanted, "Hang the Jew." As early as May, 1913, "a well-known Atlanta woman" wrote to the Georgian that this "is the first time a Jew has ever been in any serious trouble in Atlanta, and see how ready is every one to believe the worst of him." [58]

The Governor of Georgia had consulted with the commanding officer of the national guard regiment in Atlanta just before the trial ended, and had alerted him to the possible danger of a riot after the jury returned its verdict. The militia commandant said his troops would be ready if necessary. Two years later a North Georgia newspaperman, who had attended the trial, wrote, "There is no use mincing words when a human life is at stake. If the jury in the Frank case had brought in a verdict of 'not guilty' the defendant would have been lynched." [59]

CHAPTER III

An American Dreyfus

ALTHOUGH THE FRANK CASE attracted widespread attention in the South, few people in the North heard about it until after the trial ended. Very soon thereafter, however, the news spread among the most powerful and influential Jews in the country. Frank's Atlanta friends considered him the victim of a bloodthirsty anti-Semitic attack. *The Macon Daily Telegraph* reported their reaction the day after Frank had been sentenced to hang:

. . . the long case and its bitterness has hurt the city greatly in that it has opened a seemingly impassable chasm between the people of the Jewish race and the Gentiles. It has broken friendships of years, has divided the races, brought about bitterness deeply regretted by all factions. The friends who rallied to the defense of Leo Frank feel that racial prejudice has much to do with the verdict. They are convinced that Frank was not prosecuted but persecuted. They refuse to believe he had a fair trial. . . .[1]

Convinced that justice had not triumphed, Frank's Atlanta friends sought assistance from Northern Jews who might be able to suggest a future course of action. Among those consulted were members of the American Jewish Committee.

I

The American Jewish Committee had been established in 1906 for the purpose of aiding Jews "in all countries where

their civil or religious rights were endangered or denied." [2] It
had been formed by a group of wealthy Jews, of German and
American descent, who were concerned about the precarious
position of American Jewry at the beginning of the twentieth
century. For the most part, the founders of the American
Jewish Committee had either come to the United States in the
mid-nineteenth century or were descended from those Jews
who had come somewhat earlier. In their own lifetime they
had experienced no organized persecution and had found unlimited economic opportunities. As they prospered, they
moved up the social ladder, leaving many of the old-world
Jewish practices behind them. [3]

In the 1880s groups of Eastern European Jews began mi-
grating to this country. The Americanized Jews had qualms
about the influx of these people and regarded them as a threat
to their own status in this country. They feared that the
peculiar costumes and customs of the Eastern Europeans
would reflect adversely upon all Jews in this country. But
despite these feelings, no concerted effort was made to thwart
the attempts of those who insisted upon coming. Beginning in
the early part of the twentieth century, the American Jews
even encouraged immigration so that the Eastern Europeans
could obtain refuge from persecution. Once the newcomers
arrived, the Americans provided them with a good deal of
assistance. By helping the Eastern Europeans adjust to the
New World, the established Jews hoped to lessen the anti-
Semitism which, they correctly assumed, might spring up
after the new immigrants settled here. One rabbi of long resi-
dence in the United States stated the issue cogently. The
future of American Judaism will be powerfully affected by
the Russian Jews, he noted. For "our own safety [and] our
own good name" we must take them by the hand and show
them how Jews live in the United States. [4]

2

While the members of the Northern Jewish community
made efforts to assimilate the immigrant Jews, the leaders of
the New South—the railroad magnates and owners of cotton
mills and factories—in their endeavor to build an industrial
community patterned after the North, actively sought the
immigration of foreign white labor. Southern state govern-
ments established immigration bureaus in the hope of attract-
ing Northern European settlers.[5] *The Atlanta Constitution*
explained that the Georgia Immigrant Association wanted
only the "Best Type" of immigrant. "Best Type" euphemis-
tically meant Northern European stock and not "the lower-
class foreigners who have swarmed into northern cities."
Manufacturers Record, a major Southern business publication
which frequently spoke out on the South's immigrant need,
stated the position more succinctly: "The South will have
human sewage under no consideration." The Southern experi-
ment proved abortive, however, since few "desirable" immigrants came, and on at least one occasion "carefully selected
Northwest Europeans" turned out to be natives of Southern
Europe.[6]

Disillusionment with the type of foreigners arriving killed
the state government programs for selective immigration.
Except for the New South's champions, the people welcomed
an end to the policy of encouraging settlers. By the onset of
Woodrow Wilson's administration, in 1913, Southern Congressmen were practically unanimous in their opposition to
immigration from Southern and Eastern Europe.[7]

3

Between 1880 and 1915 Italians and Jews outnumbered all
other Southern and Eastern Europeans entering this country.
Several Italian settlements were established in the South dur-

ing the 1890s and invariably suffered local harassment. Nineteen Italians were lynched in Louisiana during the decade
because they seemed to fraternize with Negroes and because
many Southerners regarded them as just "another inferior
race to be disciplined." [8] Czechs and Slovaks also had difficulty in the South. Forty years after they had established a
colony south of Petersburg, Virginia, the "natives" still remained unreconciled to their presence.[9]

Jews, on the other hand, had been in the South since
Colonial times. Southern attitudes toward them had been an
amalgam of affection, tolerance, curiosity, suspicion, and re-
jection. These views, which for the most part characterized
Northerners also, might come to the fore singly, and in
combination, on different occasions. What complicated the
expression of these feelings, however, was the traditional
Southern antipathy to those whose behavior and origins
differed, even slightly, from those of the dominant group of
white, Anglo-Saxon Protestants. During periods of relative
calm Jews suffered no harm; during periods of stress, though,
ancient, and often unconscious, antagonisms became more
marked. During the great spasms of society, Jews were often
pointed to as the source of the troubles.

Some prejudice toward Jews existed in the American
colonies, but there did not seem to be much difference in
prejudice between the North and the South. Although voting
privileges were generally restricted to Protestants, the Jews,
in fact, occupied a relatively high status in Colonial times.
Merle Curti has attributed this "to the fact that they contributed to commercial prosperity. . . . The jealousy frequently occasioned by such success was offset in part by the
common assumption in a rapidly expanding economy that
there was room for everyone to get ahead." [10] Later on, after
most of the political disabilities had been abolished, the Jews
in this country still comprised an infinitesimal percentage of
the population, and until the Civil War were not subjected to
any organized persecution.

Since the main problem of the ante-bellum South revolved around slavery, Jews did not loom as a threat because, in their quest for amalgamation, they had accepted the institution. At one point this was, indeed, the test of a true Southerner. Thus Jews could rise to the highest positions in the South and often did. A South Carolina Jew served as Chief Justice of the state Supreme Court before the Civil War, and his son served as governor of the state after the war. Florida sent David Yulee to the Senate in 1845, and eight years later Louisiana elected Judah P. Benjamin to the same body. During the Civil War not only did Benjamin serve as Confederate Secretary of State, but the Quartermaster-General, the Surgeon-General, several Congressmen, and other high Confederate officials were Jews.[11]

Jews also participated actively in the professional and commercial life of the region. In Atlanta, for example, a Jew founded the city's largest department store, and Abraham Cahan, editor of a prominent New York City Yiddish language newspaper in the early part of the twentieth century, noted that it was fairly common for the large Southern law firms to have both Jewish and Gentile partners.[12]

Coexisting with this apparent acceptance of Jews, however, there remained ever-present and persisitent elements of anti-Semitic feeling. During the Jacksonian era, for example, Jews were considered "rebels against God's purpose," and many a Southern Christian mother lulled her children to sleep with fables of Jewish vices. In one popular nursery rhyme, "The Jew's Daughter" enticed a young Gentile boy into her home, "where no one would hear his call":

> She sat him on a chair of gold
> And gave him sugar sweet
> She laid him on the dresser
> And killed him like a sheep.

An incident concerning the sale of a slave girl to a Jewish woman in 1859 reveals the prevalent Judaeophobic attitudes.

On the day the slave was to be sent to her new mistress she disappeared. After a long search, her master found the child hiding under a bed. When queried about her actions, the girl pleaded that she did not want to be sold to a Jew. "I don't want to go to live with Miss Isaacs," the youngster explained. "Miss Isaacs is a Jew; and if the Jews kill the Lord and Master, what won't they do to a poor little nigger like me?" [13]

Although Judah P. Benjamin became Secretary of State in the Confederacy, during the Civil War Southern Jews aroused "pronounced anti-Semitic sentiment" for the first time. They were accused of being "merciless speculators, army slackers, and blockade-runners across the land frontiers to the North." Benjamin remained a popular target throughout the war. Almost every one of his political enemies referred to his Jewish antecedents when attacking him, and one critic applied to him the sobriquet "Judas Iscariot Benjamin." Denunciation of Jewish merchants was a common practice in many towns of Georgia, and the Southern Illustrated News observed, "All that the Jew possesses is a plentiful lot of money, together with the scorn of the world." [14]

In some quarters of the South, after the Civil War, Jews were considered worthy members of society. This opinion prevailed, primarily, among those who wished for commercial growth and those who hoped to imitate Northern industrial accomplishments. Hence one newspaper editor hailed their presence "as an auspicious sign." "Where there are no Jews," the writer continued, "there is no money to be made." Another newspaper noted that "a sober, steadier, and more industrious and law abiding class of population . . . [does] not exist." [15] In 1900 a leading Atlanta merchant was held up as "a typical exponent of the characteristics of his race [who] has happily exemplified that spirit and progressive enterprise for which his people are noted all over the world." [16]

Jews also occupied a unique social position in the South. One peddler recalled that the Christians he dealt with held him in special regard. Frequently asked about the Bible, he was often required to settle religious disputes "because I was a Jew and they all looked upon me as an authority." He also noted that some rural Southerners were so backward that they considered him as some sort of Christian. "I remember well," he reminisced, "being asked time and again 'Are you a Baptist Jew or a Methodist Jew?' " And Harry Golden, who has insisted that the South has a tradition of philo-Semitism, wrote that in the rural South people held the Jewish population almost as a private possession: "He is 'our Jew' to small-town Southerners, and they often take care of him with a zeal and devotion otherwise bestowed only on the Confederate monument in the square." [17]

Despite indications of affection, a strong anti-Semitic bias remained. In an 1878 campaign speech Senator John T. Morgan of Alabama referred to a candidate as a "Jew-dog," and the following year Senator Morgan opposed the appointment of a postmaster in Montgomery because he had been indorsed "by a parcel of Jews." In Nashville, Tennessee, in 1878, Christian mothers threatened to withdraw their children from a private school for girls after two Jews had been accepted. The principal yielded to the pressure and rescinded the enrollments. And in a Rome, Georgia, courtroom in 1873, the plaintiff's attorney declared that one cannot accept the word of a Jew "even under oath." [18] Louisiana had anti-Semitic demonstrations in the late 1880s. Then, in 1893, farmers in the Bayou state wrecked Jewish stores in a particularly harsh outburst. That same year Mississippi night riders burned Jewish farmhouses, and a Baltimore minister preached: "Of all the dirty creatures who have befouled this earth, the Jew is the slimiest." [19]

Religious teachings may have intensified these attacks and, in fact, may have generated them. Horace M. Kallen, the Jewish philosopher, believed that the roots of anti-Semitism lay in Christians teaching "that the Jews are the enemies of God and of mankind. . . ." [20] And J. F. Brown, in his study, "The Origin of the Anti-Semitic Attitude," concluded that

Christians believe "the Savior was murdered by Jews. Most enlightened adults would scoff at this as a reason for anti-Semitism. The fact that we all heard of it at an impressionable age, the fact that we heard it from parents who themselves entertained at least a latent anti-Semitism, makes it an important factor and means that we probably all harbor some anti-Semitism unconsciously." [21] The late Southern journalist, W. J. Cash, has written that "All the protests of scholars have been quite unavailing to erase from the popular mind [in the South] the notion that it was the Jew who crucified Jesus." And two other Southerners have recalled that in their childhood, "The veriest infant was made acquainted with the lapses of the ancient Jews, and all God's wrath at their behavior was thundered in his ears." [22]

Religious factors alone cannot account for the marked upsurge in anti-Semitic feelings at the end of the nineteenth century. Psychologists have found that prejudicial attacks are likely to occur among those groups that feel most uncomfortable and ill at ease with the world. Deprivation, whether it be social, economic, or emotional, seems characteristic of the bigoted person. To alleviate the built-up anger, reduce the accumulated tension, and achieve some modicum of satisfaction, the anguished individual generally attributes his plight to some vulnerable and seemingly defenseless minority group. He sees it as the harbinger of evil because consciously and realistically he cannot acknowledge the true cause of his situation. It is also the most distressed people who are aggressively hostile to those outside the pale, and fiercely proud of their own community's accomplishments. [23] In his own studies John Higham discovered that at the end of the nineteenth century anti-Semitism in this country "was strongest in those sectors of the population where a particularly explosive combination of social discontent and nationalistic aggression prevailed." [24]

To a large extent, all the above generalizations aptly characterize significant segments of the Southern population at the

beginning of the twentieth century. For the most part, as C.
Vann Woodward has pointed out, the depressed urban
workers in the South during this period were "frustrated in
their age-long, and eternally losing struggle against a hostile
industrial economy." Hence they were receptive "to exciting
crusades against more vulnerable antagonists: against anything strange, and therefore evil." [25] Southerners, fearing also
that outsiders would undermine regional mores, defended
their version of the American creed with fanatical zeal. As a
group, no people in the United States at the turn of the century was more insecure, harassed, indigent, paranoid, and nationalistic than those living below the Mason-Dixon line.
Thus the culture provided a rich soil for the fertilization of
anti-Semitic aggression.

4

In the decade before the first World War anti-Semitic outbursts throughout the country upset thoughtful American
Jews.[26] Fifteen hundred hostile workers threatened to strike
a Massachusetts shoe factory in 1906 unless the firm dismissed
its nine Jewish employees. A year later a faculty member at
Columbia's Teachers College asked a colleague to refrain
from attending a university banquet because he had invited a
friend "who does not like Jews." And during the academic
year 1913–1914 some students in Utica, New York, organized a "Kill Kyke Klan." [27]

Antagonistic attitudes toward Jews existed in Georgia also.
There had been a prosperous and tightly knit Jewish community in Georgia since Colonial times. Jews had always
occupied a relatively high occupational status,[28] and though
there had been prejudice toward them [29] no major problems
developed with Gentile neighbors—except during the Civil
War—before the twentieth century. In Atlanta the Jews
never constituted a significant percentage of the city's population, but with the influx of Russian Jews in the 1890s prob-

lems developed between the new immigrants and the established Jewish community, and between the Russians and the
working class Atlantans. The German Jews, who had come
earlier, "blackballed" the Russians from their social clubs and
did not encourage them to reside in their neighborhoods.
Eventually the older and newer immigrants did work har-
moniously in establishing some of the Jewish community's
social services, but at least through 1915 "there were constant
overtones of dissension between the leaders of the two
groups." [30]

The newly arrived Europeans came into greater contact
with Negroes than did the older Jewish community of Atlanta. This inadvertently led to conflict between Gentiles and
Jews. The newcomers purchased small businesses, including
saloons, where Negroes gathered. Sensual pictures of nude
white women allegedly decorated the walls of many of these
establishments, and rumors circulated that even the labels on
the liquor bottles were designed to incite Negro passions.
Many Atlantans assumed that the saloons "served as a gathering place and as a breeding-ground for criminals." When
Negroes got drunk and caused disturbances, the nearby
whites reproached the saloon owners for the mischief.[31]

The Jews also found themselves blamed for the chaotic
conditions in the city. They were charged with the operation
of "dope dives," gambling dens, and brothels which flourished
in Atlanta.[32] Whereas the American Jews of long standing in
this country had at one time been separated in the public mind
from the more recent immigrants, after 1900, John Higham
wrote, "the differentiation lessened in actuality and almost
vanished in popular thought." [33] This worked to the dis-
advantage of Atlanta's older Jewish residents. Adding to the
stereotyped impressions were the major muckraking stories in
national periodicals and the report of a federal government
investigating committee which concluded that Jews predom-
inated in the American white slave trade.[34] While none of
these reports named Atlanta Jews among the offenders, the

publicity, combined with white Atlantans' preconceived attitudes, led to increased antagonisms toward the Jews.[35]

The negative feelings alarmed the Jews, especially when they were expressed under the guise of objectivity or praise. In Georgia, Lucian Lamar Knight, the patrician historian of the state, ostensibly praised Jews for their commercial, and other, talents. He noted, for example, that Jews "are money makers to such an extent that the roll-call of the whole Hebrew population can be made from the tax-book." In good times and bad, he added, the Jew "has money to lend if not to burn and before he is ready to execute his will he owns the grocery-store, the meat-market, the grog-shop, the planning-mill, the newspaper, the hotel and the bank." E. A. Ross, one of the more prominent progressives, and a highly respected sociologist, stated quite clearly, in 1914: "The fact that pleasure-loving Jewish businessmen spare Jewesses, but pursue Gentile girls, excites bitter comment." [36]

One of the most outspoken anti-Semitic progressives, Burton J. Hendrick, frightened almost all Jews with his articles in *McClure's Magazine* in 1907 and 1913, on "The Great Jewish Invasion." In the first one he acknowledged that the Jews were ambitious and successful, in American terms, but he concluded by asking whether the Jew has "in himself the stuff of which Americans are made?" Hendrick's second work depicted the activities of a Jewish conspiracy seeking to seize the country. He catalogued the different industries in the United States which "the Jews absolutely control," and ominously predicted that the Jewish influence in this country within the next hundred years would "be almost preponderating." [37]

5

The growth of anti-Semitism in the United States paralleled the intensification of hostility toward Jews in France and Russia. In 1894 French military officials erroneously convicted Alfred Dreyfus, a captain attached to the general staff, of espionage. It "was not a deliberate plot to frame an innocent man. It was the outcome of a reasonable suspicion acted on by dislike, some circumstantial evidence and instinctive prejudice." [38] As more details became available, however, many people interpreted the sentence as a classic case of anti-Semitism. France eventually exonerated Dreyfus, but not until the country had been rocked by protests from both defendants and antagonists of the now celebrated Jew. The treatment accorded Dreyfus, and the fact that he had been convicted on the basis of circumstantial evidence and religious prejudice, later made his name a synonym for Jews who were unjustly accused and then persecuted because of their faith.[39]

The Dreyfus affair had barely passed from the news stories when, in 1911, a Jewish laborer in a Russian brick factory, Mendel Beiliss,[40] was arrested on the charge of having murdered a 12-year-old Christian boy so that he might use the child's blood for religious purposes. The allegation of "ritual murder" had been made against Jews as far back as 1144 in England, and records indicated that over one hundred such complaints had been made in Europe during the next eight centuries. Yet none received the worldwide attention accorded to Mendel Beiliss, who was imprisoned for two years before his court appearance in October, 1913. Ultimately, a jury of peasants acquitted him, but before the decision had been rendered, millions of people had been alerted to Beiliss' plight, had denounced the prejudicial slur, and had demanded that he be set free. In the United States mass protest meetings were held in Boston, Chicago, Cincinnati, and Milwaukee. New York's State Assembly went on record in opposition to the trial, and in the United States House of Representatives Chicago's Adolph Sabath introduced a resolution calling for the withdrawal of the "false, senseless, and unfounded charges and accusations. . . ." [41]

The attack on Dreyfus and Beiliss alarmed American Jews [42] and made them especially apprehensive about the in-

creasing number of anti-Semitic attacks in the United States.
The American Hebrew feared "that the different cases of discrimination [in this country] are not isloated instances but
part of a whole social tendency." [43] The circumstances surrounding Leo Frank's conviction filtered North shortly before Mendel Beiliss went on trial. Because of the treatment
accorded Dreyfus and Beiliss, and the accelerating hostility in
the United States, America's most prominent Jews received
the news from Atlanta with great anxiety.

6

At the beginning of September, 1913, Louis Marshall,
President of the American Jewish Committee, received three
letters from anguished Atlanta Jews. Two did not state their
problem clearly but the third spelled out what the others
mysteriously alluded to: "I would like to enlist your assistance in what is without doubt an American 'Dreyfus' case
that has just developed in Atlanta." The writer summarized
the Leo Frank case and stated his opinion that the "evidence
against Frank is purely prejudice and perjury. The feeling
against the D—— Jew is so bitter that the jury was intimidated and feared for their own lives, which undoubtedly
would have been in danger had any other verdict been
rendered." [44]

Other members of the American Jewish Committee received similar communications. Cyrus Adler, in Philadelphia,
heard that there was "violent anti-Jewish sentiment in Atlanta," and Cyrus Sulzberger, in New York, received a letter
from a resident of Columbus, Georgia, who had learned from
his Atlanta friends of the "fearful state of affairs as to this
case." [45] These letters were funneled to the American Jewish
Committee's president, and as he digested the material, he,
too, concluded "that this case is almost a second Dreyfus
affair." [46]

Marshall decided that "it would be most unfortunate if

anything were done . . . from the standpoint of the Jews. Whatever is done must be done as a matter of justice, and any action that is taken should emanate from non-Jewish sources." [47] The American Jewish Committee President understood the sensitivity that Southerners felt about Northern interference and feared that anti-Semitism would spread if Northern Jews led a campaign to overthrow the verdict against Frank. Marshall counseled that "there is only one way of dealing with this matter . . . and that is, in a quiet, unobtrusive manner to bring influence to bear on the Southern press," to use its position in creating "a wholesome public opinion which will free this unfortunate young man from the terrible judgment which rests against him." [48]

7

When the American Jewish Committee met in executive session to discuss Leo Frank for the first time, the general opinion seemed to be that Frank's conviction resulted both from an outburst of anti-Semitism in Atlanta and a newspaper campaign which forced the police to find a victim quickly. The members of the Committee interpreted the situation as another Dreyfus affair and proof of virulent anti-Semitism in the United States. They viewed what happened to Frank as a threat to the status of all American Jews. The Committee members were all the more alarmed because in recent decades anti-Semitic attacks had multiplied at a frightening pace, notwithstanding their vigorous efforts at counteraction. The conviction of Frank could not go unchallenged. American Jewry would have to fight back.

But in spite of its sympathy for Frank, and its concern over the position of the Jews in America, the American Jewish Committee did not act hastily. Jacob Schiff suggested raising a fund to help Frank, but another member thought that this would be imprudent because reports would circulate to the effect that other Jews were financing him "and the question would thus become a Jewish question. It is very important that we should prevent that." The Committee resolved to take no official action, although its members, as individuals, might do as they thought best. In explaining this action a year later, Louis Marshall noted that the American Jewish Committee did not want "to be considered as championing the cause of Jews who are convicted of crime." [49]

Frank's friends in Atlanta had been anxiously awaiting the American Jewish Committee's decision. After the Committee decided to refrain from giving any official assistance, Louis Marshall wrote to Herbert Haas, head of the legal firm defending Frank, that while the organization, as such, could not make any contributions towards a legal fund, a number of the members had indicated that if a new trial were granted, and additional finances were necessary, they would be willing to contribute "to a reasonable extent." [50] But despite the cautious tone of this letter, Marshall, in his private capacity, would provide vigorous support and would actively participate in all the legal decisions in the months to follow. Whatever efforts Northern Jews desired to make, however, would have to remain in abeyance. Legal avenues had not been exhausted and prudence dictated patience until the appeals court issued its verdict.

CHAPTER IV

The First Appeal

I

WHILE NORTHERN JEWS deliberated upon a course of action, the Atlanta attorneys prepared their appeal. They did not intend to let the jurors' verdict rest without a fight, and no sooner did the trial end than work began on the next brief. Leonard Roan, the trial judge, would be the first to hear their plea. According to a 1906 Constitutional Amendment in Georgia, an appeal in a capital case could be based only upon errors in law, and the appellate judge would not have the authority to reevaluate the evidence.[1] Frank's counsel, therefore, stressed the procedural irregularities which prevailed during the trial.

The appeal contained one hundred and fifteen points, including affidavits attesting to the alleged prejudice of two of the jurors, A. H. Henslee and M. Johenning, towards the defendant. Eight people swore that they heard Henslee express hostile sentiments towards Frank before the trial commenced, and one recalled that shortly after Frank's arrest he overheard Henslee remark: "I am glad they indicted the God damn Jew. They ought to take him out and lynch him. And if I get on that jury I'd hang that Jew sure." Three members of one family swore to having heard prejudicial remarks by Johenning.[2]

The defense also submitted affidavits from Atlantans who witnessed the trial attesting that the jury had heard the

crowds outside the courtroom and had seen the public demonstrations. Other defense motions included the assertion that
Conley's testimony, relating to Frank's alleged sexual perver-
sions, should never have been admitted into the courtroom;
and that the verdict was both without evidence to support it
and contrary to the weight of the evidence.[3]

To the charges made by the defense, Solicitor Dorsey
countered with affidavits from eleven of the twelve jurors
(the twelfth was out of town on business), who swore that
they did not hear cheering or applause from outside the
courtroom before they had rendered their verdict. They contended that they made up their minds strictly on the evidence
presented and that the public clamor did not affect their decision.[4] Henslee and Johenning made additional statements,
swearing that they entered the jury box ready to be convinced by either side. Both qualified their affidavits to some
degree. Henslee indicated that together with others he had
read about Frank in the newspapers and had discussed him
with various people but that he had never formed any opinion
"further than that 'whoever killed Mary Phagan ought to
hang.'" Johenning stated that he had at one time indicated
that the outlook for Frank, based upon newspaper accounts,
did not "seem to be very bright for him," and that he (Johenning) thought that Frank would "have a hard time in getting
loose." [5]

Once again Rosser and Arnold presented Frank's case before Judge Roan, and once again Dorsey and Hooper argued
for the state. The defense attorneys underscored their original
arguments: the evidence did not warrant the verdict and
prejudice precluded a fair trial. "It is the most horrible persecution of a Jew since the death of Christ," Arnold exclaimed.[6]

Dorsey and Hooper maintained that Frank had received a
fair trial. Hooper dismissed the defense's assertion that demonstrations might have prevented the jury from conscien-
tiously doing its duty. If such were the case, Hooper ex-

plained, the state would never get a conviction, for each defendant could arrange for his friends to demonstrate in his behalf, and this would cause an automatic mistrial. The state also contended that affirmative action by Judge Roan would put the jury system in peril and shatter the laws of the state. To grant a new trial, Dorsey concluded, would be "a slap in the face of justice."[7]

Judge Roan denied the defense's motion. Along with his decision, however, the Judge issued a most peculiar statement, one which could not help but gratify Frank's supporters and puzzle everyone else:

I have thought about this case more than any other I have tried. I am not certain of the man's guilt. With all the thought I have put on this case, I am not thoroughly convinced that Frank is guilty or innocent. The jury was convinced. There is no room to doubt that. I feel it is my duty to order that the motion for a new trial be overruled.[8]

Frank's counsel may have been disappointed with Roan's decision, but they certainly were not disheartened. "I recall your remarks upon the subject of incompetent and weak judges," Herbert Haas wrote to Louis Marshall. "The presiding officer in this case tries to do his duty, but I fear he is lamentably weak." The Atlanta attorney viewed the future optimistically. "Our Supreme Court," Haas continued in his letter, "has held more than once that it will reverse the judgment of the lower court declining a motion for a new trial where, in the bill of exceptions, it is certified that the presiding judge himself is in doubt as to the guilt of the defendant."[9]

The Atlanta Georgian found difficulty in accepting Roan's "amazing decision." "Could anything be more astonishing than this?" the *Georgian* asked in a lead editorial. If Roan does not know whether Frank is guilty, how can the people know? "It would seem that Judge Roan has written into the case an objection so large and overshadowing that the other 115 sink into insignificance and that the [Georgia] Supreme

Court will order a new trial on Judge Roan's decision, if for
no other reason." When the trial judge is in doubt, the editorial concluded, "is it not time to pause before legal murder
is added to the long list of other crimes in our State?" [10]

The *Georgian*, however, expressed a minority opinion in
the state. The *Waycross Herald* and the Greensboro *Herald-
Journal*, on the other hand, expressed what appeared to have
been the sentiment of most Georgians. The *Waycross Herald*
editorialized: "It was none of Judge Roan's business to be
convinced of Frank's guilt. . . . The jury was fully convinced and said so. It was purely up to the jury and not Judge
Roan." The *Herald-Journal*, while "surprised" at Roan's
"ignorance," sarcastically noted that "there are plenty of
people right here in Greensboro, Greene County, and else-
where that know better than that. Why, they've never heard
one word of evidence, as Judge Roan [has], but they know
absolutely that Frank is guilty. There are some mighty smart
people in the world." In the face of Roan's acknowledged
doubt, one Georgia jurist tried to explain the trial judge's
refusal to grant a new trial: "The judge must stand for reelection in a year." [11]

There is reason to surmise that Judge Roan believed Frank
innocent but feared an outburst of mob violence if he granted
another trial. He allegedly confided to a friend that had he
granted the defense's request, the Governor would "not have
enough troops to control the mob," which would certainly
have gathered as the news spread. Furthermore, in a conversation with another friend shortly after the decision, Roan
asked what people thought of his unusual comment. "I told
him," the friend later wrote to the Georgia Prison Commission and Governor John Slaton, "that some people thought it
was eminently proper for him to certify his doubts, and
others thought it highly improper. . . ." Speaking for himself, the friend claimed to have told Roan that "if I had felt as
[you] did, I certainly would have granted a new trial. [Roan]
then said, 'Well suppose I had, then that dreadful mob spirit

would have broken out again, and now when it goes to the
[Georgia] Supreme Court and comes back, maybe he can get
a fair trial.' " [12]

2

Six weeks after Roan denied the appeal for a new trial,
Rosser and Arnold argued Frank's case before the Georgia
Supreme Court. Because of the unusual nature of the case,
and its exceptionally long written record, counsel for both
sides were permitted to speak for two hours apiece, twice the
normal length. In such time Rosser and Arnold could do little
more than reiterate their oft-stated themes, that prejudice and
perjury had convicted Frank. They centered their appeal,
however, upon Judge Roan's expression of doubt. The defense attorneys mentioned half a dozen legal citations, showing that where the trial judge had expressed doubt, a new trial
had been granted. [13]

Thomas Felder, Georgia's Attorney-General, assisting
Hugh Dorsey in the presentation before the Supreme Court,
expressed the state's position that not only was the evidence
against Frank "mountain-high" but also that Judge Roan
should never have certified his doubt in the bill of exceptions. [14] After both sides completed their arguments, the attorneys retired to await the decision.

A month later the Supreme Court voted four to two to
uphold Judge Roan's ruling in denying a new trial. [15] Judge
Samuel C. Atkinson summarized the majority conclusions. He
dismissed the accusation of prejudicial jurors with the explanation that when the impartiality of the jurors is in question, the trial judge must decide the point and the Supreme
Court will not reverse the decision "unless it appears that
there has been abuse of discretion." Though spectators expressed their enthusiastic approval of events in the presence of
the jury on two occasions, this did not "impugn the fairness
of the trial." "The general rule," Judge Atkinson explained,

"is that the conduct of a spectator during the trial of a case will not be ground for a reversal of the judgment, unless a ruling upon such conduct is invoked from the judge at the time it occurs." [16]

Conley's testimony was ruled admissible not only because it explained his presence at the factory on the day of the murder but also because of the "peculiar opportunity" it afforded him to have knowledge of the crime. Although certain portions of the sweeper's testimony tended to incriminate Frank as the perpetrator of other crimes, this testimony was ruled admissible as "material and relevant" to the issue at hand. Conley's account of Frank's alleged previous conduct tended to render his tale more credible, Atkinson wrote, and also helped to explain Frank's motivation.[17]

Finally, when Atkinson came to the point concerning Judge Roan's personal expression of doubt, the Supreme Court Justice said that the rule is that even if the judge considers a case weak, if he overrules a motion for a new trial despite his own personal doubts, "his legal judgment expressed in overruling the motion will control; and if there is sufficient evidence to support the verdict, this court will not interfere because of the judge's oral expression as to his opinion." Taking the case as a whole, the Supreme Court majority found that

the evidence tended to show a practice, plan, system, or scheme on the part of the accused to have lascivious or adulterous association with certain of his employees and other women at his office or place of business. . . . It tended to show a motive on the part of the accused, inducing him to seek to have criminal intimacy with the girl who was killed, and, upon her resistance, to commit murder to conceal the crime.[18]

Justices Beck and Fish dissented from the majority but confined their argument to Conley's testimony. Using the same legal citations as the majority, they concluded that evidence as to Frank's alleged perversion should never have been admitted to the courtroom. "It is perfectly clear to us," they wrote, "that evidence of prior acts of lasciviousness committed by the defendant . . . did not tend to prove a preexisting design, system, plan, or scheme, directed toward the making of an assault upon the deceased or killing her to prevent its disclosure." To admit such evidence, they concluded, was calculated to prejudice the defendant in the minds of the jurors and thereby deprive him of a fair trial. Justices Beck and Fish made no reference to the issue of Judge Roan's expression of doubt, nor did they comment either upon the alleged prejudices of two of the jurors. They devoted their entire dissent to one main point: that evidence of any other crimes allegedly committed by the defendant was inadmissible.[19]

Six months after the trial, Frank's position seemed worse than it had been the previous August. But the prisoner's friends, who considered him to have been victimized by a gross miscarriage of justice, were not willing to accept the judgment of the Georgia Supreme Court as final. Renewed efforts would have to be made to rally support for Frank throughout the nation. And so those who were most concerned with his welfare began working harder to win his freedom.

CHAPTER V

Tom Watson
and William J. Burns

WHILE AWAITING THE Supreme Court's decision the defense prepared for the next trial. Although the lawyers had expected a ruling in Frank's favor, even an adverse decision necessitated preparation because another appeal would have to be made. The Atlanta attorneys had solicited Northern Jews for financial assistance, and with the money received they had hired additional associates, including the world-renowned detective, William J. Burns.[1] Investigators discovered new evidence, obtained new affidavits, and prevailed upon prosecution witnesses to repudiate their original testimony. Influential Jews alerted newspapers to Leo Frank's plight, and the nation's press published forceful editorials attacking Georgia justice. Mobilization of these forces required financing and leadership; Northern Jews provided both.

I

Soon after the Georgia Supreme Court had refused Frank a new trial, *The Atlanta Journal* published the results of an interview with the state biologist who had examined Mary Phagan's body shortly after her death. A microscopic study of one of the prosecution's main clues, the hair found on the lathe which Mary Phagan used, led the biologist to conclude that the hair did not belong to the dead girl. He relayed this information to Hugh Dorsey, but the Solicitor ignored it. The *Journal* confronted Dorsey with the biologist's findings and asked why he maintained that the hair belonged to Mary Phagan. "I did not depend on [the biologist's] testimony," Dorsey answered, "other witnesses in the case swore that the hair was that of Mary Phagan, and that sufficed to establish my point." [2] Atlanta's *Southern Ruralist*, which had condemned Dorsey's methods earlier, repeated its censure: "Prejudice is the mildest possible term for such conduct. Such official misrepresentation of fact . . . is the very murder of justice itself." [3]

During the next few weeks the defense released a series of affidavits from prosecution witnesses repudiating their testimony. Hearst's *Georgian* headlined the first retraction: "Plot to Hang Frank." The paper related how defense counsel obtained an affidavit from Albert McKnight, husband of the Frank family cook, stating that he had been bribed to swear that he had seen Frank act peculiarly on the day of Mary Phagan's death. McKnight now maintained that he had not seen Frank that day and summarized his retraction in one sentence: "Most everything I said on the stand was a lie." [4] When the affidavit became public, McKnight disappeared.

The next retraction came from New York. Mrs. Nina Formby, the proprietor of the "rooming house" Frank had allegedly telephoned on the night of the murder, told *The New York Times* that she wished to change her story. Mrs. Formby described how police had plied her with liquor and had encouraged her to relate an imaginary episode concerning Leo Frank. The woman stated that because of her position the police had "unduly influenced" her and had intimated that it would be prudent for her to help them.[5] Atlanta's Chief Detective, Newport Lanford, refused to believe Mrs. Formby's latest recollection: "The idea that Mrs. Formby is the author of the statement purporting to come from her is the most absurd thing I ever heard of." [6]

Shortly after Mrs. Formby's recantation, Mary Phagan's friend, George Epps, Jr., repudiated the statements that he had made at the Coroner's inquest and the trial. Epps asserted that a detective had forced him to lie but that now he wished to tell the truth. In his newest affidavit Epps recalled having seen Mary Phagan on the trolley, but since he had been seated behind her they engaged in no conversation aside from polite greetings.[7] The defense also released statements from other witnesses who told how the police, the detectives, and/or Solicitor Dorsey had manufactured the "evidence" they had given in court.[8]

Epps, McKnight, and others whom the Atlanta police could locate and reinterview repudiated their retractions. Fourteen-year-old George Epps, an inmate of the state reformatory, where he had been sent in December, 1913, for stealing, reverted to his original story within a few days after the defense had released his recantation. No explanation was given for the sudden change. A relatively unimportant witness, who repudiated statements he had given at the trial, was arrested and brought to Solicitor Dorsey's office for questioning. The man spent the night in jail, and the next day signed his name to a new affidavit stating that agents for the defense had bribed him to swear falsely, but now, he averred, the statements that he had made at the trial were true.[9]

Albert McKnight's retraction came in a peculiar fashion. He was found unconscious one night near the railroad tracks outside Atlanta. Taken to the hospital, he hovered between life and death but finally recovered. At that point he allegedly left the hospital to seek refuge in the police station where he retracted the statement he had given the defense. McKnight now claimed that Frank's lawyers had hounded him and that he had asked the police to protect him by putting him in jail! The newspapers reported that McKnight wished to remain in prison indefinitely, and the police obliged by keeping him in solitary confinement without visitors.[10]

Frank's partisans attempted to explain the peculiar behavior of the affidavit-switchers. C. P. Connolly, author of *The Truth about the Frank Case*, later suggested that Solicitor Dorsey might have reminded each witness that a Georgia statute provided the death penalty for swearing falsely in a capital case. Another explanation came from a woman who had repudiated her first affidavit but then reverted to the original statement. She confided to friends that one conducting a business in Atlanta "could not afford to antagonize the police." [11]

2

Frank's attorneys did not rely solely upon repudiated testimony in their extraordinary motion [12] for a new trial. Henry Alexander, one of the numerous lawyers working for the defense, made a careful study of the "murder notes" found near Mary Phagan's body and reached some startling conclusions. His examination showed that these notes were written on the carbons of old order pads which had been used previously by a former factory official. The dateline read "190—," indicating that the forms must have been at least four years old. The official who signed the orders left the employ of the factory in 1912, and all his office records, including pads, had been removed to the basement, near where Mary Phagan's body had been found. Alexander concluded that this proved that Conley could not have written the notes on a pad which Frank had given him *in his office*.[13]

Alexander then proceeded to examine the wording of the notes. In the second one the author had used the phrase, "play like the night witch did it." Most people automatically assumed that the expression referred to the night watchman. But Alexander pointed out that although the author of the murder notes had made many spelling errors, he had not made any in pronunciation. Therefore it seemed extremely unlikely that "night witch" would have been written if "night watch" or "night watchman" had been the author's intention. "Night

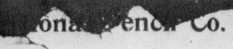
ona encil Co.

37 & 39 SOUTH FORSYTH ST.

ATLANTA, GA., _____ 190__

PUT THIS ORDER NUMBER ON YOUR BILL.

Bell Phone Main 171.   Order No. 1418

mam that negro
fire down her did
this i went to make
water and he push me
down that hole
a long tall negro i sed
that hoo it was
long sleam tall negro
i wright while i write

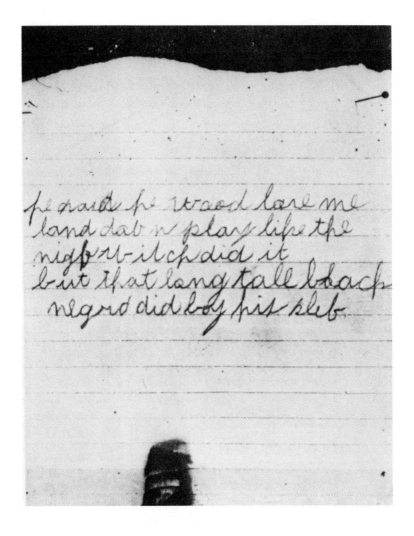

Henry Alexander, one of Leo Frank's attorneys, analyzed the "murder notes" in 1914 and made significant points about the paper used, the dateline, and the wording.

witch," Alexander wrote, meant "night witch!" He then explained that the term "night witch" referred to a peculiar
Negro superstition.[14] A Baptist minister later added that
when he had asked his Negro servant the meaning of "night
witch" she had replied, "When the children cry out in their
sleep at night, it means that the night witches are riding them,
and if you don't go and wake them up, they will be found
next morning strangled to death, with a cord around their
necks." [15] Those who believed Frank innocent agreed that it
was probable that only a Southern Negro would have known
about, and used, such an expression; therefore Frank could
not have dictated the murder notes.[16]

3

In the preparation of both the extraordinary motion and
the brief for the first appeal the previous fall, Frank's counsel
sought and received the aid of Louis Marshall, who was not
only President of the American Jewish Committee but also a
renowned constitutional lawyer. Marshall advised that, in
addition to the appeal for a new trial based upon new evidence, another motion be introduced asking for Frank's freedom on the ground that his enforced absence from the courtroom at the rendition of the jury's verdict constituted deprivation of due process of law; hence the Georgia authorities
were holding Frank in custody illegally.

The Atlanta attorneys at first hesitated to include this new
point involving a federal question because they feared it
would mitigate the effect of their extraordinary motion.
Marshall vigorously dissented from their view. He argued
that if the attorneys procrastinated until the extraordinary
motion had been disposed of before introducing the federal
question they would find both the court and the public
prejudiced against them "on the theory that [they] are apparently delaying proceedings by making one application
after another." If both were made together, Marshall argued,

then Frank's position would be strengthened "because a court which might hesitate as to the granting of a new trial on the ground of newly discovered evidence, might be induced to take a more favorable view of the proposition because of the fact that there is a serious question as to the regularity of the trial." "At all events," he added in his letter to Leonard Haas, brother and associate of Herbert Haas, "if the case should go to the Supreme Court of the United States on the question which I have discussed, it might be very useful to have in the record which goes to that court the testimony given on the extraordinary motion for a new trial, because it would impress the court that there has been an injustice done in this case." [17]

The Atlanta attorneys followed Marshall's advice and hired additional counsel to argue this federal question in the Georgia courts. At the time that the Solicitor had agreed to let Frank remain away from the courtroom, when the jury rendered its verdict, Luther Rosser and Reuben Arnold had promised Hugh Dorsey that they would not use their client's absence during part of the judicial proceedings as a basis for future appeals. Therefore Rosser and Arnold felt obliged to honor their pledge and different attorneys had to be engaged to argue this federal point in court.[18]

In addition to legal advice, the President of the American Jewish Committee used his influence in an attempt to change Southern attitudes. He induced Adolph Ochs, publisher of *The New York Times*, and also a member of the American Jewish Committee, to employ his newspaper as a weapon in the fight to exonerate Frank. The *Times* thereupon embarked on a protracted campaign to obtain another trial. Marshall cautioned Ochs that his newspaper must print nothing "which would arouse the sensitiveness of the southern people and engender the feeling that the north is criticizing the courts and the people of Georgia." The American Jewish Committee's President also "strongly urged that there should be no suggestion that the Frank case involves any element of anti-Semitism."[19] The *Times*'s articles followed Marshall's suggestions and tried to avoid offending Southern, especially Georgian, sensitivities. The campaign failed, however, because many Georgians interpreted every item favorable to Frank as a hostile act. In retrospect it seems that the attempt was doomed from the start. The Southerners who feared and resented aliens could not have been expected to heed the pleas of Northern, urban, Jewish-owned newspapers.[20]

In addition to Louis Marshall and other members of the American Jewish Committee, Albert D. Lasker, the Jewish advertising genius from Chicago, contributed his services. Lasker, too, had heard of Frank's plight and, according to his biographer, John Gunther, "Every instinct he had for justice and fair play, for racial tolerance, for dignity in the courts and good citizenship, was aroused." He went to Atlanta, interviewed Frank and his friends, and returned to Chicago determined to aid the cause. Since large sums of money were necessary to wage the legal battle, Lasker solicited wealthy friends for contributions to the "Frank Fund." It is not clear just how much money he raised at that time, but Frank personally acknowledged Lasker's "kindness and interest in my case."[21]

More important than Lasker's money was the time he devoted. For a man of his position to have written very large checks may not have been a great sacrifice, but to have neglected all other business activities for more than a year, as Lasker did, indicated what a great injustice he saw in the Frank case. Lasker made numerous trips to Atlanta, where he directed detectives and investigators while giving advice to Frank's attorneys. He also encouraged newspapers throughout the country to present Frank's case in a favorable light. He believed that as long as there was no obvious connection between the Jews and the press "their work can do no harm, but only good."[22]

Louis Marshall also sought "through various channels" to induce prominent individuals, especially Southerners, to take up the cause. To a friend in Baltimore, who asked what he could do to aid Frank, Marshall wrote: "The greatest aid that you and your friends in Baltimore can give to this cause would be to induce some of the leading newspapers in Baltimore, Richmond, Savannah, and other Southern points which you reach, to write editorials similar to that which recently appeared in *The Atlanta Journal*, and to reproduce the articles which have appeared from day to day in *The New York Times* and *The Washington Post*." The friend obviously responded to the advice, for within a few weeks he answered: "After receiving your letter, I interested all of the Baltimore papers in this matter, editorially as well as otherwise." [23]

Men like Lasker and Marshall, concerned about the miscarriage of justice, communicated their feelings to publications throughout the nation, and induced them to publicize Leo Frank's situation in the spring of 1914. A Boston newspaperman wrote of the "vigorous and well supported movement . . . to free Frank," and papers as far away as North Dakota and Utah discussed Georgia justice. In Bismarck, North Dakota, an editorialist commented: "We would have sat on that jury until this great globe hangs motionless in space and the rotting dead arise in their cerements, before we would condemn any man to death on the evidence which convicted Frank." The Baltimore *Sun* headed an appeal, "Justice Demands a New Trial for Frank," and articles urging a new trial appeared in Little Rock's *Arkansas Gazette*, Richmond's *Times-Dispatch*, and *The Mobile Tribune*.[24]

Even Georgia newspapers responded. *The Macon News* wrote that Frank's execution "under the evidence offered against him would be practically without a parallel in the annals of Georgia jurisprudence." And the *Constitution*, perhaps afraid to express any sentimental feelings toward Frank, suddenly decided to discuss a controversial conviction which had occurred in New York. In this case the *Constitution* advocated a new trial for the defendant. One could not, however, be oblivious to the obvious parallel in Georgia:

if the atmosphere of a trial or its controlling circumstances are such as to produce bias or prejudice, the accused shall have the benefit of the doubt. It is, or should be, axiomatic and impelling, that at every turn, under every condition, an environment of perfect fairness surround and characterize the trial.

Justice does not contemplate passion.

Justice does not comprehend obscure evidence, or evidence from dubious sources, especially where that evidence shall be substantiated by indirect circumstances only.[25]

The most dramatic appeal for Frank came from the *Journal*. The editors, in a scathing attack on Georgia justice, demanded that the prisoner be given another opportunity to clear himself. To hang Frank on the basis of the jury's verdict would constitute "judicial murder." The *Journal* recalled the circumstances surrounding the trial:

The very atmosphere of the courtroom was charged with an electric current of indignation which flashed and scintillated before the very eyes of the jury. The courtroom and streets were filled with an angry, determined crowd, ready to seize the defendant if the jury had found him not guilty. Cheers for the prosecuting counsel were irrepressible in the courtroom throughout the trial and on the streets unseemly demonstrations in condemnation of Frank were heard by the judge and jury. The judge was powerless to prevent these outbursts in the courtroom and the police were unable to control the crowd outside.

. . . it was known that a verdict of acquittal would cause a riot such as would shock the country and cause Atlanta's streets to run with innocent blood.[26]

The strong editorial evoked a mixed reaction. Two small-town Georgian newspapers, the Greensboro *Herald-Journal* and the *Dalton Citizen*, applauded the Atlanta paper's position.[27] The *Journal* also received a number of congratulatory letters praising the editors for their "courageous" stand. One letter, written by the court stenographer who had transcribed testimony at Frank's trial, contained the statement that "every lawyer I have talked to says that the Frank trial was simply a farce." But some people accused the *Journal* of having been "bought with Jew money," and the paper suffered a loss in circulation. Another year would pass before the *Journal* spoke out again for Leo Frank.[28]

4

The prodigious efforts made to save Leo Frank from death offended a great many Georgians. Outside influence and alien money outraged state officials and citizens alike. Many yearned for a native voice to rebut the national attack. In Tom Watson they found their spokesman.

Tom Watson had an enormous following in Georgia. From the Populist era until his death in 1921, Watson remained one of Georgia's idols. Early in his career he had fought for the yeoman farmer—both black and white—who had been oppressed by tyrannical industrialists and a compliant government. Although elected to Congress on the Democratic ticket in 1890, by 1892 he had renounced the party and had proclaimed himself a Populist. The Democratic Party in Georgia retaliated by manipulating the Congressional elections of 1892 and 1894 in such fashion as to rob Watson of reelection. The basest methods were used: bribery, ballot-box stuffing, and repeating voters. Negroes were coaxed and intimidated, by Democrats in control, to vote against Watson, who had publicly defended their political rights and who had also denounced lynchings. In 1896 the Populist Party forced William Jennings Bryan to accept a Populist vice-presidential nominee in return for endorsing his presidential aspirations. To run with Bryan, the Populists selected Tom Watson. With defeat in 1896, Watson practically retired from politics and concentrated on his law practice. At the same time he busied himself with the writing of history. Eight years later he reemerged as the presidential nominee of an almost defunct Populist Party.

Thereafter one noticed a great change in the old Populist.

He had become a self-conscious defender of Southern mores and the Lost Cause. His former understanding of, and sympathy with, Negroes changed to a more orthodox Southern outlook. He began to refer to the "bugaboo of negro domination" in Georgia politics. Furthermore, in 1906, Watson completely abandoned the Jeffersonian ideals of equalitarianism and humanitarianism which he had championed only a decade earlier. In 1910 he formally returned to the Democratic Party, and two years later his arrival at the Democratic state convention "suggested the return of some Roman conqueror." Police officers had to force a path for him, and his appearance on the floor of the convention resulted in "an outburst resembling pandemonium." [29]

Tom Watson thrived upon the ignorance and prejudices of rural Georgians. His weekly newspaper, *The Jeffersonian*, and his monthly, *Watson's Magazine*, circulated throughout the state and provided many Georgians their only contact with the outside world. Popular among illiterates, who listened to others read what Watson had written, and "crackers," Watson inspired "an almost fanatical following, many who accepted without question anything he told them." In 1891 a national periodical had described these Georgia "crackers" as people "borned in the country" who seldom, if ever, visited a neighboring town. They were frequently suspicious of strangers, and one Southerner had written that they imagined every stranger a "Yankee." It was primarily these people that Tom Watson stirred with his diatribes against the financial manipulators of the North, whom he believed had been keeping the South in economic bondage. To cater to his followers' need for vicarious excitement, and perhaps to provide himself with a satisfactory answer for why the world was "plunging hellward," Watson broadened his attack to include Catholics, the Pope, and finally Leo Frank, who turned into the greatest sales bonanza in *The Jeffersonian's* history.[30]

C. Vann Woodward has observed that Tom Watson found

his greatest satisfactions "out among the people preaching a crusade." [31] This was true in his Populist days and in his later years as well. In 1914 Watson embarked upon one of his most reckless attacks. Ironically, the "sage of Hickory Hill" aimed his thrust at another target, and touched upon what would eventually emerge as his real quarry in an oblique fashion.

Hoke Smith, Georgia's senior United States Senator in 1914, had once owned *The Atlanta Journal*. Although he had relinquished controlling interest in the paper years before, everyone recognized the *Journal* as Smith's political organ.[32] The Senator stood for reelection in 1914, and although he and Watson had at one time been allied politically, a breach had developed between the two six years earlier. The old Populist leader had his own candidate for Smith's seat, and when the *Journal* demanded a new trial for Leo Frank, Watson misinterpreted the plea as an attempt to drag the Frank case into politics.[33] Enraged by the editorial, Watson lashed back angrily.

He entitled his first salvo "The Frank Case: When and Where Shall Rich Criminals Be Tried?" and devoted most of this attack to the "personal organ" of Senator Smith, which, according to *The Jeffersonian*'s editor, was attempting "to bring the courts into disrepute, drag down the judges to the level of criminals, and destroy the confidence of the people in the orderly process of the law." Not until midway in the article, and on an inside page, did Watson switch his fire to Frank, and then he concluded "*by a process of elimination*" that either Frank or Conley, or both, had murdered Mary Phagan. Watson also asked two questions which plagued many Georgians: "Does a Jew expect extraordinary favors and immunities *because* of his race?" and "Who is paying for all this?" [34]

Although Watson aimed his assault at Hoke Smith and *The Atlanta Journal*, there were indications that readers responded more positively to his words against Frank. Watson, therefore, concentrated future articles on Frank. In April he started attacking the Jew more vehemently, without making any connection with Smith or the *Journal*. It was also in April that Watson began printing letters which commented upon his outburst against Frank. "Nothing you have written in recent years is being so widely read," wrote one admirer.[35] As the weeks passed, *The Jeffersonian* devoted more and more space to reader reactions on Leo Frank, and all the letters published praised Watson's stand. In May a correspondent confessed, "The manner in which you are handling the Frank case has opened my eyes." And the following week another thanked the editor "from the depths of my soul for the great service you are rendering. . . . I believe you are making more friends by your editorials on the Frank case than you ever did. The name Tom Watson is heard more during a conversation than it ever was." [36]

The popular response stimulated Watson. His polemics were an ingenious weaving of fact and fantasy.[37] The former Populist leader, seized upon the weakness in the defense presentation and skillfully attacked Luther Rosser, who, Watson claimed, *"strengthened the State's case enormously when he made his ludicrous failure, cross-examining that darkey."* If the "mob" influenced the trial, Watson asked, why had not a change of venue been asked for? Because of Watson's well-known legal talents, his remark that "No case can come under 'mob' influence, unless the defendant and his lawyers are entirely negligent," stung the defense while rendering Frank's attorneys helpless to retort.[38]

Watson cannily played upon the hatreds, fears, and prejudices of his readers. He wrote of the "little factory girl who held to her innocence," and further endeared Mary Phagan to his readers by characterizing her as "a daughter of the people, of the common clay, of the blouse and the overall, of those who eat bread in the sweat of the face, and who, in so many instances are the chattel slaves of a sordid Commercialism that has no milk of human kindness in its heart of stone!" [39]

Watson always stressed simple themes so that his readers

would quickly see right from wrong. "We cannot have . . . one law for the Jew, and another for the Gentile," he commented. On another occasion he concluded, "It is a bad state of affairs when the idea gets abroad that the law is too weak to punish a man who has plenty of money." With magnificent simplicity he summed up the crux of his argument, "Leo Frank is guilty of the foulest crime ever committed on a Georgia girl, and he should not be allowed to escape." [40] A contemporary publication in Georgia evaluated Watson's contributions so highly that *The Jeffersonian* reprinted the entire eulogy. "Tom Watson," *The Madisonian's* editorial began, "has added new laurels and new lustre to his fame as a writer . . . by his articles on the famous Frank case. His productions touching this case . . . are modern epics. . . . They have added a hundred thousand new friends to Mr. Watson's long list, and given *The Jeffersonian* a standing and a circulation in Atlanta and in Georgia never before enjoyed by any Watson publication." [41]

Tom Watson reinforced accepted beliefs. Emotionally Georgians "knew" that Leo Frank murdered their little girl. Yet they wanted reassurance by hearing a prominent and articulate spokesman reiterate and confirm their "knowledge." Watson supplied this need. The people had formed their opinions a year earlier. They probably forgot the specific details which led them to their conclusion. Yet they knew in their hearts that Leo Frank had murdered Mary Phagan. Not only did the courts of Georgia agree with them but Tom Watson, one of the most popular Georgians of his era, confirmed their feelings. For this the people of Georgia lionized the old Populist.

5

The Frank camp unwittingly provided material for Watson's gibes. In February, 1914, immediately after the Georgia Supreme Court rejected the bid for a new trial, Frank's

counsel announced the employment of William J. Burns to
help prove Frank innocent.[42] The appointment turned out to
be a colossal blunder.[43] In his first public statement Burns
offended the people by asserting his expectation of finding a
solution to a crime Atlantans considered already solved.
"What are believed to be mysteries," he declared, "are invariably solvable if common sense is applied." For three
months the famous detective exuded confidence and made
public statements which could not be justified in terms of his
discoveries. "I am utterly confident of success," he repeated
to newspaper reporters time after time. "The trail is very
plain," he revealed, but declined to elaborate. After six weeks
of investigation Burns announced:

I know who is the murderer of Mary Phagan. In time I will let
the public know, and I will show conclusive proof. There will
not be a single ground for the public to contradict me. . . . The
Phagan mystery is no longer a mystery. We have cleared it. I was
confident from the outset that we would have success. It was no
difficult task and our work was simple—merely the following of
the criminal trend of mind which left so many manifestations in
the Phagan tragedy.[44]

Burns's complete disdain for the public and for police
officials multiplied Frank's enemies in Georgia. If Burns knew
Mary Phagan's slayer, he should have revealed this information to the proper authorities. If his evidence was so conclusive, he should not have delayed publicizing his discoveries.
His conceited assertions led Northerners to assume that he
would "produce a confession from the real murderer, or at
least direct evidence. Failing to do that," Albert Lasker confided to Herbert Haas, "the people up here will be very disappointed, and, to be very frank with you, I fear if he does
not do something like that, it will hurt us and may do the case
more harm than if he had not entered it at all." [45]

The pent-up indignation Georgians felt toward Frank and
Burns manifested itself, on May 1, 1914, in Marietta, Georgia,
Mary Phagan's home town. A mob surrounded Burns after

his car broke down while going through the city. A crowd of people pursued the detective back to his hotel, where more than two hundred shouted out threats of "Lynch him!" "Shoot him!" "Mob him!" [46] The Mayor of Marietta pleaded with the mob to disperse, "but the crowd seemed to grow more demonstrative." Then a respected Judge asked the assemblage to let Burns get out of town. The crowd yielded, and before it could change its mind Burns was whisked into an automobile and taken back to Atlanta. As the speeding car left Marietta, the mob bombarded the vehicle with rotten eggs.[47]

The antagonism Burns created highlighted his failures, but he did manage to bring a good deal of information to light, and under other circumstances the new material would have helped Frank. The detective believed that the charge of perversion adversely affected the defendant before and during his trial and that if this could be proved erroneous the public would be willing to reevaluate new evidence. So the detective offered $1,000 reward to anyone who could submit proof of Frank's alleged perversity.[48] "If Detective Burns wants this information as badly as he pretends he wants it," Chief Detective Lanford of the Atlanta police department told reporters, "I'll certainly furnish him with what I believe to be convincing proof." [49] Burns responded to Lanford's offer, and accompanied by David Marx, the leading rabbi of Atlanta, and Henry A. Alexander, one of the lawyers working for the defense, went to the chief detective's office, prepared to turn over the reward. When they arrived Lanford refused to grant them access to the proof he claimed was locked in the police safe. He added, however, that "the state does not contend, and never has contended, that Frank is a pervert. The perversion charge was injected into the case by the attorneys for the defense, not by those for the state." [50] Lanford's remarks astonished his listeners. Leo Frank, after learning of the Chief Detective's comment, vented his wrath in a public statement: "Is there a man in Atlanta," he asked, "who would deny that

the charge of perversion was the chief cause of my conviction, or deny that the case, without that charge, would be an
entirely different question?" [51] And in the North, *The New
York Times* editorialized that "the present denial by the head
of the Police Department that either it or the State ever
charged Frank with moral perversity is incomprehensible to
anybody who has read the report of the trial and therefore
knows how directly contrary to recorded fact the denial is."
Burns then increased his reward to $5,000, but there were no
takers.[52]

The noted detective also found, although how he did so
was never made clear, letters written from jail by Jim Conley
to a girl friend, Annie Maud Carter. Copies of these letters
were furnished to the newspapers, but the *Constitution* explained to its readers that "their contents were so vile and
vulgar that their publication is impossible." [53] The letters,
according to Burns, "show beyond a peradventure of a doubt
that Conley is an abnormal man. . . . They are full of the
vilest, most abominable language, dealing with Conley's lust.
His perverted passion was aroused by her [Annie Maud
Carter] and most of the letters are full of this vile stuff." [54]
Some of Conley's expressions were indeed lewd. He also used
the words "did" and "Negro," indicating they were part of
his normal vocabulary. At the trial one of the explanations
offered by Dorsey to prove that Conley did not compose the
"murder notes" was that a Negro ordinarily uses the words
"done" and "nigger" rather than "did" and "Negro." [55]

Conley denied authorship of the letters,[56] but Annie Maud
Carter swore otherwise. Graphologists who examined the
notes confirmed that the writing compared favorably with
other material penned by Conley. Miss Carter also swore that
Conley revealed his innermost secrets to her, including a description of how he murdered Mary Phagan. According to
her statement Conley allegedly beckoned to Mary Phagan
after she left Frank's office on the fatal day. When the girl
approached he knocked her over the head, choked her, and

then pushed her down a scuttle hole in the back of the building. After following her down, he wrote the murder notes and left them near the body. Conley hoped suspicion would fall on Newt Lee, "a long tall black Negro." After writing the notes the sweeper broke the bolt on the back door of the basement and left the building. Miss Carter's narrative corroborated known facts and her explanation of how the body reached the basement seemed plausible if the elevator had not been used.[57]

Surprisingly, and inexplicably, the Atlanta press made no comment about the letters received by Annie Maud Carter aside from indicating that they were vulgar. Miss Carter's remark that Conley had confessed his guilt to her was simply reported in the news columns, but provoked no editorial comment.

The Solicitor and the detectives, however, were quite concerned with the letters. Annie Carter was in New Orleans when her affidavit was made public, but Hugh Dorsey went to court and demanded that she be subpoenaed for questioning. The presiding judge issued the order, and Frank's attorneys had her brought back to Atlanta. Dorsey immediately arrested Miss Carter and some days later produced a new affidavit from her in which she asserted that she had received only "two or three" letters from Conley, that none were vulgar, and that he had confessed no crime to her.[58] In this instance, at least, it seems quite clear that the authorities had encouraged a defense witness to deliberately tell a lie, because it was later shown that Conley had written the letters. It is impossible, at this point, to know if any others might also have been induced to swear falsely. The defense, however, believed that Dorsey and his staff had intimidated all the witnesses whom they could reach.[59]

Perhaps the most incriminating piece of information uncovered by Burns, which quickly backfired and severely damaged any chance Frank may have had for the new trial, was the evidence given by the Reverend C. B. Ragsdale, pastor of an Atlanta Baptist Church. The day after the murder, in April, 1913, Ragsdale allegedly overheard two Negroes talking. One said, "I'm in trouble. I killed a little girl at the factory the other day and I want you to help me." The other asked, "Who was there beside you?" And the first replied, "Nobody except Mr. Frank, and I'm not sure about him." Ragsdale repeated these words to a friend, who advised that he keep his own counsel. Ragsdale followed this advice. Somehow a Burns agent tracked the minister down and induced him to reveal what he knew. The defense presented the Ragsdale affidavit in court, along with one from the friend he had confided in who corroborated the minister's tale, as part of the additional evidence warranting a new trial. A few days later both men repudiated their statements and swore that they had been bribed by Burns, and others, to give false testimony. Burns denied this, but his words had no effect upon those whose confidence he lacked. Herbert Haas, however, explained the defense's position in a letter to Albert Lasker, "The charge of Ragsdale that he was bribed . . . is unqualified falsehood." Despite Haas's conviction that Burns told the truth in this matter, he readily admitted, in another letter, "It is the belief of nearly all of our friends that Burns's connection with the case has done us irretrievable damage." [60]

The Burns fiasco impaired any chance Frank may have had for a new trial. The detective's public antics also highlighted the huge sums of money being spent to save the accused, a fact which Dorsey brought to public notice when he argued against a new trial. The Solicitor came to court armed with repudiations of affidavits made for the defense. In these statements the affiants claimed that attorneys and investigators working in Frank's behalf bribed them to change their tales. The charge of corruption by so many of the prosecution's original witnesses reinforced the popular impression that the defense spent unlimited amounts of money to free Frank. [61]

Dorsey also scored brilliantly when he examined Burns in the courtroom. During the course of the interrogation the prosecutor forced the noted sleuth to admit that he had never read the testimony of the trial, only the brief prepared by the defense attorneys, and that his report to Frank's lawyers contained the opinion that "they didn't need any more evidence than was in the record." Finally Burns acknowledged that aside from the information that had already been produced in court, and the repudiated affidavits of Annie Maud Carter and C. B. Ragsdale, he had obtained no other evidence to incriminate the murderer of Mary Phagan.[62] Dorsey's interrogation of Burns appeared to the Frank camp as the final blow. "The situation is worse today than it has ever been," Haas wrote Lasker. "It is desperate. All of us feel that the situation is hopeless. Unless the Supreme Court of the United States sustains the Constitutional point, Frank is a doomed man." [63]

Within a few days Frank's attorneys concluded their petition for a new trial, and without even listening to the prosecution's summation, Judge Ben Hill denied the defense motion. He subsequently refused to set aside the verdict on the constitutional grounds that Frank's absence from the courtroom constituted denial of the federal guarantee of due process. On both counts Frank's attorneys indicated they would appeal.[64]

6

In retrospect it seems that Frank's efforts to obtain a new trial in the spring of 1914 failed, in part, because too many people tried too hard to assist him. At the same time there was no clearly established leader to coordinate affairs. Louis Marshall had attempted to guide proceedings, but he was handicapped by remaining in New York City, too far from the hub of activity, and also by the reluctance of others working for the defendant to follow his advice. Marshall did recognize, however, the cost to Frank of his well-meaning, but thoughtless, "friends." "Too many of our Jewish friends in Atlanta are assuming responsibility in this litigation," he protested to the Haas brothers, "and are conferring with Tom, Dick and Harry with regard to it." [65]

Marshall had also objected to the employment of William

J. Burns, the raising of large sums of money, and the Northern newspaper barrage which succeeded in magnifying Georgian prejudice toward Frank. As early as March 17, 1914, he had written to a friend that "the campaign in the North may be overdone." Marshall also urged that Frank's partisans deemphasize religious prejudice. "There is too much of a tendency on the part of our people to attribute everything to anti-Semitism." [66] And after Burns had barely escaped being lynched, Marshall candidly confessed to another friend that he had been opposed to hiring the detective in the first place. "I foresaw just what has happened—an attack upon him because he is a stranger and a Northerner. . . . I have been disgusted at the farcical methods to which Burns has resorted. Every one of his acts has been a burlesque upon modern detective ideas. It is deplorable that a case so meritorious as that of Frank, should have been brought to the point of distraction by such ridiculous methods." [67] Finally, the President of the American Jewish Committee hit upon one of Frank's most significant difficulties: "The lawyers in the case . . . have not at all times acted with good judgment." [68] The situation that Marshall had observed so clearly was summarized in one sentence by his law partner, Samuel Untermyer: "I am afraid the whole business has been terribly botched but the point now is to avoid further blunders." [69]

Untermyer was undoubtedly correct. The defense attorneys therefore began preparing new briefs for an appeal to the Georgia Supreme Court. But this seemed only a formality. Eventually they expected to take their case into the federal courts, and ultimately to the United States Supreme Court, where they hoped that justice might be obtained.

CHAPTER VI

Wisdom without Justice

THE SUMMER OF 1914 MARKED a calm interlude after the frenzied activity in Frank's behalf during the previous spring. American newspapers ceased condemning Georgia justice, Tom Watson vented his frustrations upon other subjects, no witnesses came forth with crucial evidence or repudiated previous testimony, the public focused its attention on the perilous European situation, and the defense counsel quietly appealed to the Georgia Supreme Court.

The repetitive arguments before Georgia's highest court lacked drama and required merely a few columns of Atlanta newsprint. The defense based its appeal upon new evidence and Frank's alleged denial of life and liberty without due process of law. The Court waited until the fall before once more thwarting the petitioner's hope for legal vindication in Georgia. The Georgia Justices unanimously agreed that Judge Ben Hill, before whom the new evidence had originally been presented, had not abused his discretion in denying the extraordinary motion for a new trial, and the Court saw no reason to reverse him.[1]

Once the Georgia Supreme Court turned down Frank's second request for a new trial, a realignment of his legal staff took place. Luther Rosser and Reuben Arnold, who had defended Frank during the trial and had argued his appeals in the Supreme Court, ended their formal association as counsel. Thereafter, the brothers Haas, Herbert and Leonard, worked with Henry Alexander, who had been hired in 1913, and the firm of Tye, Peeples, and Jordan, which had been retained in the spring of 1914 to introduce the constitutional question of whether a trial can be considered valid if the defendant had been out of the courtroom during any part of the proceedings. Louis Marshall remained in New York but continued to supervise the work of the Atlanta attorneys.

Marshall had originally suggested to the other attorneys that an attempt should be made to invalidate Frank's conviction on the technical ground that neither defendant nor counsel had the right to waive his constitutional privilege to be present in the courtroom at every stage of the proceedings. Henry Peeples, John Tye, the Haas brothers, and Henry Alexander had argued this point before Judge Ben Hill, who had denied their allegation in June, 1914. On appeal, the Georgia Supreme Court upheld Hill's decision. Five of the six Supreme Court justices [2] agreed that the defendant's enforced absence from the court was known at the time of the first appeal and the alleged lack of due process should have been brought up at that time. If it had been, the Justices intimated, then redress might have been granted.

It would be trifling with the court [however] to allow one who had been convicted of crime, and who had made a motion for a new trial on over 100 grounds, including the statement that his counsel had waived his presence at the reception of the verdict, and have the motion heard by both the superior and the Supreme Courts, and, after a denial of both courts of the motion, to now come in and by way of a motion to set aside the verdict include matters which were or ought to have been included in the motion for a new trial.[3]

Again frustrated, but not unexpectedly, Louis Marshall, commenting on the latest failure, wrote Leonard Haas, "I am not surprised [at the Georgia Supreme Court's decision], and only hope that the opinion will be on such grounds as will not increase the difficulties of procuring a review of the fundamental question by the Supreme Court of the United States." [4]

But, alas, the Georgia Supreme Court refused to grant the request of Frank's attorneys for a writ of error [5] on the grounds that the case presented only a procedural question and no constitutional point existed.[6]

The adverse judgment did not stop Frank's attorneys. Leonard Haas, Henry Peeples, Henry Alexander, and Louis Marshall appealed to the United States Supreme Court Justice Joseph R. Lamar for the writ of error. Lamar gave them "a most patient and courteous hearing," [7] but denied their application on the grounds that the point raised involved only a question of state procedure which the United States Supreme Court would not review.[8]

Frank's counsel, out of courtesy and custom, had applied first to Justice Lamar for the writ of error because Georgia was included in his circuit. After he had refused them, they let it be known that they would appeal, if necessary, to each of the other Justices, in turn.[9] The attorneys next approached Justice Oliver Wendell Holmes. Holmes, too, denied the wit because he also felt bound by the Georgia Supreme Court's decision that the motion to set aside the verdict on constitutional grounds had come too late, and was therefore a procedural question. Justice Holmes, however, doubted whether on the basis of the evidence submitted to him, Leo Frank had received due process of law. He based his conclusion upon the fact that the trial took place "in the presence of a hostile demonstration and seemingly dangerous crowd, thought by the presiding judge to be ready for violence unless a verdict of guilty was rendered." [10]

Denials of their appeal by Justices Lamar and Holmes did not daunt the determined counsel. They immediately petitioned to be heard before the entire Supreme Court and their request was granted. But their argument had no greater effect on the judges collectively than it had upon the two who rejected the earlier petitions. It took only one week for the United States Supreme Court to refuse Leo Frank a writ of error. No written opinion accompanied the denial.[11]

Holmes's explanation and the Supreme Court's refusal to issue the writ of error spawned newspaper criticism throughout the nation. Albany's [New York] *Knickerbocker Press* asked, "Is it not an amazing commentary upon our judicial system that an associate Justice of the United States Supreme Court 'seriously doubts if Frank has had due process of law,' and yet there is no means at hand by which 'due process' may be had?" [12] *The Indianapolis News* questioned, "How can the lay mind be expected to see justice in a ruling of that sort? It may be entirely legal, but it hardly seems sensible." [13]

Spurred on by editorial support and hopeful that even the United States Supreme Court might yield to the outcry, Frank's attorneys reinstituted proceedings for a hearing in the nation's highest tribunal with an appeal for a writ of habeas corpus.[14] The new plea rested upon Justice Holmes's expressed doubts and Louis Marshall's conviction "that the trial court lost jurisdiction of the case when the verdict was received in the absence of the prisoner. . . ." [15] The petition claimed that the state of Georgia illegally and unjustly held Frank in captivity because his conviction did not result from due process of law. This time, however, the basis for lack of due process was not that Frank involuntarily absented himself from the courtroom but that he did so because of the hostile attitude of the spectators at the trial. Hence mob influence constituted denial of due process.[16]

The defense attorneys asked for the writ of habeas corpus in the Federal District Court for North Georgia. The local judge denied their petition and they appealed once more to Justice Lamar. This time Lamar agreed that the United States Supreme Court should consider their petition. Justice Lamar now saw several legal issues which he believed the Supreme Court ought to rule upon, and which had not been apparent to him in the appeal for a writ of error. Among those issues he included (1) whether a defendant in a murder trial may legally waive his right to be present at all stages of the proceedings in a State Court and (2) does the failure to raise a material point in an appeal to a State Court prevent counsel from raising the question at a later date? [17] Lamar's verdict met with general newspaper acclaim. "Throughout the entire country," the Scranton (Pa.) *Tribune-Republican* declared "there was a breath of relief. . . ." [18] "Justice Lamar's decision," echoed the Portland *Oregonian*, "makes life and liberty more secure for every citizen of the United States." [19]

The opportunity to be heard by the United States Supreme Court gratified Frank and his supporters. They confidently expected success. A few days before Lamar granted the appeal, Marshall had written, "If we only get a chance for argument in open court, I feel that we should win. Our position is legally and morally impregnable." [20]

The final court presentation had to be prepared carefully. Like the writ of error, which asked to have the verdict set aside and make Leo Frank a free man, the writ of habeas corpus alleged that since Georgia held Frank illegally, he must be given his freedom at once. Louis Marshall prepared the defense brief with the realization that any court would hesitate before granting this extreme demand in light of the facts already known. "From a tactical standpoint," he wrote, "it would be far easier to succeed, if the Court were satisfied that a favorable decision would not finally discharge Frank." [21] In other words, the chance for the Supreme Court's granting the defense's request would be much greater if it could simply remand the case back to a Georgia court with instructions that a new trial be granted.[22]

Marshall's argument before the Supreme Court highlighted the irregularities of a trial dominated by hostile elements and culminating with the judge coercing the defendant's counsel to acquiesce in denying Frank the opportunity to see and face the jurors when they delivered their judgment.[23] Warren Grice, the Attorney-General of Georgia, who, along with Hugh Dorsey, represented the State of Georgia in the United States Supreme Court, rebutted Marshall's claims and partic-

ularly objected to the use of the word "coerce." "It was
simply the case of a kind-hearted Judge," Grice explained,
"suggesting to the counsel that their client remain absent." [24]

Two months passed before the Supreme Court, on April
19, 1915, rejected the defense motion by a vote of 7 to 2.[25]
Speaking for the Court, Justice Mahlon Pitney elaborated
upon the denial. Justice Pitney explained that errors in law,
however serious, committed by a court of proper jurisdiction
cannot be reviewed by habeas corpus since habeas corpus
cannot be substituted for a writ of error. Furthermore "the
allegations of disorder were found by both of the State courts
to be groundless except in a few particulars as to which the
courts ruled that they were irregularities not harmful in fact
to defendant and therefore insufficient in law to avoid the
verdict." Frank's contention of denial of due process because
he had not been present during the entire trial "has been set
aside because it was waived by his failure to raise the objection in due season when fully cognizant of the fact." The
right of the defendant to be present at the rendition of the
jury verdict, Pitney continued, "is but an incident of the right
of trial by jury; and, since the State may, without infringing
the Fourteenth Amendment, abolish trial by jury, it may limit
the effect to be given to an error respecting one of the incidents of such trial." The Supreme Court majority also acknowledged that the Georgia courts accorded Frank "the
fullest right and opportunity to be heard according to established modes of procedure. . . ." Therefore, Justice Pitney concluded, the defendant had been deprived of no right
guaranteed by the Fourteenth Amendment or any other pro-
vision of the United States Constitution.[26]

Justices Holmes and Charles Evans Hughes dissented. They
dismissed Frank's absence from the courtroom as inconse-
quential compared to the major point of whether a trial conducted in an atmosphere of overt public hostility is consonant
with due process of law. Examining the records and commenting upon Judge Roan's expressed doubt, Holmes and

Hughes thought "the presumption overwhelming that the jury responded to the passions of the mob." Therefore under no stretch of judicial imagination could they presume that Leo Frank had had a fair trial. "Mob law," they concluded, "does not become due process of law by securing the assent of a terrorized jury." [27]

Northern press commentary "was bitter against the supreme court," a Missouri newspaperman wrote to Leo Frank.[28] "The opinion of the country will be with the dissenting Justices," averred the *San Francisco Chronicle*.[29] The Muskogee (Okla.) *Democrat* lamented, "The sad part of it all is that Frank has failed to get a new trial not because the higher court believes him to be guilty but because of technical mistakes made by his lawyer." Louis Marshall wrote to a friend, "I fear that I shall never again be able to feel that reliance upon the courts in respect to the accomplishments of the ends of justice, that I had hitherto entertained." [30]

With the denial of the writ of habeas corpus all court action had been exhausted. Under the laws of Georgia only one course remained open—to petition the Governor via the Prison Commission for clemency. Frank's attorneys now set about to prepare the necessary petition.

CHAPTER VII

Commutation

A MOVEMENT TO HAVE FRANK'S sentence commuted began in the autumn of 1914, after his appeals had been turned down by the Georgia courts and the outlook in the federal courts appeared uncertain. Frank's friends hoped that national publicity might stimulate a ground swell of opposition to his conviction which would persuade the Governor of Georgia to commute the sentence. Therefore, the fall of 1914 witnessed a revived interest in Frank throughout the nation. Part of this concern may be attributed to a "sensational" new development in the case, and part may be assigned to some prominent newspapers and national periodicals which, inspired by those most concerned with the prisoner's welfare, decided to investigate the case and discover why Leo Frank had been convicted.

I

The new development which stirred Atlanta and those working to save Frank was the announcement, made on October 2, 1914, by William M. Smith, lawyer for Jim Conley, the state's key witness at the trial, that his own client had murdered Mary Phagan. This incredible admission seemed highly unethical, but Smith maintained that since Conley had already been convicted for his complicity in the crime he could not be retried. Under the circumstances, Smith felt obliged to speak up to save an innocent man's life. A careful reading of the attorney's statement, detailing the reasons for his opinion, revealed speculations, intuitions, and suspicions, but no convincing proof. He unearthed no new facts but merely juxtaposed the existing ones, to reach his conclusion. Tom Watson accused Smith of having accepted a bribe to issue his statement and asked why the lawyer had not spoken up eight months earlier, in March, 1914, when *The Atlanta Journal* published its editorial demanding a new trial for Frank.[1] Those who believed Frank guilty quickly accepted Watson's charge that Smith had been bribed; those who thought Frank innocent clung to Smith's words to bolster their thesis.

The national press used Smith's statement to reintroduce Leo Frank to their readers. From June, 1914, when a Georgia court had denied his appeal for a new trial, until October, 1914, when Smith announced his belief that Conley had killed Mary Phagan, Frank's name rarely appeared in print. But Smith's remarks gave the newspapers an occasion for reviewing the events in the case and stimulating further interest in Leo Frank.

Since many of the newspapers outside Georgia had always been sympathetic to Leo Frank, it seemed natural for them to present his case favorably again. The first of the new articles appeared in November, 1914, in the Baltimore *Sun.* Then— following in quick succession—came two articles in *Collier's,* in December, 1914, a detailed survey in *The Kansas City Star,* on January 17, 1915, and an essay in *Everybody's,* in March, 1915.[2] These stories kept material sympathetic to Frank before the public.

Two of the investigating journalists, C. P. Connolly, who wrote for *Collier's,* and Arthur P. Train, whose article appeared in *Everybody's,* were lawyers. Connolly had been a prosecuting attorney in Butte, Montana, and Train was still an assistant district attorney in New York City when he wrote. These two men, plus the other two reporters, con-

cluded that Frank was innocent. They saw the familiar ingredients of anti-industrialism, police incompetence, and newspaper sensationalism complicating the attack upon Frank. But
each stressed Atlanta's hatred of the Jew. The Baltimore *Sun*'s
reporter viewed the case as "the American counterpart of the
Dreyfus [affair]," while the essayist in *Collier's* wrote that the
cry, "Innocent or Guilty, we will 'get' the d—— Jew!" accu-
rately reflected Atlantan sentiment. By emphasizing anti-
Semitism these accounts overlooked the fact that in Georgia
many unprejudiced and impartial citizens believed Frank
guilty. Furthermore, many Georgians resented the conclusion, reached by these outsiders, that the jury had echoed the
demands of the clamoring crowds.[3]

These four articles spawned further commentary and discussion in the nation's press. The editors of the Baltimore *Sun*
reread their series and confessed that their faith in the jury
system had been shaken: "Sometimes the public is almost justified in feeling that the twelve men in the jury box deserve
hanging even more richly than the accused." Throughout the
country newspaper editorials were equally indignant. One
Pittsburgh newspaper referred to the Frank case as "the most
notorious example of the mob spirit that has invaded our
courts for many years." Frequent comparisons were made to
Russian justice. A midwestern daily declared, for example,
that "Russia, with all her benightedness, never produced anything more heinous than the case of Frank. . . ."[4]

But in Georgia there was no outpouring of sympathy.
Many Georgians considered the pro-Frank editorials as the
product of a press servile to Jewish interests. The accusations
of race prejudice and mob passions made the people of the
state more reluctant to reexamine their conclusions. Thomas
Loyless, the respected editor of *The Augusta Chronicle*,
doubted whether the Northern outcry would have been so
bitter were the victim of this alleged injustice a Gentile. A
former Governor, Joseph M. Brown, inquired indignantly,
"Are we to understand that anybody except a Jew can be

punished for crime?" One rural newspaper candidly asked if those publications which publicized Frank's situation realized that they were hurting the defendant with their continuing attacks upon Georgia justice. Whether they knew it or not, these attacks, continued daily, caused Southerners generally to believe that the publications condemning Georgia were being paid to express their opinions.[5] A despondent Louis Marshall wrote to Frank: "Apparently nothing that may be written will, under present conditions, affect public sentiment in Georgia."[6]

2

Once the newspaper protests and Georgia retaliations subsided, another quiet interlude passed while Frank's attorneys argued before the United States Supreme Court for a writ of habeas corpus in February, 1915; then they waited anxiously for the verdict. When the Supreme Court·rejected Frank's plea, on April 19, 1915, defense lawyers immediately began working for executive clemency. Marshall had been informed by Arthur Brisbane, the famous journalist in the Hearst chain, and others, that Frank would have a better chance to live if Governor Slaton, rather than his successor, received his appeal. Therefore Marshall requested the United States Supreme Court to send its mandate to the local Georgia court faster than was usual.[7] Although Leo Frank preferred a complete pardon, his attorneys cautioned that, on the basis of the numerous adverse court decisions, he would be prudent to seek commutation to life imprisonment. Counsel also hoped that sometime in the future the climate of Georgia opinion might change, and Frank's innocence would be established.[8]

While the attorneys handled legal matters, further attempts were made to create an aura of national concern over Frank. Since Jewish leaders realized that everything they did on Frank's behalf hardened Georgian attitudes, extensive efforts were made to induce prominent Gentiles to join in the crusade to save the prisoner's life.[9] The overtures succeeded. Many Gentiles had already heard of Frank's situation and doubted his culpability. They did not hesitate to express these opinions publicly.

Leo Frank's predicament appealed to an amazing variety of people. The offices of the Georgia Governor and its Prison Commission were flooded with more than 100,000 letters requesting commutation. Solicitations came from every state in the union, from Canada, and from Mexico. Included among these pleas were communications from the President of the University of Chicago; the Dean of Yale College; Charles R. Crane, the plumbing magnate; Judge Ben Lindsay of Colorado; and Jane Addams. Elmer Murphy, President of the James H. Rhodes Company, producers of industrial chemicals, sent out an appeal to every name on the mailing list of the company's publication, *Rhodes' Colossus*, earnestly requesting that each of them intercede for Frank. The Governors of Arizona, Louisiana, Michigan, Mississippi, North Dakota, Oregon, Pennsylvania, Texas, and Virginia wrote to Georgia's Governor, as did United States Senators from Connecticut, Idaho, Illinois, Indiana, Louisiana, Mississippi, and Texas, as well as scores of congressmen. The state legislatures of Louisiana, Michigan, Pennsylvania, Tennessee, Texas, and West Virginia passed resolutions urging commutation. *The New York Times* noted that the appeals by the governors and state legislatures "are said to be without precedent in the history of the United States." Mass meetings were held in Bostion, Chicago, Minneapolis, and Rochester, New York. Thousands of petitions, containing more than one million signatures, poured into Georgia from every state in the union. Chicago, alone, sent more than twenty thousand petitions with over 500,000 names, and Cincinnati, five hundred petitions. The Detroit *Times*, the Omaha *Bee*, the Cincinnati *Post*, the Louisville *Herald*, the Boston *Traveler*, and several Los Angeles newspapers printed coupons, asking clemency for Leo Frank, which readers could clip, sign, and return to the pub-

lisher's office for shipment to Georgia. Thousands responded
to these solicitations. Leo Frank, himself, received over 1,500
letters daily in May, 1915. His plight had captured the imagination of more than a million people.[10]

Georgian reaction to this fantastic display of public sympathy varied. More than ten thousand residents of the state
petitioned the Governor on Frank's behalf. Included in this
group were the state's junior United States Senator, Thomas
Hardwick, and both the son and son-in-law of the senior Senator, Hoke Smith, a political opponent of Tom Watson.
Many ministers, bankers, and lawyers also either wrote letters
or signed petitions, indicating that doubt existed as to Frank's
guilt and that, under the circumstances, the court's verdict
should be altered.[11] A number of prominent state newspapers, including *The Atlanta Journal, The Atlanta Georgian,
The North Georgia Citizen* (frequently called the *Dalton
Citizen*), and the Brunswick *News* reached the same conclusion.[12]

But a great many Georgians still wanted to see Frank hang.
None were as articulate as Tom Watson, the state's most ve-
hement opponent of commutation. He warned the Prison
Commission and the Governor not to undo what the courts
had decided; if the chief executive, who had the final authority, ignored the judicial decisions, *"there will almost inevit-
ably be the bloodiest riot ever known in the history of the
South."* [13]

The attacks upon Frank, the vulnerable antagonist, thrust
Watson, who had suffered years of setbacks, to the apex
of his popularity in Georgia. During his crusade against the
"jewpervert" *The Jeffersonian's* sales more than tripled and
profits soared. Before the Frank campaign had begun, Watson's newspaper had a circulation of about 25,000. For the
first week of September, 1915, this figure jumped to 87,000.
Thomas Loyless, the editor of *The Augusta Chronicle*, estimated that at the height of its popularity, *The Jeffersonian's*
profits exceeded $1,000 a week. Inspired by the public's re-

sponsiveness, Watson's vehemence grew more intense, more repetitive, and in the eyes of his readers, more brilliant. At the end of June, 1915, a follower rhapsodized: "It did not seem possible to me that you could improve on what you have said heretofore in the Frank case, but this last article is the best one." [14]

Tom Watson's campaign against Frank exacerbated the bitterness that Georgians harbored toward "the lustful Jew." The passions originally aroused by Mary Phagan's death and Leo Frank's trial were rekindled by essays in *The Jeffersonian* and *Watson's Magazine.* "RISE PEOPLE OF GEORGIA," the vitriolic editor demanded. He urged them to hold mass meetings and vent their feelings: "Let the Governor and the Prison Commission hear from the people." "Are you going to allow a clamorous minority, make a mockery of Justice, a farce of jury trial, a bye-word of our Laws?" Watson asked. "Are you going to provide encouragement and justification *for future lynchings,* by allowing Big Money to annul the well-weighed findings of unimpeachable jurors, whose verdict rests on unimpeachable testimony, and bears the approval of the highest court in the world?" [15]

In response to Watson's advice, protest rallies were held throughout the state. In Atlanta mass meetings, ostensibly to defend and preserve the right of trial by jury, occurred regularly in June, 1915. One gathering, held on June 5, 1915, on the grounds of the state capital, attracted thousands. *The Augusta Chronicle* characterized this group as a "mob." "We say it was 'hideous' and we call it a 'mob' because there was the bloodthirsty spirit of the mob in it. . . ." Crowds cheered the mentioning of Tom Watson and Hugh Dorsey. Leo Frank's name, on the other hand, evoked cries of "Hang him, hang him, let him hang!" The meeting ended with a hymn, and the group passed a resolution upholding the verdicts of the Georgia courts and demanding that equal justice be meted out to rich and poor alike. Subsequent gatherings attracted fewer, though equally zealous, individuals. Oftimes "Fiddling John" Carson entertained the people with verses from "The Ballad of Mary Phagan":

> Little Mary Phagan
> She left her home one day;
> She went to the pencil-factory
> To see the big parade.
>
> She left her home at eleven,
> She kissed her mother good-by;
> Not one time did the poor child think
> That she was a-going to die.[16]

3

Within hearing distance of the public demonstrations, the Georgia Prison Commission met in special session on May 31, 1915, to consider Frank's appeal for commutation.[17] Frank's plea consisted primarily of information presented before other tribunals, a letter from a prominent graphologist who believed that Jim Conley had written the murder notes without the assistance of any other person,[18] and a new letter from Leonard Roan, the judge who had presided over Frank's trial, which had been sent to the defense counsel in December, 1914. Roan had again expressed his uncertainty of Frank's guilt and acknowledged that perhaps he had shown "undue deference to the opinion of the jury." The judge agreed to repeat these doubts, at the proper time, to the Prison Commission and the Governor. Roan died before the Prison Commission met; hence the attorneys for Frank presented his views to the Commissioners. "The element of doubt, alone," one of Frank's lawyers insisted, "is sufficient to warrant commutation. And the letter of the trial justice, Judge Roan, is sufficient to establish doubt enough to warrant such action." [19]

The prosecution made no counter showing to the defense

plea. Dorsey had sent the Commission a letter expressing the state's opposition to any alteration of the death penalty, but he did not deem it necessary to appear in person.[20]

By a vote of 2 to 1, the Prison Commissioners refused to recommend clemency. Since there had been no new evidence, the majority saw no reason to intervene. Furthermore, they noted that neither the grand jurors who indicted Frank, the trial jurors who heard the testimony, nor the prosecutor for the state had interceded in Frank's behalf. The one Prison Commissioner dissenting went beyond the legalities to reach his decision. He doubted the veracity of Jim Conley's story and also seemed impressed with Judge Roan's remarks. In his minority opinion this commissioner noted that no precedent existed for hanging a man where the trial judge had expressed doubt about the defendant's guilt.[21]

The Prison Commission's decision may have pleased a majority of Georgians, but it shocked Thomas Loyless, editor of *The Augusta Chronicle*, and "greatly surprised . . . *the best thought and sentiment in Georgia.*"[22] Loyless had been led to believe that the Commissioners were going to recommend commutation, and when they did not, he intimated that they might have been intimidated by public opinion. Loyless considered this outrageous and advised, in the title of an indignant editorial, *"Let Governor Slaton Do His Duty As He Sees It, Regardless!"*[23]

4

Governor John M. Slaton had been one of the most popular chief executives in the history of Georgia. He had entered office with sixteen years of legislative experience behind him, and the esteem of all who knew him. In 1912 he had been elected Governor, "on a tidal wave of popular enthusiasm unprecedented in Georgia's annals."[24] During his two years in office Slaton fulfilled the expectations of those who had elected him, including Tom Watson who had supported him, by carrying out his duties with integrity and aplomb. In the primary of 1914 he had successfully vied for the Democratic nomination for United States Senator. Although he won a plurality of the county votes, and a majority of the popular votes, the delegates to the state convention selected Thomas Hardwick for the position.[25] In the same primary Nathaniel Harris, a "Watson man," won the nomination for Governor and was subsequently elected. He was scheduled to be inaugurated on June 26, 1915.

Because his death had been set for June 22, 1915, Leo Frank's plea for commutation would reach Governor Slaton's desk four days before Harris would take office. In June, 1915, Slaton was at the peak of his popularity. Knowledgeable Georgians assumed that on his next try he would succeed in winning a seat in the United States Senate. It is true that Slaton did expect to crown his political achievements as a Senator from Georgia. But he had not yet amassed enough strength to capture the nomination. Additional support would be necessary. Tom Watson, one of the state's leading politicians, indicated that he would be willing to throw his weight behind the Governor, if Slaton would let Frank die.[26]

Governor Slaton had an important decision to make. He had reason to believe that his political future would be jeopardized if he altered the court's decision. Since his term was about to expire, Slaton could have withdrawn gracefully from consideration of the case. He might have maintained that the pressure of last-minute business awaiting his administration prevented his giving the necessary deliberation to Frank's plea and that justice required that he defer to the next Governor, Nathaniel Harris, who would not be handicapped by lack of time and could re-examine the material judiciously before making a final decision.

Slaton also could have avoided the case by claiming "personal involvement." He had this option because he was the law partner of Leo Frank's attorney, Luther Rosser. In 1913, before the murder of Mary Phagan, but after Slaton had been elected Governor, the law offices of Slaton and Phillips had joined with those of Rosser and Brandon, to form the new firm of Rosser, Slaton, and Phillips. Slaton had done this to insure the continuity of his practice while he was Governor. For purposes of prestige he permitted his partners to use his name while he served as the state's chief executive. The merger of the offices had been agreed upon two weeks before Mary Phagan's death, but the partnership was not actually consummated until July, 1913. In the meantime Leo Frank had become Luther Rosser's client. After the new law partners commenced operations, Slaton had nothing to do with the defendant; he shared neither the burdens of the work nor the rewards of the fee. The Slaton-Rosser agreement received little publicity at the time of the merger, but in 1915 Tom Watson reminded Georgians that Governor Slaton and Leo Frank's attorney, Luther Rosser, were partners.[27] Although observers could legitimately recognize the delicacy of Slaton's position, the Governor sensed no conflict of interest. When the petition for commutation reached his desk, he assumed responsibility for the decision.

Slaton, a man with a keen sense of justice, faced the issue squarely in spite of the possible political consequences. Why he did this is pure conjecture. Perhaps he felt that he could have no self-respect if he shirked this important case. On the other hand, he might have surmised—and I have no evidence to support this contention—that he would be fairer in evaluating the evidence than his successor, Nathaniel Harris, because the latter was a close ally of Tom Watson's. Slaton may have felt—and again, this observation cannot be substantiated—that Harris would have been loath to antagonize both his patron and his constituents during his first weeks in office. And it may simply have been that Slaton felt it was his responsibility to deal with the issue, and so he did. In any case, the decision to become the judge of Leo Frank's case proved the most fateful of John M. Slaton's career.

Once having decided to consider the matter, Slaton moved

quickly. He heard arguments from both the defense counsel and the prosecuting attorney, and then he visited the pencil factory to familiarize himself with the building, its layout, and the functioning of the elevator. Since Frank's attorneys and Hugh Dorsey had differed as to the actual place of the crime —the defense had claimed that Mary met her doom in the basement, the prosecution had insisted that death overcame the girl in the metal workroom opposite Frank's office on the second floor—Slaton tried to obtain as much information as possible about the pencil plant so that he might follow the different arguments more precisely.

After the hearings ended Slaton secluded himself to consider the evidence. He had more material to cope with than anyone realized. In addition to the voluminous court hearings and judicial pronouncements, and the letters already discussed in the newspapers, the Governor had received a personal letter from Judge Roan asking him to rectify the mistake the judge realized he had made by sentencing Frank to death. The Governor had also received a secret communication from one of Hugh Dorsey's law partners, informing him that Jim Conley's lawyer had confessed to this partner that Jim Conley had murdered Mary Phagan.[28] Another communiqué which had been received by Slaton and not published until 1923 came from an inmate in Atlanta's federal penitentiary. The inmate claimed to have seen Jim Conley struggling with Mary Phagan on the day of the murder.[29] For twelve days Slaton pondered the case. "I left no stone unturned in my investigation of the case," he confessed afterwards. "I went over it again and again from every point of view."[30] While he struggled to reach a correct verdict, the Governor was bombarded with pleas for commutation or demands that the prisoner hang. More than a thousand of the petitioners threatened to kill Slaton, and his wife, if he let Frank live.

Finally the day of judgment arrived. Slaton worked all day in his library, and well into the night. At 2 A.M., on June 21, he went upstairs where his wife had remained awake, awaiting the verdict. "Have you reached a decision?" she asked. "Yes," Slaton replied, "it may mean my death or worse, but I have ordered the sentence commuted." It was said that Mrs. Slaton kissed her husband and told him: "I would rather be the widow of a brave and honorable man than the wife of a coward." [31]

Before announcing his decision Slaton made sure that Leo Frank was safe from the reach of Atlanta's mobs. He had secretly instructed the sheriff of Fulton County to deliver the prisoner to the state prison farm at Milledgeville. At about 10 P.M., on June 20, the sheriff told Frank to gather his belongings and prepare to leave the prison. Extensive security precautions had been taken. The telephone wires to the jail had been disconnected, and an automobile had been ordered to pull up in front of the building and keep its motor idling. Reporters noticed the car and watched it expectantly. While they did so, the sheriff and six deputies removed Frank from his cell, escorted him to the basement, and then to a back alley exit where another car was waiting. As soon as the group entered, the vehicle sped away. While reporters zealously guarded the other automobile, parked in front of the prison, Leo Frank and his guards headed for Atlanta's main railroad terminal. A midnight train took them to Macon, and at about 3 A.M. they reached their destination. The group drove the rest of the distance—about twenty-five miles—to the prison farm at Milledgeville. Orders were given to the warden to double the prison guard and to refuse Frank all visitors who had not received authorization from the Prison Commission in Atlanta. The following day a reporter observed, "Never in the history of Georgia's prison system had such a perfect system of secrecy been thrown around an action." [32]

With Frank safely at the state prison farm, Governor Slaton announced the commutation of Leo Frank's sentence to life imprisonment. "Feeling as I do about this case," the Governor added in an aside, "I would be a murderer if I allowed that man to hang." [33] A ten thousand word commentary, detailing the reasons for commutation, accompanied Slaton's announcement.

The Governor's explanation showed that he had given the case an exhaustive review. He appeared thoroughly conversant with the minutiae of the records. Slaton based his opinions primarily upon the inconsistencies he had discovered in the narrative of Jim Conley, who, he had concluded, "was as depraved and lecherous a negro as ever lived in Georgia."

The first significant point Slaton elaborated upon was evidence that had been overlooked by both defense and prosecution throughout the case—the human excrement found at the bottom of the elevator shaft in the pencil factory on Sunday morning, April 27, 1913, after the girl's body had been found. Conley had admitted, at the trial, that he had defecated there on Saturday morning. Conley had also sworn that he and Frank had taken Mary Phagan's body from the second floor metal room to the basement, via the elevator, on Saturday afternoon, April 26, 1913. But witnesses had testified, and the Governor himself had observed, that the elevator always touched the bottom of the shaft when it reached the basement. If Conley had indeed taken the corpse to the basement Saturday afternoon, the elevator would have mashed the excrement. But on Sunday morning, detectives, who had used the stairs to reach the basement, noticed the formed feces in the elevator shaft. Reviewing this evidence, the Governor concluded that the elevator had not been to the basement from the time Conley had defecated on Saturday morning, until Sunday morning. If one accepted the fact that the girl's body did not reach the basement via the elevator, then Conley's whole narrative fell apart, the Governor concluded.

Other points which Governor Slaton touched upon included the condition of Mary Phagan's body. She had been dealt a severe blow in the head, which had bled freely. Yet blood had not been found on the lathe her head had supposedly been bashed against, or on the floor nearby, or in the elevator, or on the steps leading downstairs. On the other hand,

Mary Phagan's nostrils and mouth had been filled with sawdust and grime, ingredients found only in the factory basement, where her body had been discovered. The Governor,
therefore, concluded that Mary Phagan had met her doom in
the pencil factory cellar, rather than on the second floor, thus
indicating another significant falsehood in Conley's story.

Slaton also commented upon the so-called murder notes.
Their syntax and phraseology showed a marked resemblance
to the letters Jim Conley had written to Annie Maud Carter
in the winter of 1913–1914. They had been unearthed by William J. Burns in April, 1914. At the time of Burns's discovery
Conley had denied authorship, but by the time the letters
reached Governor Slaton, in June, 1915, the Negro sweeper
had acknowledged authorship, but still denied having included
any of the vulgar passages.[34] The Governor observed that the
words "like," "play," "lay," "love," and "hisself" appeared
frequently, and sometimes in the same context, in the letters to
Miss Carter and in both the murder notes and Conley's oral
testimony. Slaton commented, too, upon Conley's frequent
use of double adjectives: in the murder notes, in his oral
testimony at the trial, and in his letters to Miss Carter. Expressions such as "a long tall negro, black," "He was a tall, slim
build heavy man," and "a good long wide piece of cord in his
hands" were examples the Governor selected to illustrate his
contention. The murder notes, Slaton continued, had been
written on the carbons of old order pads, found in the basement of the pencil factory. This strongly corroborated, the
Governor believed, "the theory of the defense that the death
notes were written, not in Frank's office, but in the basement. . . ."

That the pads were found in the basement, that the murder
notes resembled Conley's other writings and oral testimony,
that no blood had appeared on the lathe or the floor near the
lathe, that the elevator probably had not been used to trans-
port the body, and finally that the hair found on the lathe,
alleged to have been Mary Phagan's, could not be verified as

such when examined under a microscope led Governor Slaton to conclude that the murder of Mary Phagan might not have been committed by Leo Frank. "What is the truth?" Slaton asked rhetorically. "We may never know." But by commuting the sentence to life imprisonment, the Governor declared that he was merely expressing the same doubt about Frank's guilt as had members of every other tribunal the case had come before.[35] A few days later, in a further elucidation of his actions, Slaton said:

Two thousand years ago another Governor washed his hands of a case and turned over a Jew to a mob. For two thousand years that Governor's name has been accursed. If today another Jew were lying in his grave because I had failed to do my duty I would all through life find his blood on my hands and would consider myself an assassin through cowardice.[36]

Privately, Slaton confided to friends that he believed Frank innocent and would have granted a full pardon if he were not convinced that in a short while the truth would come out and then "the very men who were clamoring for Frank's life would be demanding a pardon for him."[37] The Governor knew certain "facts" about the case, which he did not reveal at the time, corroborating the defense's theory of the way Conley had murdered Mary Phagan. It is possible that he thought this material might convince everyone of Frank's innocence. If this were so, then Slaton erred. Eight years would pass before the information he had received privately would become public; and at that time few people besides Frank's staunchest partisans would care at all.[38]

5

Throughout the nation the press and public responded jubilantly to the commutation. In Georgia the response varied. Most of the major dailies, including *The Atlanta Georgian* and *The Atlanta Journal* [39] and about half of the rural press, commended the Governor. They restricted their remarks, however, to the courage that Slaton had exhibited rather than the accuracy of his judgment.[40] Considering that rural Georgians had appeared so hostile to Frank, it seems surprising, at first, that so many country editors applauded Slaton's deed. But when one recalls that more than ten thousand Georgians, from all over the state, had petitioned the Governor to commute, the press reaction in the state seems less noteworthy. Thomas Loyless, editor of *The Augusta Chronicle*, perhaps typified those who praised the Governor. Although he had stated on a number of earlier occasions that Frank probably had murdered Mary Phagan, Loyless admitted that he was not absolutely sure of it. Therefore he supported an alteration of the death penalty to life imprisonment. A good many people in the state either agreed with him or subscribed to the point of view expressed by the Macon *News:* "Whatever citizens may think of John M. Slaton as a man, they still owe to him, while he is Governor, the respect and deference which his office inherently commands." [41]

Others in Georgia, however, reacted more negatively. L. L. Knight later commented that what had happened after Slaton commuted Frank's sentence could not be described adequately "without the pen of Dante." [42] Hugh Dorsey denounced the Governor; and throughout the state mobs demonstrated and burned Slaton in effigy. In Marietta the dummy bore a sign, "John M. Slaton, King of the Jews and Georgia's Traitor Forever." In Columbus one man allowed each of his three daughters to take a shot at the make-believe figure as it dangled in air. In Newnan Frank, too, was burned in effigy, and then both figures were cut down, set on fire, and dragged through the streets.[43]

Blinded by fury and prejudice, many Georgians turned upon their Jewish neighbors. In Canton citizens threatened "summary vengeance" upon all Jews who were not out of the city within twenty-four hours. And north of Atlanta the "Marietta Vigilance Committee" distributed the following handbill to Jewish merchants:

NOTICE

You are hereby notified to close up this business and
quit Marietta by Saturday night, June 29, 1915, or
else stand the consequences. We mean to rid Marietta
of all Jews by the above date. You can heed this
warning or stand the punishment the committee may
see fit to deal out to you.

And Marietta's Gentiles received small business cards, printed
in red ink, which read:

(CARRY ME IN YOUR PURSE)

STOP! and *THINK!*

Before You Spend Your Money.
Shall It Go To A Fund To

PROTECT MURDERERS

To Buy Governors. Stop and
Think. Now is the time to show
your colors, to show your true
American Blood.—

IS IT STREAKED?

Can't you buy Shoes from an
AMERICAN?
Can't you buy the Necessities of
Life from an AMERICAN?

AMERICAN GENTILES,
IT IS UP TO YOU

This little card is only a little ant
hill to start with. HELP it grow
into a MOUNTAIN.

Jewish merchants were also boycotted in other sections of the
state. The New Orleans *American* predicted that these out-
rages were only the beginnings of anti-Jewish demonstrations
in Georgia.[44]

In his first issue after the commutation Tom Watson bel-
lowed: *"Our grand old Empire State* HAS BEEN RAPED!"
Endless streams of condemnation and denunciation of Governor Slaton followed. "Hereafter," *The Jeffersonian's* editor
continued, "let no man reproach the South with Lynch law:
let him remember the unendurable provocation; and let him
say whether Lynch law *is not better than no law at all.*" And
then, with the ferocity that few writers in Georgia could
equal, Watson prophesied his most diabolical fantasy:

When John M. Slaton tosses on a sleepless bed, in the years to
come, he will see a vivid picture of that little Georgia girl, de-
coyed to the metal room by this satyr-faced New York Jew: he
will see her little hands put out, to keep off the lustful beast: he
will hear her cry of sudden terror; he will see her face purpling
as the cruel cord chokes her to death—*and John M. Slaton will
walk the floor, a wretched, conscience-smitten man, AND HE
WILL SWEAT BLOOD!* [45]

Governor Slaton might have ignored the burnings in effigy,
and the poisoned pens, but he could not overlook the pandemonium which erupted in the state capital. People gathered in
downtown Atlanta as soon as the news of the commutation
had reached them.[46] Drugged by weeks of *The Jeffersonian's*
venomous commentaries, and stirred to a "white-heat" by
their own pent-up indignation, they chanted, "We Want
John M. Slaton, Georgia's Traitor Governor." And they
meant, literally, what they said. After a day of threatening,
shouting, and jeering, crowds, "armed with shotguns, rifles,
derringers, brass knuckles, heavy canes, even dynamite,"
surged past squadrons of city policemen and marched in the
direction of the Governor's mansion.

John M. Slaton lived six miles from the state capital. State
troops had already barricaded his estate and encircled it with
cordons of barbed wire. An entire battalion of the state militia
stood guard with bayonets bared, for Slaton had declared martial law within a half mile radius of his estate. When the im-

passioned mobs arrived, they threw stones, bottles, and other missiles, but the Governor's home was too far from the road for anyone inside to have been reached. The militia dutifully protected the Governor's premises and eventually dispersed the people who had come. The next night the guardsmen cornered some seventy-five men and boys in the woods behind the house. They were armed with blackjacks, guns, and dynamite. All were arrested, but the Governor refused to swear out warrants against them. Martial law, around Slaton's property, however, remained in effect until he left the state a week later.[47] Mrs. Slaton recalled afterwards the terror that haunted her throughout that trying period:

For four nights I scarcely slept at all. It was not exactly the anxiety of the moment that kept me awake, but the frequent calls of "Halt, who goes there," that kept ringing out. Every time I was aroused, in spite of myself. We live six miles in the country, and there are woods back of our house. These were full of men trying to get in.[48]

The demonstrations lasted for more than a week. News of the commutation had reached Atlantans on Monday, June 21, 1915. On Saturday, June 26, Slaton's successor, Nathaniel Harris, was inaugurated Governor of Georgia. At the inaugural ceremonies guards continued to protect John M. Slaton. After the ceremonies, as both the old and the new Governors descended the steps of the state capital, there was an immediate outburst of hisses, boos, howls, and shouts of "lynch him, lynch him!" Heavily guarded, Slaton made his way to a waiting automobile and departed the scene. A few days later, he left Georgia for an extended journey throughout the United States. After his departure, *The Atlanta Constitution* editorialized: "There must be no more mob violence in Georgia!" [49] Once again the nation's press felt impelled to comment upon the people of Georgia. *The Madison* (Wisconsin) *Journal* observed that "The public condemnation of Governor Slaton proves not so much that Georgia has besmirched her honor as that Georgia has no honor." [50]

6

Many Georgians were unwilling to believe that Governor Slaton had commuted Frank's sentence without having received some compensation for his deed.[51] For more than a generation they had been inundated with tales of wealthy plutocrats subverting justice. Tom Watson's columns reiterated the same point. He continually argued that money and influence had combined to keep a Jewish murderer alive.

To be sure, money and influence did affect the course of Frank's case. It is unlikely that a man who had not received financial assistance could have paid the expenses entailed in having his situation reviewed three times by the highest court in the state and twice by the United States Supreme Court. Certainly, a poor man would have been unable to hire additional investigators to discover new information or stimulate enough newspapers to publicize his alleged injustice. Especially when the injustice was not atypical—a man condemned for a crime that he claimed not to have committed. It is also highly unlikely that men like Louis Marshall, Albert Lasker, Jacob Schiff, et al., would have shown as much concern if someone other than a Jew had been the victim of what they considered a gross miscarriage of justice.

The efforts of Northerners and Jews had helped arouse national opinion on Frank's behalf and had won for him additional hearings. But it also weakened his case among the Southerners who tended to see "in every notion coming out of the North a menace and an abomination; to view every idea originated by the Yankee or bearing the stamp of his acceptance as containing hidden within itself the old implacable will to coerce and destroy. . . ."[52]

Law-abiding citizens knew, however, that whether they approved of the Governor's decision or not, nothing could be done about the commutation. But others recalled the words of Tom Watson. He had intimated that commutation would invoke the law of Judge Lynch. A rural Georgia newspaper, expressing the hope that people would not heed the advice of those who wished to take the law into their own hands, warned that "stranger things have happened and circumstances seem to point in that direction." [53]

CHAPTER VIII

Vigilante Justice

LESS THAN TWO WEEKS AFTER Slaton had commuted Leo Frank's sentence state newspapers prominently featured the somber pilgrimage of saddened Georgians to the unveiling of Mary Phagan's monument. The main speaker commemorated "this sainted little girl . . . who, true to her inherent high breeding and the teachings of her devoted mother, gave up her young life rather than surrender that Christian attribute —the crown, glory and honor of true womanhood into the threshold of which she was just entering." A group of one hundred and fifty men, who called themselves the Knights of Mary Phagan, then met secretly near her grave, and pledged to avenge the little girl's death. A few days afterwards rumors circulated that a plan had been devised to kidnap Leo Frank from the prison farm and lynch him. Governor Harris alerted the state police, and thereby thwarted, for the moment, a plot concocted by some of Marietta's most prominent citizens.[1]

I

For Leo Frank, life on the prison farm was a striking improvement over his two years in the Atlanta cell, where he had lost sixty pounds. At Milledgeville he spent many hours outdoors under the warm Georgia sun, and this contributed to restoring his health, which had suffered in the dank city prison.[2] His daily chores never required more than four or five hours to complete, and he then had the rest of the day free.

Frank enjoyed the leisure afforded him in prison, where he maintained a voluminous correspondence. "This is the sixteenth letter I wrote today," he told his wife, and three days later repeated, "I wrote *only* 18 letters yesterday. . . ." He wrote to his wife almost every day, and although he cautioned her that "the contents of my letters, & my life must be kept quiet," there were few items in his letters that would interest anyone but a devoted mate. In fact, his letters during the first few weeks at the prison farm resemble those from a child vacationing at a summer camp. Frank requested that his wife send or bring him handkerchiefs and pajamas, tooth paste, writing pads, a can opener, Beech Nut gum, a soap dish, fig bars ("I don't want sweet crackers, too rich") and $5 in cash.[3] If the letters to Mrs. Frank give little indication of a man under stress, other writings, to Julius Rosenwald and Supreme Court Justice Oliver Wendell Holmes, reveal Frank's continuing faith that one day truth would triumph. He believed that eventually "Right and Justice" would hold "complete sway" and his vindication would be universally acknowledged.[4]

This semi-idyllic life did not last long. Only four weeks after his arrival, a fellow convict, William Creen, crept up to Frank's cot, plunged a butcher knife into the sleeping figure, and proceeded to slash his victim's throat.[5] By the time the guard, and two other convicts, reached the pair, blood flowed freely from a seven and a half inch wound. Fortunately, two other prisoners were doctors, and they quickly clamped the gushing jugular vein and stopped the hemorrhage. Frank was then removed to the prison hospital, where the two convict-doctors, along with the prison physician, stitched the wound, and then secured his head in a metal surgical brace to prevent the stitches from falling out. Days passed, however, before anyone would predict whether the operation would be successful. The doctors feared that blood poisoning might set in, making death a certainty.[6]

Governor Nathaniel Harris ordered an immediate investigation of the attack, but the warden's inquiry failed to satisfy him. Harris then went to the prison farm to review recent events and personally interviewed prison officials, Leo Frank, and William Creen, the assailant. Creen told Harris that he had been called "from on high" to murder the Jew, and explained further that he had tried to kill Frank to prevent other prisoners from being harmed, should an attempt be made to storm the prison and abduct its most notorious inmate. When Harris returned to Atlanta, he found petitions demanding that William Creen be pardoned as a reward for his noble deed.[7]

In the prison hospital Frank showed remarkable resiliency, calmness, and fortitude. Although doctors feared that he might not survive, Frank told one of them, "I am going to live. I must live. I must vindicate myself." When finally on the road to recovery, which "was little short of miraculous!" Frank wrote to a friend, "Certainly my escape was providential, and the good Lord must sure have in store for me a brighter and happier day when that honor, justly mine now, will be restored to me. I have been victorious in my struggle with death & I await impatiently for the day of vindication and liberty." [8]

The attack upon Frank brought further denunciation of Georgia, in both the Northern and Southern press, as editorial writers condemned state authorities for their laxity. Frank would not have been attacked, newspapers argued, had he been properly protected. In Georgia Thomas Loyless, of *The Augusta Chronicle*, castigated the "mob spirit" which culminated in Creen's savagery. He asked: "Who can doubt the psychological connection between such crazy acts as that of William Creen and the inflammatory articles and speeches of such *professional agitators and apostles of hate* as afflict Georgia?" And *The New Republic* looked back centuries for a parallel to Frank's experiences:

In ancient times when a man was treated as Leo Frank has been treated people felt that an obscene God was pursuing him. No mortal could be so relentless. No mortal could surround another with such ingenious cruelty. Only a conspiracy of fate could make horror so massive. We try nowadays to think differently, but in the case of Frank it is not easy.[9]

2

One month after the attempt on Frank's life, a band of twenty-five men stormed the prison farm shortly after 11 P.M. Five went directly to the warden's house, while several cornered the prison superintendent; both men were handcuffed, but otherwise unharmed. There were only two guards on duty that night, and they were easily overpowered. (One of them had heard several automobiles approaching the prison farm and had pleaded in vain with his chief to move their famous prisoner to a safer place.) Four of the intruders went directly to Frank's hospital room and met with no obstacles. As soon as they opened his door, one of the men said, "We want you to come with us." Frank got out of bed and made a feeble attempt to dress himself, but one of the men commanded: "Don't bother with the clothes; come just as you are." The abductors then handcuffed their charge, and led him out of the building. Frank, stoically calm, as was his wont, looked neither terrified nor surprised; nor did he make any attempt to resist. In all, the intruders spent less than five minutes in the prison; when they left, no one pursued them.[10]

The men who kidnapped Leo Frank had begun to plan their adventure after Governor Slaton had commuted his sentence. These men represented the "best citizens" of Marietta, Georgia, the hometown of Mary Phagan. In fact, the so-called riffraff had been deliberately excluded. A clergyman, two former Superior Court justices, and an ex-sheriff were included among the planners and executioners who were later described, by the Dean of the Atlanta Theological Seminary, as "a sifted band of men, sober, intelligent, of established good name and character—good American citizens." The leader bore "as reputable [a] name as you would ever hear in a lawful community. He was a man honored and respected." The abductors were the same men who, a month earlier, had postponed their plans to kidnap and lynch Frank when news of the conspiracy had reached Governor Harris. On August 16, 1915, however, they carried out their task with order, precision, and dispatch.[11]

The kidnapping of Leo Frank showed that careful preparations had been made. Two scouts had been sent in advance to reconnoiter and cut the telephone and telegraph wires leading to the prison, while other men had departed, at intervals, from Marietta earlier that afternoon. To avoid drawing attention to themselves, each small group traveled a different route in the 175-mile trip to Milledgeville. After converging at a prearranged spot, the men proceeded to the prison. To mask their identity, they wore goggles and kept their hats pulled down over their faces. After seizing Frank, they drove all night before finally stopping in a grove, just outside Marietta. The original plan had called for hanging Leo Frank near Mary Phagan's grave, but dawn broke earlier than anticipated. The kidnappers, wishing not to be seen, selected another site for the execution.

In the automobile that had taken Frank to his final destination, the prisoner sat, apparently unruffled,[12] between two guards in the rear seat. The kidnappers tried to get their prisoner to confess, but he would not do so. Some of the abductors even offered to let him live if he would confess, but Frank would not yield. In fact, on the few occasions that the prisoner spoke, he sounded so sincere that two of his listeners thought that perhaps he really had not murdered Mary Phagan, and that he should be returned to the prison farm. But when all the automobiles stopped, and this suggestion was made, the passengers of the other cars were shocked. Then Frank began to talk. When he had finished, he had convinced others in the group of his sincerity, and all but four indicated their willingness to forgo the lynching. But then someone pointed out that it was too late to drive back to Milledgeville, that posses were out all over the state, and that there was no time left to change their plans. So the men once again concerned themselves with their intended task. But "at least one of [the] self-appointed executioners mutinied, urged that Frank be returned to prison, and refused to take part in the final scene of the drama." [13]

Those that remained finished what they had set out to do. Frank was escorted to a large oak tree. Along the way he muttered, "I think more of my wife and my mother than I do of my life." As members of the party professionally tied a Manila rope into a hangman's knot, Frank was again asked if he had murdered Mary Phagan; but he did not reply. The leader then spoke: "Mr. Frank, we are now going to do what the law said to do—hang you by the neck until you are dead. Do you want to make any statement before you die?" Frank said that he did not wish to say anything else, but then changed his mind and requested that his wedding ring, which he then removed from his finger, be delivered to a newspaperman with the instructions that the reporter return it to his wife. (Frank's last wish was obeyed.) The executioners tied the knot around their prisoner's neck, flung the rope over a limb of the oak tree, placed Frank upon a table, and proceeded, after checking to see that everything had been done properly, to kick the table from under the feet of the suspended figure. Without waiting to see their victim dead, the lynchers left. One of the members of the lynching party confided afterwards that the hangmen did not go about their work with "a spirit of lawlessness or vindictiveness. They felt it [the lynching] to be a duty to the State and a duty to the memory of Mary Phagan. . . ." [14,*]

* There is an ironic footnote to this story. One of the members of the lynching party, known as D. B. (Bunce) Napier in 1915, but called Fred Lockhart nineteen years later, was himself almost lynched on April 17, 1934 —the fiftieth anniversary of Leo Frank's birth—by a mob in Shreveport, Louisiana. He told reporters then that he had driven the car in which Frank

Crowd milling about after the lynching. Frank is suspended from the tree.

3

News of Frank's abduction had spread quickly. Those who had been assigned to cut the telephone wires in Milledgeville had missed one connection, so that within an hour after the kidnapping state officials knew of the affair. Governor Harris alerted the sheriff of every county between Milledgeville and Marietta to watch for a caravan of automobiles passing swiftly through their territories. A resident of Marietta had also seen the lynching party pass by and walked into town to announce his observation. Somehow Mariettans had no difficulty in finding the exact location of the lynching shortly after the executioners had completed their work. Hordes of people made their way to the oak tree where the lifeless figure, with its gaping red throat wound, swayed in the wind. Souvenir hunters tore pieces of cloth from the sleeves of the nightshirt which covered the body, and snipped strands of the rope.[15] Others took pictures or milled about happily, as if at a holiday barbecue. Wild-eyed people gaped; women and children examined the dead man closely. One man ran up to the swaying corpse and shouted: "Now we've got you! You won't murder any more little innocent girls! We've got you now!! We've got you now!!!" Shouts and yells echoed in the wind.

One man who wanted to mutilate and burn the body was stopped by the intervention of a respected Marietta judge, Newton Morris. Morris had rushed to the scene as soon as he heard of the lynching. When he arrived, he saw the half-

had taken his final journey after being whisked away from the prison hospital. Lockhart said that he now understood how Frank must have felt that night. Lockhart explained that he had changed his name after escaping from a Georgia chain gang on August 19, 1931. He had been sentenced to prison for criminally assaulting a young girl. (*Author's Note.* The Baltimore Morning *Sun*, April 20, 1934, p. 1; clipping, *Atlantic City Evening Union*, April 20, 1934, located within the Alexander Brin scrapbooks. Mr. Brin permitted me to see his collection when I interviewed him on August 19, 1964 in Boston.)

crazed man screaming and demanding a bonfire. The Judge interceded and pleaded with everyone to permit Frank's remains to be sent home to his parents for a decent burial. He convinced the onlookers and quickly arranged for two undertakers to carry the corpse away. As Frank's body was being removed, the man who had originally wanted to burn him struck the body, and it fell to the ground with a thump. Then he "stamped upon the face, and ground his heel into the dead flesh, and stamped again, and again, until the crowd, stricken silent and motionless by the horror of the sight, could hear the man's heel as it made a crunching sound." "Stop him! Stop him!" Judge Morris implored, while signaling the undertakers to remove the dead man. They responded as ordered, swiftly lifted the corpse into their wagon, and headed straight for Atlanta.[16] This maniacal incident, however, seemed to have escaped the notice of *The Marietta Journal and Courier*, which praised the onlookers for their good conduct: "We are proud, indeed, to say that the body hanged for more than two hours amid a vast throng and no violence was done. Cobb county people are civilized. They are not barbarians."[17]

In Atlanta thousands surrounded the undertaking establishment and threatened to force their way in. Their morbid appetites would not be satiated until they, too, could see the body of this devil incarnate. The police succumbed to their wish and permitted an orderly viewing of Frank's remains before the undertakers shipped it to New York, for burial at Mt. Carmel Cemetery. Fifty policemen stood guard as more than 15,000 persons passed by the bier. The acting Mayor appeared on the scene and urged everyone "to be orderly and quiet, and thus protect the good name of our great city," but he pleaded to no avail. Boisterous crowds pressed against the police, and each other, in their eagerness to see the corpse. Men and women filed by the casket in separate lines. "Scores of women [passed] without so much as a look of horror on their faces as their eyes fell upon the dead man's body." Cameramen photographed the corpse, the crowds, the guards, the funeral parlor, and everything else that caught their eye.[18]

Outside the undertaking establishment souvenir hunters purchased pictures of Frank's body dangling from the tree, and hundreds bought pieces of the rope. (As late as 1917, pictures of the lynching could still be purchased in Marietta.) The traffic in souvenirs alarmed city officials. Four days after the lynching the Atlanta City Council "unanimously passed an ordinance making it unlawful to sell in Atlanta a photograph of the body of a person who has been hanged illegally."[19]

Several affluent Georgians offered as much as $250 for the tree from which Leo Frank had been hung, but the owner refused to sell. Instead he encouraged loyal citizens of Marietta to guard the big oak. Townspeople made pilgrimages to the hallowed oak and, according to the owner, "hugged and patted that old tree and then they stood still and looked upward for a long time. I think they must have been praying." Plans were made to build a concrete wall around the tree, calling forth the sardonic comment from a Wisconsin newspaper: "If the prison in which Frank was kept had been so surrounded, the tree would not need to be now imprisoned."[20]

Governor Harris expressed shock and grief at the lynching and ordered an investigation. Everyone knew, though, that the search would prove fruitless. The lynchers had carried out the will of the people, and the local Marietta newspaper praised their deed: "We regard the hanging of Leo M. Frank in Cobb county as an act of law abiding citizens." With public sentiment so favorable, an indictment was impossible. The Greensboro (Georgia) *Herald-Journal* cannily observed that "the lynchers could confess, publish their confession in the Atlanta papers, and they would never be molested." The killers were generally known throughout Marietta—some of them, in fact, gave interviews to reporters;[21] but after an inquest, the Coroner's jury concluded that Leo Frank died at the hands of persons unknown. *The Pittsburgh Gazette* inter-

preted this announcement for its readers: "What the coroner's jury really meant was that Frank 'came to his death by
hanging at the hands of persons whom the jury wishes to remain unknown.' " [22]

The press of the nation denounced the state of Georgia
while the press of Georgia—with the exception of *The Jeffersonian, The Marietta Journal and Courier*, two Macon papers,
and a Baptist weekly—upbraided the lynchers. The opinion
of the *Richmond Times-Dispatch* was representative of those
horrified by the act: "[Frank's] lynching constitutes the most
vicious blow struck at organized government in a century,
and the South, in particular, must suffer." Even *The Atlanta
Constitution*, which had heretofore remained editorially silent
on Leo Frank, headed its arraignment: "Georgia's Shame!"
and began its charge: "No word in the language is too strong
to apply to the deliberate and carefully conspired deed of the
mob." [23]

There were, however, accolades for the lynchers. The editor of Georgia's most prominant Baptist journal, *The Christian Index*, observed that an "orderly mob" had carried out
the judicial verdict. "He deplored the fact," however, "that
the mob had to administer the justice which the courts should
have administered." [24] Tom Watson, naturally, praised the
doers and the deed. The Mayor of Atlanta announced, to a
conference in California, that Frank suffered a "just penalty
for an unspeakable crime." L. L. Knight, the chronicler of
Georgia's history, wrote in 1917: "There is something inherently fine in the passionate desire of a people to keep inviolate
the honor of womanhood and to visit swift punishment upon
a wretch who dares to stain the purity of a child's life. . . ." [25]

Judge Newton Morris, the man who had prevented Frank's
corpse from being burned, explained to a reporter that "the
very best people" had permitted Frank's appeal to go through
all of the courts, but after the judges had turned down his
successive requests, they were "outraged" by Slaton's action.
Many people believed that Frank's lawyer, Louis Marshall,

had deliberately speeded the judgment of the United States Supreme Court back to the Georgia courts, so that his client's clemency petition would reach Governor Slaton and not Governor Harris. (It is true that Frank's lawyers had expedited the process because they wanted Slaton to act, but there is no evidence that they had bribed him or that they had expected him to act favorably because Rosser was his partner.[26]) A great many Georgians, the Judge continued, were aggrieved at how much money had been spent to buy the Northern press. While Frank's position had been clearly and emphatically restated in these newspapers, Judge Morris bitterly observed, the Georgian side had been ignored. The Judge concluded: "I believe in law and order. I would not help lynch anybody. But I believe Frank has had his just deserts." [27]

CHAPTER IX

Aftermath

I

FRANK'S FATE COULD, perhaps, have been forecast. Personal responsibility for the enforcement of the law—deplored by many yet accepted by significant numbers—was part of the Southern heritage. In ante-bellum days the master had almost total power over the dispensation of justice to his slaves. And when he dealt with equals, the Southern plantation dweller would sooner resort to a duel than request any third party—a law officer, for example—to intercede on his behalf. Poor whites had absorbed the mores of the upper classes, and the tradition of individual law enforcement has retained its potency well into the twentieth century. The defense of a woman's honor was also part of every Southerner's creed, and the culture dictated swift punishment to anyone who violated a kinswoman. In the closed Southern society, where fourth and fifth cousins were regarded as blood relations, whole communities felt responsible for their women.

Violence had characterized the Old South to some extent, but it flourished even more in the New South. Gun fights, duels, lynchings, family feuds, and the like were part of everyday living for many Southerners.[1] Georgians had been especially notorious in following this infamous tradition. From 1889 through 1928, for example, more people were lynched in their state than any other state in the Union.[2] Two weeks after Georgians had attempted to mob him, John M. Slaton readily acknowledged that "there are some offenses to which [Southerners] take the law into their own hands." Slaton then elaborated: "In the South we generally punish by lynching for one offense"—assaulting a white woman.[3]

To those small-town Southerners who pondered the Frank case lynching seemed the most appropriate action. Georgia's major Baptist publication, *The Christian Index*, had observed as early as 1892 that the great majority of lynchings came about because Southerners were imbued with "a high sense of honor and [the] highest regard for female character." Seven years later it repeated: "By common consent, lynching for rape has been made an offense to be condoned." Tom Watson's bellowing, therefore, merely encouraged an accepted procedure; and the "best citizens" of Marietta did not hesitate to fulfill their moral obligations.[4]

But the death of Leo Frank did not dissipate the wrath of disgruntled Georgians. Ironically, in fact, the lynching left a void—the despondent and the vengeful had lost their whipping boy. In the autumn of 1915 Colonel William J. Simmons stepped into this vacuum with a new answer to an insoluble problem: a new fraternal organization dedicated to the everlasting exaltation of Southern heroism, chivalry, and Anglo-Saxon splendor; an organization that would work for the revival of rural, Protestant culture; an organization which shunned the alien, put the Negro in his place, and elevated the Anglo-Saxon American to his rightfully superior niche in American society. This new fraternity would revive the glorious name and hallowed memory of the well-remembered paragon of Southern heroism—the Knights of the Ku Klux Klan [5] —that was active in the Reconstruction days after the Civil War.

Simmons, a professional fraternalist who belonged to six or seven other lodges, had, as an adolescent, envisioned the day when he would inaugurate a new order to memorialize the old Ku Klux Klan.[6] His opportunity came during the hullabaloo which ended with Leo Frank's hanging from a large oak tree.

After Frank's death, Simmons found in Georgia a receptive group, which had been mobilized by Tom Watson and now needed new direction.[7] Simmons answered the call. His new Ku Klux Klan opposed everything that Frank had personified: urbanization, industrialization, and foreigners. The Klan staunchly defended American, small-town, Protestant values such as sexual morality, religious orthodoxy, and traditional economic individualism, and deplored all the modern innovations which had compromised the accepted virtues of Southern life.

Had it not been for Leo Frank, Simmons would probably have had to wait before launching his venture. But he found in the Knights of Mary Phagan, already organized but with its sense of purpose vanished, a suitable nucleus for the new Klan. In the autumn of 1915 Simmons and thirty-three of the Knights of Mary Phagan met on a mountain top just outside Atlanta and brought the Klan into being with elaborate ritual.[8]

2

The Frank case revealed how weak were the safeguards of our judicial system against police loquacity, journalistic license, and politically ambitious prosecutors. The police have often shared their findings and assumptions with newspapermen whose papers reported—and sometimes distorted—the semi-official version of events. Sensational cases often have been tried in the newspapers long before they reached the courtroom. Under such circumstances it is often difficult for the most conscientious juror to attempt an impartial evaluation of the facts presented during a trial. Juries, too, have been notorious for their responsiveness to community sentiment.[9] Certainly Leo Frank was tried before he ever appeared in court.

The process of selecting American public prosecutors—not unique to Georgia—clearly contributed to Frank's undoing.

More frequently elected than appointed, the state's attorney is dependent upon the good will of his constituents for both his position and subsequent political advancement. To further their careers, politically ambitious prosecutors frequently seek popular and dramatic convictions to publicize their own talents. In 1913, when Hugh Dorsey prosecuted Leo Frank, he convinced many people that his primary concern was with his political reputation and not with obtaining justice.[10]

Since Frank's death the United States Supreme Court has revamped its standards for fair trials. Beginning in 1923, the Court overruled numerous criminal convictions which came about, in its estimate, because community sentiment had entered the jury box or because pretrial publicity precluded an impartial hearing. Prosecutors have also been censured for misconduct and states have been condemned for using perjured testimony.

The first significant change occurred in 1923, when Oliver Wendell Holmes, who had dissented from the majority viewpoint in *Frank* v. *Mangum*, practically restated the same opinion as spokesman for the Court. The case, *Moore* v. *Dempsey*, involved five Arkansas Negroes who, in the words of Justice Holmes, "were hurried to conviction under the pressure of a mob, without any regard for their rights, and without according to them due process of law." Such circumstances, Holmes concluded in a doctrine which has been accepted by the federal courts ever since, interfere with the course of justice, depart from due process of law, and hence are not coincident with the preservation of constitutionally guaranteed rights.[11] Louis Marshall commented afterwards that the Supreme Court "adopted the principle for which I contended." [12]

Another subject on which justices of the Supreme Court have expressed concern has been coerced confessions. In 1913 an Atlanta jury relied primarily upon Jim Conley's testimony to convict the factory superintendent. Yet Conley had been questioned by the police and had given certain statements, without having had the benefit of counsel. Conley had also incriminated himself in affidavits which he signed after having undergone a series of intensive interrogations. Because Conley's charges had received extensive publicity, they provided another difficult hurdle which Leo Frank had to overcome before his trial officially began.

In the 1930s, however, the Supreme Court began to overrule convictions which had been based on what it interpreted as coerced confessions. In *Brown* v. *Mississippi*, a unanimous Court ruled that confessions obtained after the accused had been whipped into submission were void.[13] In the case of *Chambers* v. *Florida*, in 1940, Justice Hugo Black, speaking for another unanimous court, reinforced this judgment. Black declared that confessions obtained after the accused had been subjected to five days of questioning, without having had recourse to counsel, were presumed to be coerced confessions, hence a denial of due process of law.[14] Six years later, in *Ashcraft* v. *Tennessee*, the Supreme Court overruled the conviction of a man who had given a confession "after thirty-six hours [of] continuous grilling by investigating officers, who were holding him incommunicado in the county jail."[15] In similar cases, in 1957 and 1963, the Court continued to strengthen the right of a defendant against self-incrimination. In *Fikes* v. *Alabama*, Chief Justice Earl Warren held a confession invalid which had been made after a prisoner had been kept in isolation for a week "except for sessions of questioning."[16] In 1963 Justice Arthur Goldberg stated, in a significant ruling, that the United States Constitution favors "the right of the accused to be advised by his lawyer of his privilege against self-incrimination."[17] And finally, in 1966, the Court set new and more stringent standards for police interrogations. Under the most recent rulings, "the prosecutor cannot use in a trial any admissions or confessions made by the suspect while in custody unless it first proves that the police complied with a detailed list of safeguards to protect the right against self-incrimination." These include the defendant's right to be informed that he may remain silent, that anything he says may be used against him, and that he is entitled to consult with an attorney before making any comment at all.[18]

There are other reasons which indicate that today's Court would not consider Frank's trial in accord with due process of law. In 1951 a majority of the high court's justices overruled a conviction which had been obtained after considerable pretrial publicity. In the opinion of Justices Felix Frankfurter and Robert Jackson, "prejudicial influences outside the courtroom . . . were brought to bear on this jury with such force that the conclusion is inescapable that the defendants were prejudged as guilty and that the trial was but a legal gesture to register a verdict already dictated by the press and public opinion which it generated." [19] In 1963 the Supreme Court restated this position in the case of *Rideau* v. *Louisiana*. Justice Potter Stewart, speaking for the majority, observed that after a community had been exposed to extensive publicity about an alleged criminal, "any subsequent court proceedings . . . could be but a hollow formality." [20] And more recently, in 1966, the Court considered the case of Dr. Samuel H. Sheppard, a Cleveland osteopath, who had been convicted, in 1954, of murdering his wife. Justice Tom Clark noted that the trial had been preceded by months of "virulent publicity" as "charges and countercharges were aired in the news media besides those for which Sheppard was called to trial." The Supreme Court assumed that some of the inflammatory assertions "reached at least some of the jury." The trial was then conducted in a "carnival atmosphere." Justice Clark, speaking for all but one member of the Court,[21] asserted that Sheppard's rights had been adversely affected by "the inherently prejudicial publicity which saturated the community." Justice Clark observed further, that every tribunal which had considered the case, "save the court that tried it, has deplored the manner in which the news media inflamed and prejudiced the public." Newspapers had given undue emphasis to material which tended to incriminate Dr. Sheppard, and in one account a detective " 'disclosed that scientific tests at the Sheppard home have definitely established that the killer washed off a trail of blood from the murder bedroom to the downstairs section.' " This "evidence" was never presented in court. The following excerpt from the Supreme Court's opinion is also reminiscent of the circumstances surrounding Leo Frank's trial in Atlanta:

Much of the material printed or broadcast during the trial was never heard from the witness stand, such as the charges that Sheppard had purposely impeded the murder investigation and must be guilty since he had hired a prominent criminal lawyer; that Sheppard was a perjurer; that he had sexual relations with numerous women; that his slain wife had characterized him as a "Jekyll-Hyde"; that he was "a bare-faced liar" because of his testimony as to police treatment; and, finally, that a woman convict claimed Sheppard to be the father of her illegitimate child. As the trial progressed, the newspapers summarized and interpreted the evidence, devoting particular attention to the material that incriminated Sheppard, and often drew unwarranted inferences from testimony. At one point, a front-page picture of Mrs. Sheppard's blood-stained pillow was published after being "doctored" to show more clearly an alleged imprint of a surgical instrument.

The trial judge also came in for censure because of his failure "to control disruptive influences in the courtroom." "The fact is," Justice Clark stated, "that bedlam reigned at the courthouse during the trial." The opinion concluded that because of the enumerated violations, Dr. Sheppard had not been accorded all of his legal rights and hence the State of Ohio had incarcerated him unjustly.[22]

In our own day, the methods employed by Solicitor Dorsey might also be subject to judicial scrutiny. Not only did he engage in conduct unbecoming a state official, but he also suppressed evidence and misrepresented important items. In 1935 Justice George Sutherland censured an attorney for being "guilty of misstating the facts in his cross-examination of witnesses; of putting into the mouths of such witnesses things which they had not said; of suggesting by his questions that statements had been made to him personally out of court, in respect of which no proof was offered . . . of assuming prejudicial facts not in evidence; of bullying and arguing with witnesses; and in general conducting himself in a thoroughly indecorous and improper manner." [23] And eight years later, Chief Justice Harlan F. Stone severely criticized the closing remarks of a federal prosecutor which, in the opinion of a majority of the Supreme Court, were calculated "to arouse passions and prejudice." In fact, the Chief Justice said that the conduct of the prosecutor "prejudiced petitioner's right to a fair trial and . . . might well have placed the judgment of conviction in jeopardy." [24] In 1967, moreover, the Supreme Court upset a criminal conviction because the prosecutor had "deliberately misrepresented the truth." He had repeatedly referred to a pair of men's undershorts, which "constituted a vital link in [the] circumstantial evidence on which defendant was convicted," as "bloody shorts" even though he "knew at [the] time of the trial that the shorts were stained with paint. . . ." "More than 30 years ago," Justice Potter Stewart concluded, "this Court held that the Fourteenth Amendment cannot tolerate a state criminal conviction obtained by the knowing use of false evidence. . . . There can be no retreat from that principle here." [25]

The Supreme Court has also ruled against the use of perjured testimony to obtain a conviction. Although none of the witnesses in the Frank case was ever convicted of perjury, many of them changed their statements, and then reverted to the originals, in the spring of 1914. Many people also thought that Jim Conley's testaments, each one modifying remarks sworn to previously, debarred him as a useful witness. It is unlikely that any court today would consider testimony made after the retraction of four successive affidavits worthy of consideration. In only one case, however, that of Annie Maud Carter, the woman who had received letters from Jim Conley, was it possible to prove that an affidavit was incorrect. With so many state witnesses contradicting their trial testimony, and then reverting to their original statements, the present Court might consider the possibility that the state influenced some of them to testify falsely. In a landmark decision, in 1935, the Supreme Court decided that if a state knowingly used witnesses whose testimony was falsified, the proceedings violated due process and hence were void.[26] This dictum was repeated by Justice Frankfurter in 1942, when he wrote, "If a state, whether by the active conduct or the connivance of the prosecution, obtains a conviction through the use of perjured testimony, it violates civilized standards for the trial of guilt or innocence and thereby deprives an accused of liberty without due process of law." [27] In 1957 the Court threw out a conviction obtained after the prosecutor had encouraged the key witness to withhold vital information—which, if known, almost certainly would have altered the jury's opinion—unless the defense attorney specifically asked for it.[28] And in the same vein Justice Warren, speaking for a majority in 1959, overruled a judgment in a criminal prosecution because the state's attorney promised to recommend a lighter sentence for a witness if he fabricated his testimony.[29]

With the Supreme Court so zealous in its defense of civil liberties today, it is extremely unlikely that another Frank case could occur. Although local communities and ambitious prosecutors may still wink at rigid standards of justice, the nation's highest court no longer tolerates a loose interpretation of the Fourteenth Amendment's directive that no state may "deprive any person of life, liberty, or property, without due process of law; nor deny to any person within its jurisdiction the equal protection of the laws."

3

To many prominent Jews, Leo Frank's trial and conviction seemed another instance of the anti-Semitic assaults which had become increasingly obvious for almost a generation. Mem-

bers of the American Jewish community therefore resolved to
take remedial action. Four weeks after Frank's trial ended, the
B'nai B'rith, a Jewish fraternal order founded in 1843, established its Anti-Defamation League to combat prejudice in the
United States. Plans for the organization had been discussed
for years, and each succeeding anti-Semitic outburst strengthened the hand of the proponents of the new group. But it
took Atlanta's condemnation of Leo Frank to give final impetus to the League. In the founding statement, Adolph
Kraus, President of the parent organization, commented
upon the abundance of prejudice and discrimination in this
country. "Remarkable as it is," one paragraph began, "this
condition has gone so far as to manifest itself recently in an
attempt to influence courts of law where a Jew happened to
be a party to the litigation. This symptom, standing by itself,
while contemptible, would not constitute a menace, but form-
ing as it does but one incident in a continuing chain of occasions of discrimination, it demands organized and systematic
effort on behalf of all right-thinking Americans to put a stop
to this most pernicious and un-American tendency." [30]

In Georgia hostility toward Jews and disapproval of their
intervention in the Frank case continued to echo long after
Frank's demise. A minister noted in October, 1915, that the
"masses" resented the power of money which had been used
"to protect criminals from the punishment which our laws
provide for their deeds." [31] Less than a year after the lynching, Senator Hoke Smith refrained from stirring up memories
of things past by withholding his announcement, until the last
minute, that he would vote to confirm Louis Brandeis, a Jew,
for a position on the United States Supreme Court.[32] And in
1925 Herbert Asbury, an Atlanta newspaperman, wrote: "If
the Jews had been content to regard Frank as a man suspected
of murder, entitled to a fair trial and nothing more, instead of
as a Jew on the threshold of martyrdom, hounded by Christians thirsting for his blood, there would have been little or no
anti-Semitic feeling in Atlanta." [33]

Whether Asbury was correct or not, however, is less sig-

nificant than the continued hostility which frightened Atlanta's Jews and made them fearful of further repercussions.
In 1923, at the height of the Ku Klux Klan's power, a foreign
journalist, working for *The Atlanta Constitution*, became interested in Leo Frank and went back to study the records of
the case. He came across some x-rays showing teeth inden-
tations in Mary Phagan's left shoulder and compared them
with x-rays of Frank's teeth; but the two sets did not corres-
pond. On the basis of this, and other insights garnered from
his investigation, the newspaperman wanted to write a series
"proving" Frank's innocence. One anonymous correspondent
sent him a printed note: "Lay off the Frank case if you want to
keep healthy," but this did not deter him. What did thwart
publication, however, was the effort of prominent Atlanta
Jews, fearing repercussions, who prevailed upon the *Constitution*'s editor to refrain from printing the articles.[34] Even in
1942 one of Atlanta's rabbis refused a Jewish graduate student
permission to examine his extensive files, detailing the efforts
which had been made to save Frank, on the grounds that anything written would only stir up trouble.[35]

4

The reverberations of the Frank case touched a number of
individuals who had become connected with the affair: Jim
Conley, John M. Slaton, Hugh Dorsey, and Tom Watson.
Jim Conley, the Negro sweeper who proved to be the key
witness against Frank at the trial, passed into oblivion; and
aside from his obituary notice in 1962, appeared in the newspapers again only when in jail. In 1919 he was shot in an attempt to burglarize an Atlanta drug store. For this offense he
received a twenty-year sentence in the state penitentiary, although for the assistance allegedly given to Frank in remov-
ing Mary Phagan's body, Conley had spent only a year on the
chain gang. In 1941 he was among a group picked up by the
Atlanta police for gambling; and in 1947 he was again ar-

rested, on a charge of drunkenness. There is no record of his ever having revealed anything more about his role in the Phagan murder case.[36]

Governor John M. Slaton remained in exile from his native state for a number of years. After the First World War he resumed his law practice in Atlanta but was never again elected to public office. In 1928, however, the Georgia Bar Association honored him by unanimously electing him its president. In 1953 Slaton granted Samuel Boorstin, a good friend and contemporary of Leo Frank, an interview and reminisced about the Frank case. Slaton recalled that Judge Roan had said to him that if Hugh Dorsey's predecessor in the office of Solicitor-General of the Atlanta circuit had been alive, Frank would never have been prosecuted on the evidence that the state had amassed. Slaton also told Boorstin that, as Governor, he had received word, indirectly, that Jim Conley's lawyer believed his client guilty. Toward the end of his life John Slaton expressed the opinion that the passage of time had, indeed, established Frank's innocence. Upon Slaton's death in 1955, the flags of the state capitol flew at half staff, and Ralph McGill, of *The Atlanta Constitution*, eulogized: "A giant of his day, it was one of destiny's mocking ironies that his great integrity should have cost him his political life. . . ."[37]

Hugh Dorsey reaped great political rewards from prosecuting Frank and emerged as one of the influential Georgians of his day.[38] In 1916 the demand for his entrance into the gubernatorial race was so great "that it swept the state like a prairie fire, rolling from the mountains to the sea."[39] In the primary that year Dorsey received more votes than the combined total of his three opponents, as he scored one of the greatest electoral victories in Georgia's history. Dorsey remained Governor until 1921, when he retired to private life. In 1920 Tom Watson thwarted the Governor's attempt to obtain a seat in the United States Senate by decisively defeating both Dorsey and Hoke Smith in a three-cornered primary race. Later on Dorsey served as Judge of Atlanta's City Court and of the Fulton County Superior Court. He died in 1949.[40]

Tom Watson's political power increased as a result of his activities against Frank. In the election of 1916, when he supported Dorsey for chief executive, all his candidates won decisive victories. Two years later Watson once again ran for Congress but was narrowly defeated in a contested election which the state authorities refused to review. The campaign had been marked by overtones of loyalty and patriotism. Watson had denounced President Woodrow Wilson and had opposed American entry into the war; his paper, *The Jeffersonian*, had been suspended for violating the espionage act. Watson's opponent, Carl Vinson, had gone down the line with the administration. After the war Watson continued to strike out at Wilson, opposed American entry into the League of Nations, and denounced the United States Attorney-General, A. Mitchell Palmer, for his raids upon Socialists.

By 1920 Georgians had become less enthusiastic about the administration in Washington, and Tom Watson capitalized upon this change in feeling. In the presidential primary, in which the former Populist had barely campaigned, he nosed out A. Mitchell Palmer, the administration's candidate, and Hoke Smith, and he carried a plurality of Georgia's counties. But Palmer had won the county unit vote and therefore went into the national convention with all Georgia's votes behind him. Watson then entered the primary race for the United States Senate. This time he trounced both opponents, Smith and Dorsey, and easily walked off with the victory. The Georgian did not serve long in the Senate. On September 26, 1922, he died from a bronchial attack in Washington, D.C. The Ku Klux Klan sent a cross of roses, eight feet high, to his funeral.[41]

5

A large number of people have familiarized themselves with the Frank case, but their views concerning his guilt or innocence have varied considerably. This is true not only of contemporaries but of more recent chroniclers as well. Immediately after the lynching, one scribe prophesied: "Future writers . . . will unanimously admit that Leo M. Frank was the victim of a biased sentiment, that his judicial rights were denied him and that his hanging on a lonely oak was the climax of a series of flagrant violations of justice which ignominiously but undoubtedly will raise him to the position of the first American martyr." [42] With the perspective of a decade behind him, however, Herbert Asbury, who worked as a reporter for *The Atlanta Georgian* during the crisis over Mary Phagan's murder, wrote, "Frank's trial could hardly have been fairer." [43] And one of the newspapermen who witnessed the trial from the press table, MacLellan Smith, still remained adamant in his belief, fifty years later, that Leo Frank had murdered Mary Phagan. [44] Not quite convinced about either the defendant's guilt or innocence, Francis X. Busch, author of *Guilty or Not Guilty*, wrote: "One simply cannot, with evidence supporting reason, declare unequivocally that [Frank] was guilty or that he was not guilty. There is evidence and reasonable probability to support either conclusion." [45]

Yet Harold Ross, who reported the case for *The Atlanta Journal*, and C. Vann Woodward, who familiarized himself with the facts while writing his biography of Tom Watson, have reached different verdicts. Ross, who later founded *The New Yorker* magazine, commented in 1915 that the evidence "did not prove [Frank] guilty beyond that 'reasonable doubt' required by law." [46] And in his penetrating study, Woodward wrote, "A fateful weight of irrelevant but prejudicial fact dogged Frank's case to the end," and then added that a Negro suspect was "later implicated by evidence overwhelmingly more incriminating than any produced against Frank." [47]

The more recent investigators, however, have been the most vocal in decrying the verdict of the courts. Charles and Louise Samuels, authors of *Night Fell on Georgia*, ended their work with the statement: "Leo Frank was the victim of one of the most shocking frame-ups ever perpetrated by American law-and-order officials." John Roche, who chronicled the development of civil rights in this century, stated, "As one who has read the trial record half a century later, I might add . . . that Leo Frank was the victim of circumstantial evidence which would not hold up ten minutes in a normal courtroom then or now." And Harry Golden echoed Roche's opinion that no one would be convicted today on the evidence which doomed Leo Frank.[48]

6

In retrospect, it seems that the Frank case illuminated the shape of historical forces long at work. It threw into dramatic relief the pressures, the frustrations, and the realities of the South's struggle to adjust to new ideas while still reluctant to part with the old. It mobilized the American Jews into a concerted defensive action without precedent in the annals of our country, and it quickened the establishment of a new Ku Klux Klan. But above all, the Leo Frank case showed as clearly as possible that, if the laws of civilization are to be respected, societies must eradicate the conditions which turn men into beasts. For if they do not, other Leo Franks will continue to appear, and suffer punishment for crimes for which no single individual can ever be wholly responsible.

Excerpt from the Appeal of Frank's Lawyers for a New Trial

IN THEIR PETITION for the new trial before the Georgia Supreme Court, Frank's lawyers included the following argument. It is reproduced from *Frank* vs. *State of Georgia, Brief and Argument for Plaintiff in Error*, in the Supreme Court of Georgia, October Term, 1913, pp. 300–2.

JUDGMENT OF THE COURT OVER-RULING THE MOTION FOR A NEW TRIAL

After hearing extensive argument on the motion for a new trial, the same was over-ruled. In over-ruling the motion the Court rendered a judgment denying the same, and in rendering said judgment, stated "that the jury had found the defendant guilty; that he, the judge, had thought about this case more than any other he had ever tried; that he was not certain of the defendant's guilt; that with all the thought he had put on this case, he was not thoroughly convinced that Frank was guilty or innocent, but that he did not have to be convinced; that the jury was convinced, and that there was no room to doubt that. That he felt it to be his duty to order that the motion for a new trial be over-ruled."

In the original motion for new trial, it was alleged that the verdict was contrary to the evidence and without evidence to support it. In passing upon this ground of the motion, the duty devolved upon the Judge of exercising his discretion, and in doing so, he ought to have applied to the task the best of his brain, heart and conscience.

If after so doing, the verdict met with his approval, it was his duty to over-rule the motion, but if it did not meet [with] his approbation, it was his duty to grant a new trial.

This is a duty that no trial judge can fairly shirk. The danger of doing so is appalling; the temptation to do so is very great.

This Court, keeping in mind the danger and the temptation, has repeatedly reversed the Court below when it appeared from the record that the trial Court, from timidity or from misapprehension as to the law, failed to exercise his own discretion and substituted the verdict of the jury for that discretion which it is his solemn duty to exercise.

It is, of course, true that in determining whether the Court exercised or failed to exercise his legal discretion, this Court will look solely to the record, giving full force to the presumption that the Court has exercised his discretion and that the verdict does in fact meet [with] his approbation.

In the present case, the Court rendered an oral judgment, as will be seen from the bill of exceptions. The whole of the judgment was not incorporated in the order over-ruling the motion for new trial, but the whole of that judgment was fully set out in the bill of exceptions. In determining just what was the judgment of the Court in over-ruling the motion, this Court will look to the whole record. If the record itself and the bill of exceptions are irreconcilably inconsistent, of the two, the record will prevail.

When, however, there is no such inconsistency and it is legally possible to reconcile the record and the recitals in the bill of exceptions, this court will do so and give full force, not only to the record but to the recitals in the bill of exceptions, as well. Doing so, there can be no doubt that Judge Roan did not sanctify this verdict by exercising that discretion which the law demands. The words of his judgment portray on his part a state of mind wholly inconsistent with that settled conviction which a trial judge ought to possess in denying a motion for new trial. He was not thoroughly convinced that Frank was guilty. He was not thoroughly convinced that he was innocent. He did not have to be convinced. Conviction was not a part of his duty; that was the province of the jury. They were convinced, and their conviction was to determine the matter, although he was still unconvinced.

What must have been the state of mind of the trial judge when he denied this motion? What a turmoil of mental doubt and vacillation must have overwhelmed him! Think of the case as he might and as much as he said he did, he was still unable to find one single yard of solid, fixed conviction upon which to stand. Try as earnestly as he could, he reached and could reach no conviction that satisfied his heart and conscience. Unsettled and perturbed, with no hope for peace or rest, he cast the whole burden upon the jury. Undoubtedly they had been convinced—he was unable to become so, and in his dilemma, he put forward the discretion of the jury as an excuse for not exercising his own. *Merchants & Miners Transportation Company* v. *Corcoran*, 4 Ga. App. 654; *Rogers* v. *State*, 101 Ga. 561; *Central of Ga. Ry. Co.* v. *Hardin*, 113 Ga. 453; *Thompson* v. *Warren*, 118 Ga. 644; *McIntyre* v. *McIntyre*, 128 Ga. 67; *Griffin* v. *State*, 12 Ga. App. 622.

The Ballad of Mary Phagan

Franklyn Bliss Snyder, "Leo Frank and Mary Phagan," *The Journal of American Folk-Lore*, XXXI (1918), 264–66.

Little Mary Phagan
She left her home one day;
She went to the pencil-factory
To see the big parade.

She left her home at eleven,
She kissed her mother good-by;
Not one time did the poor child think
That she was a-going to die.

Leo Frank he met her
With a brutish heart, we know;
He smiled, and said, "Little Mary,
You won't go home no more."

Sneaked along behind her
Till she reached the metal-room;
He laughed, and said, "Little Mary,
You have met your fatal doom."

Down upon her knees
To Leo Frank she plead;

The Ballad of Mary Phagan

The Ballad of Mary Phagan

He taken a stick from the trash-pile
And struck her across the head.

Tears flow down her rosy cheeks
While the blood flows down her back;
Remembered telling her mother
What time she would be back.

You killed little Mary Phagan,
It was on one holiday;
Called for old Jim Conley
To carry her body away.

He taken her to the basement,
She was bound both hand and feet;
Down in the basement
Little Mary she did sleep.

Newtley was the watchman
Who went to wind his key;
Down in the basement
Little Mary he did see.

Went in and called the officers
Whose names I do not know;
Come to the pencil-factory,
Said, "Newtley, you must go."

Taken him to the jail-house,
They locked him in a cell;
Poor old innocent negro
Knew nothing for to tell.

Have a notion in my head,
When Frank he comes to die,
Stand examination
In a court-house in the sky.

Come, all you jolly people,
Wherever you may be,
Suppose little Mary Phagan
Belonged to you or me.

Now little Mary's mother
She weeps and mourns all day,
Praying to meet little Mary
In a better world some day.

Now little Mary's in Heaven,
Leo Frank's in jail,
Waiting for the day to come
When he can tell his tale.

Frank will be astonished
When the angels come to say,
"You killed little Mary Phagan;
It was on one holiday."

Judge he passed the sentence,
Then he reared back;
If he hang Leo Frank,
It won't bring little Mary back.

Frank he's got little children,
And they will want for bread;
Look up at their papa's picture,
Say, "Now my papa's dead."

Judge he passed the sentence
He reared back in his chair;
He will hang Leo Frank,
And give the negro a year.

Next time he passed the sentence,
You bet, he passed it well;
Well, Solister H. M. [Dorsey]
Sent Leo Frank to hell.

APPENDIX C

Freeman's Tale

AN ALTERNATE EXPLANATION for the murder of Mary Phagan was published in 1923 when alleged data about Jim Conley's participation in the mystery came to light. The information had been received eight years earlier by Governor Slaton, from a questionable, but perhaps important, source. In 1915 a Negro prisoner, identified only by the name "Freeman," thought that he was dying in the federal penitentiary located in Atlanta, and revealed what he claimed to have know about Mary Phagan's death. Freeman made his statement to a prison doctor, who relayed it to Governor Slaton.

The narrated story follows: Freeman recalled playing cards with Jim Conley in the basement of the pencil factory on the day of the murder. Shortly before noon Conley went up the ladder to the main floor. After a short while Freeman heard muffled screams. Inquisitive, he climbed to the first floor and saw Conley struggling with someone. Frightened, Freeman returned to the basement and left the building through a rear door. Later that afternoon, Conley went to Freeman's home and said that he needed $3 but was short $1.80. In return for the money, Conley offered his friend a woman's mesh handbag. Freeman obliged. The following day, however, he read about the murder and Mary Phagan's missing mesh bag which contained her $1.20 wage. Fearing involvement, Freeman gave the mesh bag to a friend and admonished her to hide it in a safe place. He then fled the city. Within two months, however, he was convicted of a federal crime and imprisoned in Atlanta.*

* The Baltimore *Sun*, October 2, 1923, "Frank's Prophesy of Vindication Comes True 10 Years After Georgia Mob Hangs Him as Slayer," *The*

Why newspapers published Freeman's story for the first time in 1923, or how they obtained this information, was never explained. But former Governor Slaton, the ex-prison doctor, and one of the Georgia Prison Commissioners verified, in 1923, that they had heard the tale in 1915.* An *Atlanta Constitution* report noted "that proven inaccuracies in [Freeman's] story had discredited it." † Unfortunately the *Constitution* did not elaborate.

Amazingly, *The Atlanta Georgian* had also received part of Freeman's tale, although not identified as such, in June, 1913, before Frank had gone to trial. On June 6, the *Georgian* headlined a front page account: "REPORT NEGRO WHO SAW PHAGAN ATTACK," and related how a federal prisoner was about to be returned to Atlanta by a Pinkerton detective. The Negro in question, according to the *Georgian*, had allegedly been shooting craps with Conley in the factory basement on the day of the murder. Conley, having lost his money and in a half-drunken stuper, then allegedly left the basement and attacked Mary Phagan, who had just come down from Frank's office after collecting her pay. The *Georgian* could not verify the report and subsequently dropped the story.‡

Additional corroboration for Freeman's tale came in 1959 when an Atlanta attorney published his memoirs. Relating how he knew of Frank's innocence, the attorney, A. L. Henson, claimed that Conley had confessed to his lawyer that he had been drinking in the factory basement on the day of the murder. According to Henson, Conley had also recalled having seen a girl approach him on the main floor, remembered struggling with her, and then his mind went blank. When Conley revived he was sitting opposite a dead girl in the factory basement, but he could not remember anything that had transpired in the previous few hours.§ Hen-

---

Jewish Advocate (Boston), XLII (October 18, 1923), 20; AJ clipping, n.d., probably October 1 or 2, 1923, Frank Papers, Brandeis.

* AC, October 2, 1923, p. 7.

† *Ibid.*

‡ AG, June 6, 1913, p. 1; June 10, 1913, p. 1.

§ Allen Lumpkin Henson, *Confessions of a Criminal Lawyer* (New York, 1959), p. 63. Other facts reported by Henson vary from contemporary reports, and I cannot vouch for his accuracy. In an interview with Samuel A. Boorstin, on October 12, 1953, John Slaton admitted that he had been

son's narrative fits well with Freeman's tale and the story published in the *Georgian*.

---

told by one of Hugh Dorsey's law partners that Jim Conley's lawyer
believed that Conley committed the murder. Memorandum of a conversation had by Boorstin with Slaton, Anti-Defamation League files, Leo
Frank folder, New York City.

APPENDIX D

A Georgian's View

THE LETTER REPRINTED BELOW is located among the Julius Rosenwald Papers at the University of Chicago. It was written at the end of 1914 or the beginning of 1915 by a newspaper reporter for *The Atlanta Georgian,* identified solely as the "Old Police Reporter." The recipient of the letter is unknown. If it was not Julius Rosenwald, it might have been Albert Lasker or some other Northern Jew interested in obtaining Frank's freedom.

This letter is significant because it represents the views of a considerable number of knowledgeable Georgians who reached their conclusions on the basis of the evidence printed in the newspapers and related at the trial. The author, however, was particularly familiar with the case. He attended the trial, had a number of personal interviews with Leo Frank, and also had access to the prosecutor.

Dear Mr.————

My personal opinion is that Leo M. Frank is guilty of the murder of Mary Phagan, committed after an attempted seduction—probably successful, and most likely of a perverted type. This opinion was formed during a close attendance at the trial and in the course of ten or twelve conversations with Frank after the dust of action had had some six months to settle.

As to the trial itself, our town seems to be getting in pretty bad with *Collier's,* the *Chicago Tribune,* and certain other publications. It seems we are pistol-toters and browbeaters of juries and all that sort of thing . . . . I do not think Atlanta is getting a square deal in this matter. It is true there was a lot of excitement here during the trial. It is true there was a popular clamor

for a "goat." I think that is true in every city where any crime
of especial horror is committed. It also is true there was some
race prejudice in evidence; that the trial judge was a weak sister;
that he was bullied lamentably by both sides during the trial, but
notably by the defense; that the entire trial was under tension,
so to speak. It has even been said that the Solicitor's closing
speech was stopped early on Saturday afternoon and the case
continued until Monday because a verdict was expected almost
as soon as the jury got the case—and, it being Saturday, the town
was well jammed with country people, who really were more
worked up over the case than the city folk, if that is possible.

I am not certain of this last statement; but it is certain there
was a lot of excitement; you recall the first Hyde trial, of course.
Well, this was much like that, except for a more pronounced
animosity against Frank than was in evidence against Hyde.

On the other hand, the *Tribune* and *Collier's* are guilty of gross
exaggeration, particularly in detailing the conduct of the courtroom crowd. To my mind, the crowd was commendably quiet.
The only break in the uniform good order was a ripple of applause, perhaps twice, when Dorsey, the Solicitor, entered the
room toward the end of the trial. It was rebuked promptly. As to
the "hands moving toward hip-pokets," and the "cries of 'If you
let the Jew go, we'll hang him and you, too' "—there simply was
none of that, and no excuse for the injection of such stuff into
any account of the case.

The jury was unusually high-class in intelligence and in pre-
sumptive character. We have the sworn statements of each that
his conclusion was the result of his own unbiased consideration
of the evidence—but of course they would say that. They all
maintain that they heard nothing of the so-called "demonstrations" outside the courthouse—cheering in the streets the last
day of the trial, and so on. But it would be nearly impossible and
out of reason that those men should not have sensed the public
sentiment. Still, the Supreme Court said Frank had a fair trial;
and the trial judge said so—qualifying his statement with his
peculiar remark, which I heard him make, and which was clipped
from the *Georgian* as I wrote it, and made into part of the court
record:

"I am not convinced of the guilt or innocence of the defendant;

but I do not have to be convinced. The jury was convinced, and that is enough."

My impression at the time was that Judge Roan was merely trying to placate Luther Rosser, chief lawyer for the defense, to whom it is said the judge is a political debtor of some kind. The remark was part of Judge Roan's denial of a motion for a new trial before the case got up to the Supreme Court; and it was used for all it was worth in the plea to that body.

So you see it is ticklish business, when the trial judge himself is not convinced, but says the defendant had a fair trial according to law.

Frank is a well educated young man; a graduate of Cornell; a smooth, swift, and convincing speaker. If you have seen any good pictures of him, you will understand what I mean when I say that he looks like a pervert. It is a slightly significant fact, I think, that I sized him up as one the first time I saw him, before a whisper of the perversion testimony came out. . . . Others have told me they were impressed the same way. In strict confidence (that is, so far as any publication is concerned) Solicitor Dorsey told me of a fearful mass of testimony with which he said he was prepared to prove the perversion of the accused in the event the defense tried to back its character case to a finish, which it did not, refusing in every instance to cross-examine the witnesses put on by the state, who were (under the Georgia law) permitted on direct examination to answer no more than "Bad," to the state's question as to the character of the defendant.

As to Frank's being convicted on the unsupported testimony of a "black brute"—I think that is peculiarly unfair to a section of which it has been the stigma that the negro could never get a fair deal in a court of law.

I really am convinced that the State's case would have stood up without the negro Conley's testimony; and I know it to be a fact that Dorsey had practically finished what was to be his indictment case to the grand jury before Conley spilled a word. Whether Frank would have been indicted (Dorsey revised his case after Conley loosened up) is another question. At any rate, it is worth while to note these points:

1. That Leo Frank tried to fasten suspicion on two other negroes first, and never mentioned Conley until fairly pushed to it.

2. That Leo Frank knew Conley could write all the time, and was silent while knowing that Conley was denying he could write; the inference being that Frank was shielding Conley lest Conley should open up on him.

3. That the several untrue statements of Conley, of which so much is made by *Collier's,* were simply the efforts of the untutored Afro-American to shield his boss—and get the $200 promised him by Frank. As soon as Conley saw he was getting into it himself, he promptly threw Frank overboard and came through with the goods.

4. That Frank never was able to account for his time during the half hour the state contends he was engaged with Mary Phagan.

That Frank, after seeing the girl's body the morning after the murder, and hearing the name, said he did not know if such a girl worked at the factory, and would have to look it up on the rolls, whereas it was shown that he had spoken to Mary Phagan frequently calling her by name.

These are only a few points. The "murder notes" are a queer business all to themselves. For my part, I do not undertake to say or guess if Frank dictated them to Conley, who certainly wrote them; or if the negro being ordered to dispose of the body by burning it, changed his mind and wrote the notes of his own volition.

But I will say that I heard Conley's evidence entire, and was impressed powerfully with the idea that the negro was repeating something he had seen; that was photographically fixed on his mind; perhaps you know something of the remarkable capacity for observing and recalling details exhibited by crude minds, especially in negroes . . . . Conley's story was told with a wealth of infinitesimal detail that I firmly believe to be beyond the capacity of his mind, or a far more intelligent one, to construct from imagination . . . . For example . . . . "And when we run the elevator back up to the office floor, it didn't quite get to the level, and Mr. Frank, he stumbled and like to fell down, and cussed, and brushed his pants off, this way." That sort of thing, all the way.

And the next day, with upwards of fifty typewritten pages of solid testimony to check him by, Luther Rosser tore into that nigger, hour after hour, up and down and sidewise, misquoting his testimony, skipping about—every trick of a trained lawyer—and he did not shake that nigger once or make him contradict himself. It just stuck in my craw, Mr. X, that that nigger was telling something he had SEEN. . . . . . .

Well, I've no idea you wanted all this stuff, but it's easy to write and maybe you will find something of interest in it. I have thought about it a good deal, and have come to the conclusion stated in Paragraph I; but I must say honestly that I am one of those persons who find it easier to hold a man guilty until he proves himself innocent than the vice versa laid down in our wonderful system of jurisprudence . . . . To go the whole route, my theory of the crime is that Frank is a pervert; that he kept after Mary Phagan until he dated her up, for that Decoration Day afternoon, in the "metal room" of the factory; that he frightened her by his unnatural behavior; and that either in the fright, or in the revulsion following the performance she began to cry and became hysterical, probably insisting, louder and louder, that she was going to "tell on him"—she was only a little girl, you know. . . . Then I can imagine Frank trying to pacify her; perhaps backed up against the locked door, imploring her to be quiet; perhaps she even attacked him in her frenzy to be away. Anyway, I imagine he tried to hold her, and she wrenched herself violently away, falling against a lathe and knocking herself unconscious . . . . Frank may have thought her dead; anyway, it was his last chance, for nothing but death would stop her story now . . . . So he made sure by strangling her . . . . And then, in the ghastly jangle of his nerves, he sought aid from his Man Friday—Jim Conley, who was watching below, as he testified he had watched many another Saturday afternoon while Frank "chatted" with women in the deserted factory.

It may be all wrong, Mr. X, but that's my honest opinion. It amounts to a conviction. I believe Frank to be guilty, and I think he had as fair a trial as could have been had with all the public stress of the case, which could not have been avoided in any way that I can see. Anyway, the Supreme Court said he had a fair trial, and so far as we poor mortals are concerned we have to take the findings of our highest courts as the ultimate truth. Leo Frank and Jim Conley and God know the truth of this thing.

Frank says one thing; Conley says another and more probable thing. God hasn't said anything yet—unless He speaks through juries and Supreme Courts. . . . Anyway, this is just my humble personal opinion, as you asked for it—and if I have been tiresome, I apologize heartily.

With best wishes to yourself and all the boys for the coming year, and all the rest of them, I am

Sincerely yours,

Notes

I. THE MURDER OF MARY PHAGAN

1. *The Atlanta Constitution* "extra," April 27, 1913, pp. 1, 2; April 28, 1913, pp. 1, 2; *The Atlanta Journal,* April 28, 1913, pp. 1, 2; cited hereafter as AC and AJ.

2. AC, May 8, 1913, p. 2.

3. AC, April 27, 1913 "extra," pp. 1, 2; April 28, 1913, pp. 1, 2.

4. Henry A. Alexander, *Some Facts about the Murder Notes in the Phagan Case* (privately published pamphlet, 1914), pp. 5, 7.

5. A. B. Macdonald, "Has Georgia Condemned an Innocent Man to Die?" *The Kansas City* [Mo.] *Star,* January 17, 1915, p. 1C.

6. *Frank v. State, Brief of the Evidence,* pp. 15, 43.

7. *Ibid.,* pp. 38, 43.

8. *The Atlanta Georgian,* April 28, 1913, p. 2; April 29, 1913, p. 2; cited hereafter as AG.

9. Macdonald, *The Kansas City Star,* January 17, 1915, p. 2C; AG, April 29, 1913, p. 2; *The Savannah Morning News,* April 30, 1913, p. 1; cited hereafter as SMN.

10. AG, April 28, 1913, p. 1; AJ, April 28, 1913, p. 1. Careful newspaper readers, however, might have noticed in the *Constitution* that same morning: "The deed, apparently, was committed upon either the first or second floor. No blood or marks of scuffle can be found, however, on either." AC, April 28, 1913, p. 2. The state biologist later stated that he could not identify the hair as Mary Phagan's. See pp. 84–85.

11. AG, April 28, 1913, p. 1; April 30, 1913, p. 1; AJ, April 29, 1913, p. 1. This information was later proved to be false.

12. Quoted in SMN, April 30, 1913, p. 1.

13. *The New York Times,* August 26, 1913, p. 18; February

18, 1914, p. 3; AC, June 1, 1915, p. 4; AG, May 13, 1913, p. 2; interview with Alexander Brin, a Boston reporter who covered the later stages of the Frank case, August 19, 1964; Charles and Louise Samuels, *Night Fell on Georgia* (New York, 1956), p. 21.

14. AC, April 30, 1913, p. 2.

15. Elmer R. Murphy, "A Visit with Leo M. Frank in the Death Cell at Atlanta," *Rhodes' Colossus*, March, 1915, p. 3. Murphy added, however, that when he learned to know Frank, he found him a very fine person. Mrs. Samuels told me that in the course of her research she spoke with reporters who covered Frank's trial. They found him to be a cold person, and difficult to like. Alexander Brin, on the other hand, thought Frank a very warm, friendly person.

16. AG, April 29, 1913, p. 2; AC, April 30, 1913, p. 1. That Mrs. Frank tried to visit her husband appeared quite insignificant on April 29. Hugh Dorsey, the prosecuting attorney, would argue at Frank's trial, however, that Mrs. Frank waited two weeks before visiting her husband, and he concluded that this proved Mrs. Frank knew her husband was guilty.

17. SMN, May 1, 1913, p. 1; *The Augusta Chronicle*, May 2, 1913, p. 6; cited hereafter as TAC.

18. C. P. Connolly, *The Truth about the Frank Case* (New York, 1915), pp. 55–56.

19. Atlanta's population soared from 89,872 in 1900 to 173,713 in 1913. AC, January 18, 1915, p. 1.

20. William D. Miller, *Memphis during the Progressive Era, 1900–1917* (Memphis, 1957), p. 8.

21. A United States government survey reported in 1910 that 90 per cent of the children in Georgia earned less than $6 a week. U.S. Congress, Senate, *Report on Conditions of Woman and Child Wage-Earners in the United States*, 61st Cong., 2d sess., 1910, Senate Document 645, Serial 5685, I, 310; "Dixie Conditions Stir Unionists—Description of Actual State of Atlanta Textile Workers Make Delegates Weep," *The Textile Worker*, III (December, 1914), 21. The cost of living in 1913, in Atlanta, was the second highest in the nation (Boston was first), and wages lagged behind those paid in the northern cities, *The Atlanta Journal*, September 17, 1913, p. 1; cited hereafter as AJ. See also W. J. Cash, *The Mind of the South* (New York, 1941), p. 247. C. Vann

Woodward reported that in 1912 and 1913 hourly earnings in New England averaged 37 per cent above those in the South. *Origins of the New South* (Baton Rouge, 1951), pp. 420–21. U.S., *Report of the Industrial Commission,* 1901, VII, 56, 57. A few years later the U.S. Senate's *Report on . . . Wage-Earners . . . ,* noted that the average work week in Georgia cotton mills in 1908 was 64 hours, which was longer than the work week in Virginia, North Carolina, South Carolina, Alabama, and Mississippi. Of the 31 establishments that the Commission investigated, 16 had a 64-hour week; 40 minutes was the average lunch time, p. 261. A. J. McKelway, "Child Labor in the South," *The Annals,* XXXV (January, 1910), 163.

22. Lenora Beck Ellis, "A New Class of Labor in the South," *Forum,* XXXI (May, 1901), 307; S. A. Hamilton, "The New Race Question in the South," *Arena,* XXVII (April, 1902), 356; C. Vann Woodward, *Tom Watson: Agrarian Rebel* (New York, 1938), pp. 219, 223–24, 418; Edmund De S. Brunner, *Church Life in the Rural South* (New York, 1923), p. 21; *Annual Report of the Atlanta Chamber of Commerce,* 1909, p. 5; *The Textile Worker,* III (December, 1914), 21; *The Journal of Labor,* XV (November 7, 1913), 4; *Report of the Comptroller of the City of Atlanta, for the Year Ending 1911,* pp. 15, 16, 20, 32, 41, 42; U.S. Bureau of the Census, *General Statistics of Cities: 1909,* pp. 88, 148.

23. Dewey W. Grantham, Jr., *Hoke Smith and the Politics of the New South* (Baton Rouge, 1958), pp. 149, 150, 178; Woodward, *Tom Watson, pp.* 374–78; Glenn Weddington Rainey, "The Race Riot of 1906 in Atlanta" (unpublished Master's thesis, Department of History, Emory University, 1929), chap. 5 (no pagination); Ray Stannard Baker, "Following the Color Line," *The American Magazine,* LXIII (April, 1907), 563, 569.

24. U.S. Bureau of the Census, *Statistics of Cities for 1905,* p. 324; *Statistics of Cities: 1907,* pp. 102, 107, 410. I have been unable to find an exact census of Negroes in Atlanta for 1905. The census of 1900 listed 45,532 Negroes residing in Fulton County (Atlanta comprised 85 per cent of the county), and the census of 1910 listed the figure as 57,985. I assume, therefore, that Atlanta had about 50,000 Negroes in 1905. Similarly, I have not found a breakdown between the number of whites and Negroes

arrested in Atlanta in 1905. But according to the census of 1910, 9,717 Negroes were committed to prison in Georgia that year, against 2,684 whites. U.S. Bureau of the Census, *Negro Population, 1790–1915* (Washington, 1918), pp. 437, 779.

25. Hugh C. Weir, "The Menace of the Police: II. The Bully in the Blue Uniform," *World To-day*, XVIII (1910), 174; Philip Weltner, "Municipal and Misdemeanor Offenders," *The Call of the New South*, edited by James E. McCulloch (Nashville, 1912), pp. 110, 111.

26. G. W. Dyer, "Southern Problems That Challenge Our Thought," *The Call of the New South* (McColloch, editor), p. 27.

27. AG, April 28, 1913, p. 3.

28. Cash, p. 118.

29. *The Memphis Commercial Appeal*, June 7, 1904, as quoted in William D. Miller, p. 25.

30. Broadus Mitchell, *The Rise of Cotton Mills in the South* (Baltimore, 1921), p. 195. To some extent, this attitude existed in the North also.

31. *Ibid.*, p. 194.

32. Arthur G. Powell, *I Can Go Home Again* (Chapel Hill, 1943), p. 287.

33. Quoted in AG, April 28, 1913, p. 3.

34. *Journal of Labor*, XV (May 2, 1913), 4. The opinions of the working classes might have had a greater influence in Atlanta than in a city with a different power structure. An economist has commented upon the influence of labor in Atlanta. He noted that the Mayor of Atlanta in 1913 was a member of the typographical union, and that two-thirds of the city's wards were dominated by workingmen. This fact was reflected in the composition of Atlanta's city council. Mercer G. Evans, "The History of the Organized Labor Movement in Georgia" (unpublished Ph.D. dissertation, Department of Economics, University of Chicago, 1929), p. 289.

35. AC, April 28, 1913, p. 3; AG, April 28, 1913, p. 2; AJ, July 30, 1913, p. 4.

36. AG, April 28, 1913, p. 5; April 29, 1913, p. 1; AJ, July 27, 1913, p. 1; SMN, April 30, 1913, pp. 1, 5.

37. N. W. Ayer and Sons, *American Newspaper Annual and*

Directory (Philadelphia, 1911, 1912, 1913, 1914), listed the following circulation figures:

	1910	1911	1912	1913
AC	35,454	41,519	41,405	42,405
AG	42,858	40,000	38,000	60,000
AJ	52,035	51,827	52,000	54,000

38. W. A. Swanberg, *Citizen Hearst* (New York, 1963), p. 232.

39. Herbert Asbury, "Hearst Comes to Atlanta," *The American Mercury*, VII (January, 1926), 87–88.

40. See n. 37, *supra*.

41. Asbury, *The American Mercury*, VII (January, 1926), 89.

42. *Ibid.*, p. 87; William Curran Rogers, "A Comparison of the Coverage of the Leo Frank Case by the Hearst-Controlled Atlanta *Georgian* and the Home-Owned Atlanta *Journal*, April 28, 1913—August 30, 1913" (unpublished M.A. thesis, University of Georgia, 1950), p. 66; Paul Rosenblum, printer for *The New York Times*, told me that there are 176 inches in each page of the newspaper.

43. AG, April 28, 1913, pp. 1–5; clipping in Boston *Herald-Traveler* newspaper morgue, June 8, 1915.

44. Miller, p. 29; Richard Hofstadter, *The Age of Reform* (New York, 1960, Vintage edition), pp. 188–89.

45. W. I. Thomas, "The Psychology of the Yellow Journal," *American Magazine*, LXV (March, 1908), 492.

46. AC, April 30, 1913, p. 2.

47. AJ, April 28, 1913, p. 1; April 29, 1913, p. 1; AG, April 29, 1913, p. 1.

48. AG, April 29, 1913, p. 1, extra No. 5.

49. AC, April 30, 1913, p. 1; AJ, April 30, 1913, p. 1.

50. SMN, May 1, 1913, p. 3.

51. SMN, May 2, 1913, p. 2.

52. TAC, May 2, 1913, p. 1.

53. AC, April 29, 1913, p. 4.

54. Among the seven, two were quickly released because there was no evidence against them. Two others were Negroes, and after the police questioned them, the two were put in cells and the police forgot about them for a while. Both were eventually released. Newt Lee, Leo Frank, and Jim Conley, a Negro sweeper in the pencil factory, were the only three who received serious

press attention after the first two or three days following the murder.

55. AC, May 11, 1913, p. 1.

56. AC, May 16, 1913, p. 1; May 17, 1913, p. 4.

57. Burns, in fact, did not reach Atlanta until 1914. And at that time, he was in the employ of Leo Frank's attorneys. The reason for this is that shortly after his agents began working for the city of Atlanta, Solicitor Dorsey satisfied himself that he had enough evidence to convict one of his suspects, and that the services of the Burns agency would no longer be necessary. See below, p. 23.

58. Macdonald, *The Kansas City Star*, January 17, 1915, p. 1C; Connolly, p. 40; Murphy, *Rhodes's Colossus*, March, 1915, p. 6; Samuels, p. 19.

59. Murphy, *Rhodes's Colossus*, March, 1915, p. 6.

60. Quoted in Samuels, p. 20.

61. AC, May 1, 1913, p. 1. A few days earlier an *Atlanta Georgian* reporter interviewed young Epps and the boy told the reporter that he sometimes rode into town with Mary Phagan but did not mention that he had done so on the fatal day. Connolly, pp. 28–29.

62. AC, May 8, 1913, p. 2; AG, May 9, 1913, pp. 1, 2.

63. AC, May 9, 1913, p. 1.

64. AC, May 11, 1913, p. 1.

65. AC, May 23, 1913, pp. 1, 2.

66. AJ, May 3, 1913, p. 1; Anon., "Why Was Frank Lynched?" *Forum*, LVI (December, 1916), 686.

67. AC, April 29, 1913, p. 3; AG, May 7, 1913, p. 1; Macdonald, *The Kansas City Star*, January 17, 1915, p. 1C; Manning Jasper Yeomans, "Some Facts about the Frank Case" (unpublished thesis, Emory University, n.d., *ca.* 1915), p. 4.

68. Abraham Cahan, *Blätter Von Mein Leben* (5 volumes; New York, 1931), V, 494. The section on Leo Frank was translated for me by my father, Abraham Dinnerstein; Connolly, p. 14. Samuels, p. 26.

69. Interview with McLellan Smith in Washington, April 2, 1964. Mr. Smith covered the trial of Leo Frank as a cub reporter for *The Atlanta Georgian*. Samuels, p. 26; *The New York Times*, December 20, 1914, IV, 9; AC, March 14, 1914, p. 2; AJ, May 12, 1913, p. 1; The Baltimore Morning *Sun*, November 19, 1914,

p. 3; Macdonald, *The Kansas City Star*, January 17, 1915, p. 1C; Yeomans, unpublished thesis, p. 5; Sam P. Maddox to Luther Rosser, June 10, 1915, John M. Slaton Manuscripts, Brandeis University (cited hereafter as Slaton, Brandeis); Wytt E. Thompson, *A Short Review of the Frank Case* (Atlanta, 1914), p. 25.

70. Thompson, p. 26.

71. Even though newspapers reported that Mary Phagan had been raped, doctors could not find any evidence to substantiate this point.

72. SMN, August 31, 1913, clipping in Leo Frank Papers (American Jewish Archives, Cincinnati), cited hereafter as Frank Papers. Since all newspaper references to the Frank Papers are clippings, the word "clipping" will not be repeated.

73. AC, May 18, 1913, p. 2.

74. AC, May 27, 1913, p. 1.

75. AJ, May 18, 1913, p. 1.

76. *The Frank Case: Inside Story of Georgia's Greatest Mystery* (Atlanta, 1914), pp. 39–40.

77. AC, May 25, 1913, p. 1; *The New York Times*, November 20, 1914, p. 5; Connolly, p. 40.

78. AJ, May 24, 1913, p. 1.

79. In subsequent affidavits, Conley would acknowledge that he had written both the murder notes, but in his statement of May 24 he maintained that Frank had written the other.

80. AG, May 1, 1913, p. 1; AC, October 4, 1914, p. 1.

81. John D. Lawson (ed.), *American State Trials* (10 vols.; St. Louis, 1918), X, 245; AJ, May 24, 1913, p. 1; AC, May 25, 1913, p. 1; AG, May 24, 1913, p. 1; May 25, 1913, p. 1.

82. AC, August 6, 1913, p. 2; Arthur Garfield Hays, *Trial by Prejudice* (New York, 1933), pp. 312–13; The Baltimore Morning *Sun*, November 21, 1914, p. 1; Macdonald, *The Kansas City Star*, January 17, 1915, p. 2C.

83. Lawson (ed.), X, 236.

84. AJ, May 29, 1913, p. 1; AG, August 7, 1913, p. 1.

85. AG, May 19, 1913, p. 2.

86. The Grand Jury had not been informed of Conley's statement. Like everyone else, the jurors read about it in the newspapers after they had indicted Frank.

87. Lawson (ed.), X, 237; AG, May 24, 1913, p. 1.

88. AJ, May 23, 1913, p. 7; AC, May 25, 1913, p. 1; May 27, 1913, pp. 1, 2; AG, May 25, 1913, p. 2; May 26, 1913, p. 1.

89. The following items appeared in successive editions of *The Atlanta Georgian*, May 28, 1913, p. 2: (1) "Despite the new developments, the detectives, of course, stand firmly by their theory of Frank's guilt. They assert that they have the testimony of four handwriting experts that the writing on the notes found by the body of Mary Phagan positively is that of Frank. This evidence is lessened in importance by the fact that three other handwriting experts have declared as positively that the writing is that of Newt Lee. . . ." (2) The same officials who "had announced that they had conclusive evidence 'by experts' . . . that Frank wrote the notes," now say that Conley has written them. See also AJ, May 28, 1913, p. 1.

90. AJ, May 26, 1913, p. 1.

91. *Frank* v. *State, Brief of the Evidence*, p. 81.

92. Lawson (ed.), X, 245–48; AJ, May 29, 1913, p. 1.

93. AG, May 28, 1913, p. 1; May 29, 1913, p. 1; May 30, 1913, p. 2; AJ, June 2, 1913, p. 9.

94. AJ, May 29, 1913, p. 24.

95. AG, May 30, 1913, p. 2.

96. AJ, May 30, 1913, p. 4.

97. AC, May 30, 1913, p. 1.

98. Lawson (ed.), X, 248–50.

99. AJ, May 30, 1913, p. 4.

100. AG, May 30, 1913, p. 1.

101. AC, June 1, 1913, p. 1.

102. *Ibid.*, p. 2.

103. AJ, June 1, 1913, p. 1.

104. AC, July 19, 1913, p. 1.

105. AC, June 3, 1913, p. 1.

106. AG, June 5, 1913, p. 1.

107. AJ, June 4, 1913, p. 1; AG, June 4, 1913, p. 1; AC, June 5, 1913, p. 3.

108. AG, June 5, 1913, p. 2; AJ, June 6, 1913, p. 9.

109. AG, June 5, 1913, p. 1; AJ, June 5, 1913, p. 1. AC, June 6, 1913, p. 2.

110. AG, June 5, 1913, p. 1; AJ, June 5, 1913, p. 1; the wording of Dorsey's reply varies slightly in the two publications.

111. AG, June 19, 1913, p. 1.

112. AG, June 21, 1913, p. 1.

113. Quoted in AJ, June 22, 1913, p. 1.

114. AG, July 10, 1913, p. 1.

115. AG, July 11, 1913, p. 1.

116. AC, July 22, 1913, p. 1.

117. AJ, July 18, 1913, p. 1.

118. AC, July 22, 1913, p. 1. The minutes of this meeting are not available.

119. During the first week after the murder there was a great deal of confusion in the city, and this was reflected in the newspapers which published rumor and hearsay, information and misinformation, indiscriminately. My comments concerning the newspapers' handling of the case, therefore, refer to the treatment given after May 5 or 6, 1913.

120. The *Constitution*, for example, published a full-page article the day before the trial opened, lauding the detectives who "solved" the murder case. AC, July 27, 1913, magazine section.

121. The statements from the policeman who thought he had seen Frank alone in a park with a young girl the previous year and from the proprietor of the "rooming house" that Frank had allegedly phoned on the night of the murder were both published first in the *Constitution*.

122. Harold Ross wrote this for a San Francisco newspaper in June, 1915. It is reprinted in Harry Golden, *A Little Girl Is Dead* (Cleveland, 1965), pp. 355–58.

123. AG, May 11, 1913, p. 2.

124. AG, June 22, 1913, p. 2.

125. AJ, May 8, 1913, p. 1.

126. AC, May 23, 1913, p. 2.

127. AG, June 11, 1913, p. 2.

128. AC, May 30, 1913, p. 2.

129. AJ, July 18, 1913, p. 1.

130. AC, July 19, 1913, p. 1.

131. Even an astute observer like C. Vann Woodward accepted, uncritically, the views of Northern journalists. In his biography, *Tom Watson*, Woodward wrote, "The Atlanta press immediately assumed the guilt of Frank . . . ," p. 435.

132. See below, pp. 79–80 and 94.

133. The impression of the Jew as alien existed in the South even though his ancestors might have served in the Confederate army. Cash, pp. 305, 342.

134. Arnold Rose, "Anti-Semitism's Root in City-Hatred," *Commentary*, VI (1948), 375–77; Jacob J. Weinstein, "Anti-Semitism," in Oscar I. Janowsky (ed.), *The American Jew* (New York, 1942), pp. 187, 188; Oscar Handlin, "American Views of the Jew at the Opening of the Twentieth Century," *Publications of the American Jewish Historical Society*, XL (June, 1951), 344; John P. Roche, *The Quest for the Dream* (New York, 1963), p. 88; Howard M. Sachar, *The Course of Modern Jewish History* (Cleveland, 1958), p. 139. For a more extensive discussion of Jews and anti-Semitism, see chapter III.

135. Arthur Train, "Did Leo Frank Get Justice?" *Everybody's*, XXXII (March, 1915), 317.

136. Thompson, p. 29.

137. "The Case of Leo M. Frank," *The Outlook*, CX (May 26, 1915), 167.

138. John Higham, *Strangers in the Land* (New Brunswick, 1955), p. 185.

139. *The Jeffersonian*, April 9, 1914, p. 8. (Italics in original.)

140. L. O. Bricker, "A Great American Tragedy," *The Shane Quarterly*, IV (April, 1943), 90.

141. DeWitt H. Roberts did a study of the Frank case for the Anti-Defamation League in 1953. He wrote to me that in 1931 he had been present during a "heated but good-natured argument" on the subject of Frank's guilt. At that time one of Dorsey's assistants still maintained that Frank had been guilty. Roberts to Leonard Dinnerstein, February 19, 1964. See also Appendix D.

142. AG, May 30, 1913, p. 1. DeWitt H. Roberts to Leonard Dinnerstein, February 19, 1964.

143. AG, July 27, 1913, p. 1.

144. AJ, July 26, 1913, p. 1.

II. PREJUDICE AND PERJURY

1. AC, August 4, 1913, p. 2; August 17, 1913, p. 2A; AG, July 27, 1913, p. 1.

2. SMN, August 10, 1913, p. 3; AC, August 4, 1913, p. 2.

3. AG, July 27, 1913, p. 2.

4. *Ibid.*

5. Herbert Haas and Co. was the legal firm retained by Frank. Rosser and Arnold, however, directed the presentation in court. AC, July 27, 1913, p. 2; June 22, 1913, p. 1; AJ, June 22, 1913, p. 1.

6. AC, July 27, 1913, p. 1.

7. Lawson (ed.), X, 197, 201, 242; AJ, August 2, 1913, p. 5.

8. AC, August 5, 1913, p. 2; August 13, 1913, p. 2; SMN, August 6, 1913, p. 1; AJ, August 3, 1913, p. 1; AG, July 27, 1913, p. 2; August 3, 1913, p. 1; TAC, August 11, 1913, p. 1.

9. AJ, August 4, 1913, p. 6.

10. Lawson (ed.), X, 202.

11. *Frank v. State, Brief of Evidence*, pp. 54–58.

12. AG, August 4, 1913, p. 2; AC, August 5, 1913, p. 2; SMN, August 6, 1913, p. 1.

13. *Frank v. State, Brief of the Evidence*, pp. 59–73, *passim.*

14. AG, August 5, 1913, p. 4; August 6, 1913, p. 3; AJ, August 4, 1913, p. 6; August 10, 1913, p. 1.

15. *The Memphis Commercial Appeal*, January 3, 1915, p. 5; see also Macdonald, *The Kansas City Star*, January 17, 1915, p. 2C; Hal Steed, *Georgia: Unfinished State* (New York, 1942), p. 238.

16. Interview with McLellan Smith, April 2, 1964, Washington, D.C.

17. Quoted in AC, August 6, 1913, p. 2.

18. AC, August 6, 1913, p. 2; August 7, 1913, p. 2; AG, August 21, 1913, p. 3.

19. AC, August 7, 1913, p. 3; AG, August 7, 1913, p. 3; *Chattanooga Daily Times*, August 7, 1913, p. 1. Technically Arnold could not ask for a mistrial at the point that he jumped up because the jury had been excused for a few moments and had not been present to hear the demonstration. Other grounds for a mistrial had presented themselves earlier in the trial, before Conley testified. The jury observed Judge Roan reading a copy of *The Atlanta Georgian.* Roan held the paper so that every juror could read the headline emblazoned in red: "STATE ADDING LINKS TO CHAIN." The defense attorneys asked Roan at that time to caution the jurors about ignoring newspaper headlines when they

reached their conclusion and did not press for a mistrial. Roan did as he was asked. AG, August 3, 1913, p. 1; AC, August 3, 1913, p. 1; SMN, August 3, 1913, pp. 1, 3; AC, December 17, 1913, p. 1.

20. "The Prosecution of Leo M. Frank," *Frost's Magazine*, I (August, 1913), 1, 2.

21. *Frank* v. *State, Brief of the Evidence*, pp. 26, 41, 54, 83–84, 103–17, 153–54, 229–32; Lawson (ed.), X, 220; AC, August 7, 1913, p. 3.

22. AC, August 17, 1913, p. 2A.

23. Lawson (ed.), X, 227, 237; AG, August 21, 1913, p. 3; AC, August 19, 1913, p. 1.

24. AC, August 9, 1913, p. 1; August 17, 1913, pp. 2A and 4A; August 18, 1913, pp. 1, 2.

25. AJ, August 15, 1913, pp. 6, 20; August 14, 1913, p. 6; AG, August 18, 1913, p. 2.

26. *Leo M. Frank* v. *State of Georgia, Motion for a New Trial*, p. 107.

27. Quoted in AC, August 14, 1913, pp. 1, 3. *The Atlanta Journal* and *The Atlanta Georgian* reported Mrs. Frank's outburst but did not include the words "you dog" as part of her remark. AJ, August 13, 1913, p. 1; AG, August 13, 1913, p. 1. The New York *Sun*, on the other hand, quoted Mrs. Frank as saying, "No, nor you either—you Christian dog!" October 12, 1913, p. 6.

28. AC, August 13, 1913, p. 1; Thompson, p. 25.

29. Lawson (ed.), X, 238, 239, 242; AJ, August 21, 1913, p. 2.

30. Lawson (ed.), X, 264, 266.

31. AC, August 24, 1913, p. 1.

32. AC, August 24, 1913, p. 1; AG, August 23, 1913, p. 1; Lawson (ed.), X, 302, 303, 312. The windows of the courtroom were constantly open because of the heat. Since the room was on the main floor of the building some of the voices traveled clearly to the outside. At times Dorsey's summation was so impressive that murmurs of applause could be heard inside of the courtroom from those assembled outside of the building.

33. Lawson (ed.), X, 319.

34. *Ibid.*, p. 321.

35. This is one of the rumors that traveled through Atlanta

after Frank's arrest. It is not without foundation, however. Although Mrs. Frank rushed to the police station as soon as she heard of her husband's arrest, the police refused her permission to see him. Mrs. Frank did not visit her husband again until May 11 —reportedly because he expected to be released at any moment and did not want to have her humiliated by visiting him in jail. AG, April 29, 1913, p. 1; AC, April 30, 1913, p. 1; AG, May 12, 1913, p. 1.

36. Lawson (ed.), X, 395.

37. AJ, August 23, 1913, p. 1; AG, August 24, 1913, p. 1.

38. AG, August 22, 1913, p. 1; August 23, 1913, p. 1; August 24, 1913, p. 1; AC, August 23, 1913, p. 1; AJ, August 24, 1913, p. 1; AC, October 24, 1913, p. 7.

39. *Frank v. Mangum*, 235 *Supreme Court Reporter* 594 (1914).

40. *Frank v. State, Motion for a New Trial*, p. 130.

41. AC, October 25, 1913, p. 14; 235 *Supreme Court Reporter* 594 (1914).

42. AC, August 26, 1913, pp. 1, 2.

43. The twelve men included one bank teller, one bookkeeper, one real estate agent, one manufacturer, one contractor, one optician, one railroad claims agent, one mailing clerk, two salesmen, and two machinists. Franklin M. Garrett, *Atlanta and Environs* (3 vols.; New York, 1954), II, 622.

44. AC, August 26, 1913, p. 1. Conley was tried as an accessory to the crime in February, 1914. He was found guilty and sentenced to a year on the chain gang.

45. AC, August 26, 1913, p. 1.

46. SMN, August 26, 1913, p. 1. Different newspapers gave varying figures for the size of the crowd. *The Atlanta Georgian* reported it as 3,500 in one edition and 4,000 in the next, August 25, 1913, p. 1; *The Marietta Journal and Courier* also gave the figure of 4,000, August 29, 1913, p. 2; the Associated Press figure was 2,000 plus and this was reported on August 26, 1913, p. 1, in each of the following newspapers: New Orleans *Times-Democrat*, Columbia (S.C.) *State, Chattanooga Daily Times*, Raleigh (N.C.) *News & Observer*, and *The Birmingham Age-Herald;* the New York *Call* estimated the size of the crowd as 5,000, August 26, 1913, p. 1.

47. AC, August 26, 1913, pp. 1, 4.

48. AG, August 25, 1913, p. 1; Bricker, *The Shane Quarterly*, IV (April, 1943), p. 90.

49. *The Marietta Journal and Courier*, August 29, 1913, p. 2; *The Herald-Journal* (Greensboro, Ga.), August 29, 1913, p. 4; SMN, August 26, 1913, p. 6.

50. AC, August 27, 1913, p. 1.

51. *Ibid.*, p. 2.

52. Cahan, *Blätter Von Mein Leben*, V, 416.

53. See pp. 84–85, below.

54. DeWitt H. Roberts to Leonard Dinnerstein, February 14, 1964; DeWitt H. Roberts, "Anti-Semitism and the Leo. M. Frank Case" (unpublished essay, files of the Anti-Defamation League, New York City, n.d., ca. 1953), p. 15.

55. Louis Joughin and Edmund M. Morgan, *The Legacy of Sacco and Vanzetti* (Chicago, 1964), p. 196.

56. Quoted in William H. Nichols, *Southern Tradition and Regional Progress* (Chapel Hill, 1960), p. 300.

57. TAC, August 26, 1913, p. 2. The Atlanta race riot occurred in September, 1906. This is probably the "reign of terror in 1907" referred to in the final sentence of the quotation.

58. AG, May 28, 1913, p. 3; *Minutes* of the American Jewish Committee's Executive Commmittee (American Jewish Committee Archives, New York), November 8, 1913 (hereafter cited as *Minutes*); W. F. Eve to Governor John Slaton, May 27, 1915 (Prison Commission files, State of Georgia Archives, Atlanta) (hereafter cited as PC Records); interview of John Slaton by Samuel A. Boorstin, October 12, 1953 (files of Anti-Defamation League, New York City); DeWitt Roberts, "Anti-Semitism and the Leo M. Frank Case" (unpublished essay, *ibid.*, n.d., ca. 1953), pp. 12–13; *The Evening World* (New York City), August 26, 1913, p. 6; Macdonald, *The Kansas City Star*, p. 3C; AC, October 25, 1913, p. 14; Thompson, p. 31; Connolly, pp. 11, 18; *The North Georgia Citizen* (Dalton, Ga.), May 27, 1915, p. 4 (*The North Georgia Citizen* is frequently referred to as "The Dalton Citizen"); *The New Castle* [Pa.] *Herald* published the following item on June 22, 1915: an Atlantan, interviewed the previous day, said, "A mob as infuriated and unworthy of credence as that which clamored for the crucifixion of Jesus Christ . . . was in Atlanta during the Leo M. Frank trial and all hands were crying 'Hang

the Jew!' " Clipping, John M. Slaton Scrapbooks, Georgia State Archives (Atlanta, Ga.). (Hereafter cited as Slaton Scrapbooks.)

59. *The New York Times*, June 22, 1915, p. 6; *The North Georgia Citizen*, May 27, 1915, p. 4.

III. AN AMERICAN DREYFUS

1. *The Macon Daily Telegraph* (Georgia), August 27, 1913, Frank Papers.

2. *Minutes*, I (November 11, 1906), 69.

3. Yonathan Shapiro, "Leadership of the American Zionist Organization, 1897–1930" (unpublished Ph.D. dissertation, Columbia University, 1964), p. 26.

4. Nathan Schachner, *The Price of Liberty: A History of the American Jewish Committee* (New York, 1948), pp. 5–6, 49–53; Shapiro, Ph.D. dissertation, pp. 21–22; Marshall Sklare, *Conservative Judaism* (Glencoe, Ill., 1955), pp. 163–64; Morton Rosenstock, "Louis Marshall and the Defense of Jewish Rights in the United States" (unpublished Ph. D. dissertation, Columbia University, 1963), p. 67. Rosenstock's work has been published under the title, *Louis Marshall, Defender of Jewish Rights* (Detroit, 1966).

5. Robert De Courcy Ward, "Immigration and the South," *The Atlantic Monthly*, XCVI (November, 1905), 611. See also AC, February 20, 1907, p. 1.

6. Higham, *Strangers in the Land*, p. 113; Walter L. Fleming, "Immigration to the Southern States," *Political Science Quarterly*, XX (June, 1905), 282, 290; AC, February 20, 1907, p. 3; "Phases of Immigration," *Manufacturers' Record*, XLVII (June 15, 1905), 497; *The Independent*, XI (August 17, 1911), 395.

7. Grantham, p. 157; Joseph D. Herzog, "The Emergence of the Anti-Jewish Stereotype in the United States" (unpublished thesis, Hebrew Union College, 1953), p. 42; Rowland T. Bertoff, "Southern Attitudes toward Immigration," *The Journal of Southern History*, XVII (August, 1951), 360.

8. Higham, *Strangers*, p. 169; Bertoff, *The Journal of Southern History*, XVII, pp. 343–44. The lynchings created an international incident, and President Benjamin Harrison even found it necessary to comment upon them in his State of the Union address to

Congress in 1891. Charles H. Watson, "Need of Federal Legislation in Respect to Mob Violence in Cases of Lynching of Aliens," *Yale Law Journal*, XXV (1916), 569, 577, 578; see also "Southern Peonage and Immigration," *The Nation*, LXXXV (December 19, 1907), 557.

9. Bertoff, *The Journal of Southern History*, XVII, p. 344.

10. Merle Curti, *The Growth of American Thought* (New York, 1943), p. 51.

11. Lawrence H. Fuchs, *The Political Behavior of American Jews* (Glencoe, Ill., 1956), pp. 37–40; Alfred O. Hero, Jr., *The Southerner and World Affairs* (Baton Rouge, 1965), p. 494. Hero has an excellent historical discussion in his chapter "Southern Jews." See also Bernard Postal, "Jews in the Ku Klux Klan," *The Jewish Tribune*, XCIII (September 14, 1928), 60.

12. Henry Givens Baker, *Rich's of Atlanta* (Atlanta, 1953), p. 225; Cahan, V, 353.

13. John Higham, "Social Discrimination against Jews in America, 1830–1930," *Publications of the American Jewish Historical Society*, XLVII (1957–1958), 4; Nina Morais, "Jewish Ostracism in America," *The North American Review*, XCCCIII (1881), 271; "The Jew's Daughter," *Journal of American Folklore*, XV (1902), 196. See also *ibid.*, XIX (1906), 293–94; XXIX (1916), 166; XXV (1922), 344; and XXXIX (1926), 212–13. *Harper's New Monthly Magazine*, XIX (1859), 860.

14. E. Merton Coulter, *The Confederate States of America* (Baton Rouge, 1950), p. 226; Eaton, *Freedom of Thought in the Old South* (New York, 1951), p. 233; Bertram Wallace Korn, *American Jewry and the Civil War* (Philadelphia, 1951), pp. 158, 177, 179; Rudolph Glanz, *The Jew in the Old American Folklore* (New York, 1961), p. 54.

15. E. Merton Coulter, *The South during Reconstruction* (Baton Rouge, 1947), p. 203.

16. Baker, p. 225.

17. Harry Golden, *Forgotten Pioneer* (Cleveland, 1963), pp. 66–67; Golden, *A Little Girl Is Dead*, p. 226; Golden, "Jew and Gentile in the New South: Segregation at Sundown," *Commentary*, XX (November, 1955), 403–4.

18. *The American Israelite*, December 5, 1873, p. 6; January 28, 1876, p. 6; November 15, 1878, p. 6; December 6, 1878, p. 5; March 12, 1879, p. 6.

19. Higham, *Strangers*, pp. 92, 113; A. H. Tuttle, D.D., "The Jew," a sermon delivered in Baltimore, January 22, 1893.
20. Horace M. Kallen, *Judaism at Bay* (New York, 1932), p. 149.
21. J. F. Brown, "The Origin of the Anti-Semitic Attitude," in Isaque Graeber and Stewart Henderson Britt (eds.), *Jews in a Gentile World* (New York, 1942), pp. 134–35.
22. Cash, p. 342; Broadus Mitchell and George Sinclair Mitchell, *The Industrial Revolution in the South* (Baltimore, 1930), p. 273.
23. Daniel Bell, "The Dispossessed," in *The Radical Right*, edited by Daniel Bell (Garden City, 1963), pp. 2–3; Eric Hoffer, *The True Believer* (New York, 1958), p. 92; Israel S. Wechsler, "The Psychology of Anti-Semitism," *The Menorah Journal*, XI (April, 1925), 164; Else Frenkle-Brunswick and R. Nevitt Sanford, "Some Personality Factors in Anti-Semitism," *The Journal of Psychology*, XX (1945), 277, 283, 285; Gordon W. Allport and Bernard M. Kramer, "Some Roots of Prejudice," *ibid.*, XXII (1946), 29–30; Bruno Bettelheim, "The Dynamism of Anti-Semitism In Gentile and Jew," *The Journal of Abnormal and Social Psychology*, XLII (1947), 163; John Dollard, Neal E. Miller, Leonard Doob, O. H. Mowrer, and Robert R. Sears, *Frustration and Aggression* (New Haven, 1939), p. 1; David Riesman, "The Politics of Persecution," *Public Opinion Quarterly*, VI (Spring, 1942), 45; Bruno Bettelheim and Morris Janowitz, *Social Change and Prejudice* (New York, 1964), pp. 54–55, 58, 278; Isaac A. Hourwich, "Is There Anti-Semitism in America?" *The American Hebrew*, XCIII (October 17, 1913), 683–84; Gerhart Saenger, *The Social Psychology of Prejudice* (New York, 1953), pp. 110–11; David W. Petegorsky, "The Strategy of Hatred," *The Antioch Review*, I (September, 1941), 377; Selma G. Hirsh, *The Fears Men Live By* (New York, 1955), pp. xi, xviii, 64–65; "Leo Frank," *The New Republic*, III (July 24, 1915), 300; Gustov Icheisen, "Fear of Violence and Fear of Fraud," *Sociometry*, VII (November, 1944), 378; Isaque Graeber, "An Examination of Theories of Race Prejudice," *Social Research*, XX (August, 1953), 278, 281; Otto Fenichel, "Psychoanalysis of Antisemitism," *The American Imago*, I (March, 1940), 31; and Arnold Rose, "Anti-Semitism's Root in City-Hatred," *Commentary*, VI (1948) 374.

24. John Higham, "Anti-Semitism in the Gilded Age: A Re-interpretation," *Mississippi Valley Historical Review*, XLIII (March, 1957), 572. See also Nancy Carter Morse, "Anti-Semitism: a Study of It's Causal Factors and Other Associated Variables" (unpublished Ph.D. dissertation, Department of Psychology, Syracuse University, 1947), p. 422.

25. Woodward, *Tom Watson*, pp. 418–19.

26. Albert I. Gordon, *Jews in Transition* (Minneapolis, 1949), p. 46; Stuart E. Rosenberg, *The Jewish Community in Rochester, 1843–1925* (New York, 1954), pp. 118–19; E. A. Fischkin, "Jewish Problems in Chicago," *The Reform Advocate*, XXXII (January 26, 1907), 830; David Herman Joseph, "Some More of It, and Why," *The Temple*, I (December 10, 1909), 3; B. H. Hartogensis, "Religious Intolerance in Maryland," *The Jewish Exponent*, XLV (April 12, 1907), 8; Ida Libert Uchill, *Pioneers, Peddlers, and Tsadikim* (Denver, 1957), pp. 157–58. Indications of the growing anti-Semitism in the United States can also be garnered from Rev. F. F. Ellinwood, "The Duty of Christendom to the Jews," *The Missionary Review of the World*, III, New Series (November, 1890), 801–7; Josephus, "The Jewish Question," *The Century*, XLIII (1891–1892), 395–98; "Classical Anti-Semitism," *The Nation*, LXI (1895), 50–51; "A Gross Injustice," *The Jewish Messenger*, LXXVIII (July 12, 1895), 4; Major W. Evans Gordan, M.P., "Where Come Our Immigrants?" *The World's Work*, V (April, 1903), 3276–81; Richard Hayes Mc-Cartney, *That Jew!* (Chicago, 1905); "The Jews in the United States," *The World's Work*, XI (January, 1906), 7030–31; "Is a Dreyfus Case Possible in America?" *The Independent*, LXV (November 12, 1908), 1105–8; Sydney Reid, "Because You're a Jew," *ibid.*, LXV (November 26, 1908), 1212–17; "Race Prejudice against Jews," *ibid.*, LXV (December 17, 1908), 1451–56; "Will the Jews Ever Lose Their Racial Identity?" *Current Opinion*, L (March, 1911), 292–94; J. G. Wilson, "The Crossing of the Races," *The Popular Science Monthly*, LXXIX (November, 1911), 486–95; Nathum [*sic*] Wolf, "Are the Jews an Inferior Race?" *The North American Review*, CXCV (April, 1912), 492–95; Burton J. Hendrick, "The Great Jewish Invasion," *McClure's Magazine*, XXVIII (January, 1907), 307–21; Hendrick, "The Jewish Invasion of America," *ibid.*, XL (March, 1913), 125–65;

Heywood Broun and George Britt, *Christians Only: A Study in Prejudice* (New York, 1931), p. 57; Mark Twain, "Concerning the Jews," *Harper's Magazine*, XCIX (1899), 530, 532; and Joseph D. Herzog, "The Emergence of the Anti-Jewish Stereotype in the United States" (unpublished thesis, Hebrew Union College, 1953), p. 68.

27. *American Jewish Year Book*, VII (1905–1906; Jewish year, 5666), 235; David Herman Joseph, "Some More of It, and Why," *The Temple*, I (December 10, 1909), 3; *The American Israelite* (September 17, 1914), p. 1.

28. Solomon Sutker, "The Jews of Atlanta: Their Social Structure and Leadership Patterns," (unpublished Ph.D. dissertation, Department of Sociology, University of North Carolina, 1950), pp. 80, 81.

29. AG, October 29, 1913, Leo Frank Papers.

30. Sutker, unpublished Ph.D. dissertation, pp. 30–31, 120, 143, 159.

31. Rainey, "The Race Riot of 1906 in Atlanta" (unpublished Master's thesis, Emory University, 1929), chap. 3; the Baltimore Morning *Sun*, November 23, 1914, p. 3.

32. AC, March 4, 1907, p. 3; Garrett, II, 574; The Baltimore Morning *Sun*, November 23, 1914, pp. 1, 3. See also Thomas Gibson, "The Anti-Negro Riots In Atlanta," *Harper's Weekly*, L (October 13, 1906), 1457–59.

33. Higham, "Social Discrimination against Jews in America, 1830–1930," *PAJHS*, p. 14.

34. George Kibbe Turner, "The Daughters of the Poor," *McClure's Magazine*, XXXIV (November, 1909), 45–61, *passim;* S. S. McClure, "The Tammanyizing of a Civilization," *ibid.*, pp. 122–23; Maurice Fishburg, "White Slave Traffic and Jews," *The American Monthly Jewish Review*, IV (December, 1909), 4, 23; "The Trade in White Slaves," *The American Review of Reviews*, XXXIX (March, 1909), 371; *The Immigration Commission* (61st Cong., 2nd Sess., Senate Document 196, Serial 5662, 1909–1910), pp. 23–24. George Kibbe Turner, whose original revelations caused a public sensation, told a New York Grand Jury, under oath, "that he had no personal knowledge of the things he wrote." "It is by such worthless evidence that the impression has been created in the minds of the people that the traffic in girls is

largely in the hands of Jews." "Jews in the White Slave Traffic," *The Temple*, II (February 25, 1910), 176. This stereotype was not restricted to Atlanta. In the 1920s an Ohioan told a sociologist, "Why, a young girl is no longer safe on our country roads! They are picked up by men in automobiles. The Jews get them and sell them as white slaves. They have a regular price list and the business is carried on from New York to San Francisco." Frank Bohn, "The Ku Klux Klan Interpreted," *The American Journal of Sociology*, XXX (January, 1925), 388.

35. The Baltimore Morning *Sun*, November 23, 1914, p. 1.

36. Lucian Lamar Knight, *Reminiscences of Famous Georgians* (2 vols.; Atlanta, 1907), I, 512; E. A. Ross, "The Hebrew of Eastern Europe in America," *The Century Magazine*, LXXXVIII (September, 1914), 787.

37. Hendrick, *McClure's Magazine*, XXVIII (January, 1907), 314, 319–20; XL (March, 1913), 125, 126, 136, 153, 156, 158.

38. Barbara Tuchman, *The Proud Tower* (New York, 1966), p. 173.

39. Leslie Derfler, *The Dreyfus Affair* (Boston, 1963), vii-xvi.

40. Beiliss is frequently spelled with only one "s." I have adopted the spelling used by Maurice Samuel in his book *Blood Accusation* (New York, 1966).

41. Handbill, "Mendel Beilis Protest Meeting" (American Jewish Archives, Cincinnati); *The New York Times*, October 15, 1913, p. 3; October 16, 1913, p. 16; October 17, 1913, p. 6; October 18, 1913, p. 4; October 20, 1913, p. 4; October 21, 1913, p. 4; October 24, 1913, p. 5; October 27, 1913, p. 8; October 28, 1913, p. 10; October 30, 1913, p. 10; Samuel, pp. 6–8, Chapter 19; "The 'Ritual Murder' Case in Kiev," *The Outlook*, CV (November 1, 1913), 113; "Russia's Christianity on Trial," *The Literary Digest*, XLVII (November 8, 1913), 877.

42. Rose A. Halpern, "The American Reaction to the Dreyfus Case" (unpublished Master's thesis, Department of History, Columbia University, 1941), chapter 3; Louis Marshall to Edward Menkin, November 1, 1913, Louis Marshall Papers (American Jewish Archives, Cincinnati). All letters to and from Louis Marshall are in this collection unless otherwise stated; therefore the expression "Marshall Papers" will not be repeated. Louis Marshall will be cited hereafter as LM. See also E. Lifshutz, "Repercussions

of the Beilis Trial in the United States," *Zion*, XXVIII (1963), 206–22.

43. Hourwich, *The American Hebrew*, XCIII (October 17, 1913), 684.

44. Milton Klein to Louis Marshall, September 4, 1913; David Marx to Louis Marshall, August 30, 1913; Leonard Haas to Louis Marshall, August 30, 1913.

45. Cyrus Adler to Herman Bernstein, September 2, 1913; E. B. M. Browne to Cyrus Sulzberger, September 21, 1913, "The Leo Frank Correspondence Folder" (The American Jewish Committee Archives, New York City).

46. LM to Irving Lehman, September 9, 1913.

47. *Ibid.;* LM to Milton Klein, September 9, 1913; LM to Simon Wolf, September 27, 1913.

48. LM to Adolph Kraus, September 27, 1913; LM to Irving Lehman, September 9, 1913.

49. *Minutes*, II (November 8, 1913), 180; LM to William Rosenau, December 14, 1914.

50. LM to Herbert Haas, December 27, 1913. The initial expenses had been taken care of by Frank's immediate family and a well-to-do uncle. By the beginning of November, 1913, they already had spent about $30,000. *Minutes*, November 8, 1913.

IV. THE FIRST APPEAL

1. Connolly, *The Truth about the Frank Case*, p. 16.

2. *Frank v. State, Motion for a New Trial*, p. 125; AJ, October 4, 1913, p. 1.

3. *Ibid.*, pp. 1, 2; *Frank v. State*, 141 *Georgia* 283 (1914).

4. AJ, October 21, 1913, p. 1.

5. AC, October 22, 1913, p. 9.

6. AC, October 26, 1913, p. 1.

7. AC, October 28, 1913, p. 1.

8. Quoted in AG, November 1, 1913, p. 1, Frank Papers.

9. Herbert Haas to LM, October 31, 1913. See Appendix A.

10. AG, n.d. (November 1, 1913?), Frank Papers.

11. *Waycross-Herald*, November 5, 1913, Frank Papers; Greensboro *Herald-Journal*, November 7, 1913, p. 6; "The Real Case," *Southern Ruralist*, XX (January 15, 1914), 20. Poor health

prevented Judge Roan from seeking renomination in 1914. AJ, May 13, 1914, p. 5.

12. J. J. Barge to Georgia Prison Commission and Governor John Slaton, May 31, 1915, PC Records. See also Allen Lumpkin Henson, *Confessions of a Criminal Lawyer* (New York, 1959), p. 65. A Georgian, familiar with the facts in the case, has written, "Friends of Judge Roan . . . felt that he expected an acquittal by the jury, and would have granted a new trial had he not been sure that the Supreme Court would do so." DeWitt H. Roberts to Leonard Dinnerstein, February 19, 1964.

13. AJ, December 11, 1913, pp. 1, 7; December 15, 1913, pp. 1, 19, 20; AC, December 16, 1913, pp. 1, 4, December 17, 1913, pp. 1, 5. See Appendix A.

14. AC, December 17, 1913, p. 1. Felder seemed less concerned with the legality of Roan's action than with winning his case. He said nothing about the precedents covering cases where the trial judge did so certify.

15. The justices of the Georgia Supreme Court at that time were William H. Fish (Chief Justice), Beverly D. Evans, Joseph Henry Lumpkin, Marcus W. Beck, Samuel C. Atkinson, and Hiram Warner Hill. Justices Fish and Beck dissented from the majority.

16. *Frank* v. *State*, 141 *Georgia* 246–47, 281, 283.

17. *Ibid.*, pp. 253–54, 256, 260.

18. *Ibid.*, pp. 266–67, 284.

19. *Ibid.*, pp. 285–307.

V. TOM WATSON AND WILLIAM J. BURNS

1. Burns had been brought into the case a year earlier when a public subscription had been raised to pay for the famous detective's services in helping Atlanta find the culprit. After Conley's affidavits, however, toward the end of May, 1913, Solicitor Dorsey informed the Burns agency in the city that its services would no longer be needed. The Burns agent, who had investigated the murder for about two weeks, had announced in May, 1913, that he, too, believed Frank guilty. But William J. Burns had never come to Atlanta, nor did he have any hand in the investigation undertaken by his agents in 1913. Once Dorsey had informed his

agency that its services would no longer be necessary, the Burns people dropped all association with the case. Therefore when William J. Burns was again solicited, in February, 1914, he felt free to accept the assignment from the defense. See AC, May 27, 1913, pp. 1, 2.

2. AC, February 21, 1914, p. 1.

3. *Southern Ruralist*, March 15, 1914, p. 21.

4. Quoted in AG, February 22, 1914, p. 1; Frank Papers.

5. *The New York Times*, February 26, 1914, p. 1.

6. Quoted in AC, February 27, 1914, p. 2.

7. AJ, March 4, 1914, p. 1. At the trial, however, the motor-man who had conducted the trolley that Mary Phagan had come to town on, said he also knew George Epps, Jr. and that the boy had not been on the trolley with Mary Phagan. *Brief of the Evidence*, p. 84.

8. AC, February 24, 1914, p. 7; March 13, 1914, p. 1; March 15, 1914, p. 2A; March 28, 1914, p. 1. See also affidavits in Frank Papers.

9. AJ, March 5, 1914, pp. 1, 2; AC, May 4, 1914, p. 1; AJ, May 3, 1914, p. 1.

10. AC, March 15, 1914, p. 1; April 19, 1914, p. 1; AJ, April 19, 1914, p. 1.

11. AJ, May 1, 1914, p. 22; May 3, 1914, p. 1; May 4, 1914, p. 1; Connolly, p. 65; Macdonald, *The Kansas City Star*, p. 2C.

12. An "extraordinary motion" was needed to place Frank's case before the Georgia courts again because the ordinary procedures had already been exhausted. The "extraordinary motion" was based on new information, not available at the time of the trial.

13. *The New York Times*, March 9, 1914, p. 1; March 17, 1914, p. 3; *The Washington Post*, March 9, 1915, p. 5; AJ, March 8, 1914, p. 1; March 9, 1914, p. 2.

14. Henry A. Alexander, p. 7.

15. L. O. Bricker, "A Great American Tragedy," *The Shane Quarterly*, IV (April, 1943), 91.

16. Macdonald, *The Kansas City Star*, p. 2C; Connolly, p. 88; *The New York Times*, March 15, 1914, III, 10; Cahan, V, 502.

17. LM to Leonard Haas, March 25, 1914.

18. *The New York Times*, October 26, 1914, p. 1.

19. LM to Adolph Ochs, January 8, 1914; LM to Judge Julian Mack, March 17, 1914.

20. Tom Watson would eventually remind his readers that the Northern periodicals leading the fight to exonerate Frank—*Puck*, *The New York Times* and *The Evening World* (New York)—were all owned by Jews. "What is the purpose of this continued and systematic crusade in behalf of one convicted Jew whose connections command unlimited wealth?" Watson later asked. And then he added, touching on one of the themes he frequently made reference to when discussing the influence of the Jews: "The Frank case is enough to depress the most hopeful student of the times. It has shown us how the capitalists of Big Money regard the poor man's daughter. It has shown us what our daily papers will do in the interest of wealthy criminals. It has shown us how differently the law deals with the rich man and the poor." *The Jeffersonian*, December 5, 1914, pp. 1, 8.

21. Albert D. Lasker's secretary, C. M. Langan, to Julius Rosenwald, December 10, 1913. Julius Rosenwald Papers, University of Chicago; hereafter cited as Rosenwald papers. Leo Frank to Albert D. Lasker, December 18, 1913, *ibid.*; Albert D. Lasker to Julius Rosenwald, June 26, 1915, *ibid.*; John Gunther noted that over a two-year period Lasker contributed $100,000 out of his own pocket. *Taken at the Flood* (New York, 1961), pp. 82–83. Harry Golden, on the other hand, estimated that Lasker and his father had spent $160,000 between them, and that an uncle of Frank's had spent $50,000 (*A Little Girl Is Dead*, p. 230); on June 19, 1915, Herbert Hass acknowledged that "Mr. Frank's defence [*sic*] for the past fifteen months has been assisted financially by and through Mr. A. D. Lasker, of Chicago." Hass to Jacob Schiff, Jacob Schiff Papers, American Jewish Archives; cited hereafter as Schiff Papers. People such as Louis Marshall, Jacob Schiff, and Julius Rosenwald also contributed substantial sums to Frank's cause. If the estimate is based on the entire list of contributors, it seems conservative to say that at least a quarter of a million dollars was spent in order to free Leo Frank. Albert D. Lasker to Herbert Hass, April 20, 1914, Schiff Papers; Schiff to Herbert Hass, June 21, 1915, *ibid.*; Julius Rosenwald's secretary, "WCG," to Julius Rosenwald, March 9, 1914, March 13, 1914, March 14, 1914, Rosenwald Papers; Albert Lasker to Louis Wiley, April 20, 1914, April 22, 1914, Schiff Papers.

22. Gunther, p. 83; "WCG" to Julius Rosenwald, March 14, 1914, Rosenwald Papers; Julian Mack to LM, March 16, March 19, 1914.

23. LM to Siegmund B. Sonneborn, March 13, 1914; Siegmund B. Sonneborn to LM, April 2, 1914.

24. Clipping, April 18, 1914, Boston *Herald-Traveler* Library; *The American Israelite*, May 21, 1914, p. 1; The Baltimore Morning *Sun*, March 17, 1914, p. 8; *Arkansas Gazette*, April 15, 1914, Richmond *Times-Dispatch*, March 24, 1914, *The Mobile Tribune*, March 21, 1914, Frank Papers. *The Salt Lake City Tribune* thought it "somewhat remarkable that the conviction was obtained on the negro's testimony in the first place." Clipping, March 19, 1914, Frank Papers.

25. *The Macon News*, March 9, 1914, p. 11, Frank Papers; AC, February 26, 1914, p. 4.

26. AJ, March 10, 1914, p. 8.

27. *The Greensboro Herald-Journal*, March 20, 1914, p. 8; *The North Georgia Citizen*, March 12, 1914, p. 4.

28. AJ, March 15, 1914, pp. 5, 6; Macdonald, *The Kansas City Star*, p. 3C. A Georgia woman wrote to a Northern newspaper, "No one has yet dared publicly to express his belief in Frank's innocence without being accused of having been bought with Jewish money," *The New York Times*, November 28, 1914, p. 5. Berry Benson also indicated at the beginning of his presentation, "I have not received one cent from Frank's people, nor from anybody. I make this statement to anticipate the low jibe of any vicious or crazy person, or any person both crazy and vicious, who may say I am in the pay of the Jews." "Five Arguments in the Frank Case" (n.p., n.d., *ca.* June, 1914), p. 1.

29. Woodward, *Tom Watson*, pp. 176, 177, 187–89, 223, 332, 348–49, 357, 371, 402, 408, 419; Woodward, *Origins of the New South*, pp. 188, 257, 262; Lucian Lamar Knight, *A Standard History of Georgia and Georgians* (6 vols.; Chicago, 1917), II, 1127; Mary Richards Colvin, "Hoke Smith and Joseph M. Brown, Political Rivals" (unpublished M.A. thesis, University of Georgia, 1958), p. 70. See also Gustavus Myers, *History of Bigotry in the United States* (New York, 1943), p. 261.

30. Mercer G. Evans, "The History of the Organized Labor Movement in Georgia" (unpublished Ph.D. dissertation, Department of Economics, University of Chicago, 1929), p. 291; Clare

de Graffenried, "The Georgia Cracker in the Cotton Mills," *The Century Magazine*, XLI (February, 1891), 477–78, 495, 496; Ward Greene, *Star Reporters and 34 of Their Stories* (New York, 1948), p. 132; Oscar and Mary Handlin, *Danger in Discord* (New York, 1948), pp. 22–23; Woodward, *Tom Watson*, p. 442.

31. Woodward, *Tom Watson*, p. 248.

32. Louis Turner Griffith and John Erwin Talmadge, *Georgia Journalism: 1763–1950* (University of Georgia Press, 1951), p. 138; Colvin, "Hoke Smith and Joseph M. Brown, Political Rivals" (unpublished M.A. thesis, University of Georgia, 1958), p. 16.

33. Woodward, *Tom Watson*, p. 437; Griffith and Talmadge, p. 139; Garrett, II, 625–26; Steed, p. 239.

34. *The Jeffersonian*, March 19, 1914, pp. 1, 8. Albert Lasker acknowledged privately, "If it had not been for the energy, influence and money expended, Frank—innocent though he is—would have been hung long ago." Lasker to Louis Wiley, April 20, 1914, Schiff Papers.

35. *The Jeffersonian*, April 2, 1914, p. 2.

36. *Ibid.*, May 7, 1914, p. 5; May 14, 1914, p. 3. Praiseworthy letters on this subject were published in every issue from April 16 through May 28, 1914. No unfavorable comments were printed.

37. "Tom Watson fell on the Frank case with the lust of a starved tiger and the cunning of a political opportunist. By the time . . . national names . . . were blazoned among Frank's supporters Watson was feeding his 'woolhats' a diet of 'Wall Street plot, Jewish gold and Yankee meddlers' in language careless of truth or decency and always inflammatory." Greene, p. 132.

38. *The Jeffersonian*, April 9, 1914, p. 1. Louis Wiley wrote LM: "While I can understand the clamor and mob feeling which led to the unjust verdict in the Frank case, I am strongly inclined to believe that the prisoner was not adequately defended. If he had been it seems to me the dreadful situation now before us might have been prevented." April 3, 1914.

39. *The Jeffersonian*, April 9, 1914, p. 8; April 30, 1914, p. 10.

40. *Ibid.*, April 9, 1914, p. 1; May 7, 1914, p. 1; April 23, 1914, p. 10.

41. Quoted in *The Jeffersonian*, May 28, 1914, p. 5.

42. AJ, February 18, 1914, p. 9.

43. Herbert Asbury, "Hearst Comes to Atlanta," *The American Mercury*, VII (January, 1926), 91; Steed, p. 239; Knight, *A Standard History of Georgia*, II, 1165.

44. AJ, February 19, 1914, p. 1; March 16, 1914, p. 1; March 18, 1914, p. 1; AG, March 22, 1914, Frank Papers, Box 693; AC, March 20, 1914, p. 2; April 5, 1914, p. 1.

45. Lasker to Herbert Hass, April 20, 1914, Schiff Papers.

46. AC, May 2, 1914, pp. 1, 2.

47. AC, May 2, 1914, p. 2.

48. AJ, April 12, 1914, p. 3.

49. Quoted in AC, April 12, 1914, p. 2A.

50. Quoted in AJ, April 24, 1914, p. 1. See also *The New York Times*, April 25, 1914, p. 8.

51. AJ, April 28, 1914, p. 20.

52. *The New York Times*, April 25, 1914, p. 8; April 27, 1914, p. 10.

53. AC, April 26, 1914, p. 1.

54. Quoted in AC, April 26, 1914, p. 3.

55. AJ, April 26, 1914, p. 7; *supra*, pp. 53–54.

56. AC, April 25, 1914, p. 3. In June, 1915, he inexplicably changed his mind. At that time he admitted writing the letters but claimed that someone else must have put in the vulgar expressions because he had not done so. AJ, June 14, 1915, p. 1. None of the Atlanta papers commented about Conley's admission in 1915.

57. AJ, April 24, 1914, p. 8; AC, May 6, 1914, p. 5; *The New York Times*, April 25, 1914, p. 20. Frank's attorneys maintained at the trial that the elevator had not been used to take the body to the basement; the prosecution argued otherwise. Lawson (ed.), X, 210.

58. AJ, May 5, 1914, p. 2; AC, May 6, 1914, p. 5; *The New York Times*, May 6, 1914, p. 3.

59. Herbert Haas to A. D. Lasker, April 30, 1914, May 2, 1914, Rosenwald Papers.

60. *The New York Times*, April 25, 1914, p. 8; May 1, 1914, p. 5; AC, April 30, 1914, p. 5; May 1, 1914, p. 1; Haas to Lasker, April 30 and May 2, 1914, Rosenwald Papers.

61. *The New York Times*, May 6, 1914, p. 3; AC, May 2, 1914,

p. 2; May 4, 1914, p. 1; May 5, 1914, p. 10; May 6, 1914, p. 1; AJ, May 5, 1914, p. 2.

62. AJ, May 2, 1914, p. 3.

63. Herbert Haas to Lasker, May 2, 1914, Rosenwald Papers.

64. AJ, May 6, 1914, p. 1; AC, June 7, 1914, p. 1. In 1913 the Georgia General Assembly created a new judgeship for the Atlanta circuit to which Judge Benjamin H. Hill was appointed. At the same time, Judge Roan, who had presided at Frank's trial and had denied the motion for a new trial, was transferred to the State Court of Appeals. Therefore the subsequent appeals in the Atlanta circuit were heard by Judge Hill. Knight, *A Standard History of Georgia*, II, 1135–36.

65. LM to the Messrs. Hass & Hass, April 13, 1914.

66. LM to Julian W. Mack, March 17, 1914.

67. Burns's connection with the case did, in fact, have dire consequences for Frank. Louis Marshall wrote to an editor of a New York newspaper, "It is nevertheless the fact, that people of the highest standing in Georgia, some of whom prior to the advent of Burns were strong believers in Frank's innocence, have turned against him and have deduced an argument of guilt from the very fact that Burns has been identified with the case. It is also a very significant fact that, since that time, all people who are connected with trade unions and the working classes generally, have been more vituperative in their animosity to Frank than ever before." LM to Keats Speed, January 13, 1915. LM to Louis Wiley, May 5, 1914, Schiff Papers.

68. LM to Louis Wiley, May 5, 1914, Schiff Papers.

69. Samuel Untermyer to Louis Wiley, May 5, 1914, *ibid.*

VI. WISDOM WITHOUT JUSTICE

1. *Frank v. State*, 83 *Southeastern Reporter* 234.

2. The sixth justice was ill and did not participate in the decision.

3. 83 *Southeastern Reporter* 654.

4. LM to Leonard Haas, November 14, 1914.

5. Writ of error: a writ issued for an appeals court to the judge of court of record requiring him to remit the record in order that an examination may be made of certain errors alleged to have been committed so that judgment may be reversed, corrected, or af-

firmed. Frank's counsel wanted the Georgia Supreme Court to grant the writ of error so that the United States Supreme Court would review the evidence and remand the case back to the Georgia courts for another trial. Even though technically the lawyers asked to have the verdict set aside, in reality they did not want, or expect, the judges to do this. But they did expect a new trial. Louis Marshall and Albert Lasker agreed that "if a new trial were to take place, with the entire nation looking on and with newspaper correspondents from all parts of the country in attendance, there would be no likelihood of a conviction, especially in view of the fact that the facts of the case are now much better understood than they were at the time of the trial." LM to Lasker, January 30, 1915.

6. AC, November 21, 1914, p. 4.

7. LM to Chief Justice Edward D. White, November 24, 1914, Reznikoff (ed.), *Louis Marshall: Champion of Liberty* (Philadelphia, 1957), I, 300.

8. AJ, November 26, 1914, p. 4.

9. AC, November 24, 1914, p. 1.

10. Quoted in AC, November 27, 1914, p. 5; see also *The New York Times*, November 27, 1914, p. 1.

11. AJ, December 7, 1914, p. 1.

12. Reprinted in *The New York Times*, December 1, 1914, p. 7.

13. Reprinted in *ibid.*, December 2, 1914, p. 8. *The New York Times* reprinted other newspaper comments on the case regularly. Most newspaper commentary seemed to express the feeling that Frank did not have a fair trial and that some way of obtaining one should be found. There are literally hundreds of clippings to this effect scattered among the Frank Papers, Boxes 694–701. Albert Lasker wrote to Jacob Billikopf, of Kansas City, Mo.:

"Outside of the State of Georgia, the press of the United States, including the leading papers of every city in the South, save Georgia, are editorially not only commenting on the case, and agitating a public sentiment for the unfortunate Frank, but daily hundreds of papers, including the leading Southern papers, are editorially crying that Frank's execution would amount to judicial murder, and that in this case, the State of Georgia is more at bar than Frank. I do not exaggerate when I state that hundreds of such editorials are appearing daily."

December 28, 1914, Rosenwald Papers.

14. Writ of habeas corpus: to get a person released from un-lawful punishment. Only issue under consideration is whether prisoner's liberty has been denied without due process of law.

15. LM to Meier Steinbrink, December 19, 1914, Rezinkoff (ed.), *Louis Marshall*, I, 300, 303.

16. *The New York Times*, December 18, 1914, p. 6.

17. *The New York Times*, December 29, 1914, p. 1; AJ, De-cember 31, 1914, p. 5.

18. The Scranton (Pa.) *Tribune-Republican*, December 30, 1914, Frank Papers.

19. Reprinted in *The American Jewish Review*, IV (January, 1915), 2, Frank Papers.

20. Copy of letter from LM to Haas (Leonard or Herbert not stated), December 24, 1914, Rosenwald Papers.

21. LM to A. D. Lasker, January 30, 1915.

22. LM to A. D. Lasker, January 30, 1915, February 5, 1915, LM to Henry A. Alexander, February 19, 1915.

23. Reznikoff (ed.), *Louis Marshall*, I, 304–11, *passim; The New York Times*, February 21, 1915, II, 11.

24. Quoted in *The New York Times*, February 27, 1914, p. 8.

25. The majority included Edward D. White, Chief Justice, and Associate Justices Joseph McKenna, William R. Day, Willis Van Devanter, Joseph R. Lamar, Mahlon Pitney, and James C. McReynolds. Justices Holmes and Charles Evans Hughes dis-sented.

26. *Frank* v. *Mangum*, 237 U.S. 326, 333, 343, 344, 345 (1915).

27. *Ibid.*, pp. 347, 349. "In *Frank* v. *Mangum*, Hughes worked with Holmes on his dissenting opinion, and in circulating it Holmes wrote a note saying, 'I think it would be fairer to say (if you agree) that you and I think the judgment should be re-versed and to put *we* for I all through.' The opinion came down that way after Hughes had replied, 'I shall be proud to be as-sociated with you in this opinion.'" Merlo J. Pusey, *Charles Evans Hughes* (2 vols.; New York, 1951), I, 289.

28. Letter from A. B. Macdonald to Leo Frank, Slaton, Brandeis.

29. *San Francisco Chronicle*, April 21, 1915, p. 18; see also *Washington Post*, April 21, 1915, p. 6; *Galveston Daily News*, April 23, 1915, p. 4.

30. Muskegee *Democrat*, April 29, 1915, Frank Papers. LM to Judge Julian Mack, April 24, 1915. Chief Justice White later insisted that he knew not one word of the evidence in the case, nor anything about its merits, and that the question of guilt or innocence did not come before him at all, "but solely the dry, technical question . . . as to whether there was such Federal question involved as to require the Federal Courts to wrest the case from the State tribunals." John M. Slaton, "Governor Slaton's OWN Defense in the Frank Case," The New York *World*, July 4, 1915, editorial section, p. 1.

VII. COMMUTATION

1. AC, October 3, 1914, p. 1; October 4, 1914, p. 1. *The Jeffersonian*, October 8, 1914, p. 9.

2. The Baltimore *Sun*, November 19, 1914, p. 1; November 23, 1914, p. 3; C. P. Connolly, "The Frank Case," *Collier's*, LIV (December 19, 1914), 6–7; LIV (December 26, 1914), 18–20; Macdonald, *The Kansas City Star*, January 17, 1915, pp. 1C–3C; Arthur Train, "Did Leo Frank Get Justice?" *Everybody's*, XXXII (March, 1915), 315–17. Arthur Brisbane also investigated the case for the Hearst newspapers, and the New York *World* and Chicago *Tribune* sent reporters to Atlanta for further information. *The New York Times*, February 2, 1915, p. 6.

3. The Baltimore *Sun*, November 19, 1914, p. 1; *Collier's*, December 19, 1914, p. 6; *The Kansas City Star*, January 17, 1915, pp. 1C–3C; *Everybody's*, March, 1915, pp. 315–17. For the view of a Georgian who believed Frank guilty and who was exceedingly familiar with the facts, see Appendix D.

4. The Baltimore *Sun*, November 26, 1914, p. 4. The Pittsburgh *Index*, December 26, 1914, Duluth *Herald*, December 17, 1914, Frank Papers. There are more than one hundred clippings among the Frank papers expressing these ideas. See also opinions of other American newspapers reprinted in *The New York Times*, December 1, 2, 4, 9, 11, 12, 13, 15, 22, 23, 1914.

5. *The New York Times*, December 10, 1914, p. 6; *The Augusta Chronicle*, December 27, 1914, p. 3. Then there are the following newspaper clippings from small town Georgia papers, all from the Frank Papers: Brunswick *News*, November 29, 1914,

Waycross *Journal,* January 16, 1915, and the Macon *Telegraph,*
January 16, 1915.

   6. LM to Leo Frank, January 30, 1915.

   7. None of the letters that I have seen spell out the reasons it
was thought that Slaton would be more likely to commute. LM
to Herbert Haas, May 7, May 21, May 28, 1915.

   8. *The New York Times,* April 22, 1915, p. 1.

   9. William Howard Taft to Julius Rosenwald, May 17, 1915;
Julius Rosenwald to Senator L. Y. Sherman, May 18, 1915; Senator L. Y. Sherman to Julius Rosenwald, May 21, 1915; Rosenwald Papers. Simon Wolf to Woodrow Wilson, June 10, 1915;
William J. Burns to Joseph P. Tumulty, May 29, 1915; Woodrow Wilson Papers, Library of Congress (Washington, D.C.),
Series VI, File 3658. LM to Herbert Haas, LM to Harry Frieden-
wald, both May 15, 1915. Also LM to Daniel Guggenheim and
to A. D. Lasker, both May 10, 1915. LM to Herbert Haas, May
21, 1915, May 28, 1915.

   10. Harvey Judson, President of the University of Chicago, to
the Georgia Prison Commission, May 9, 1915; Charles R. Crane
to Georgia Prison Commission, May 29, 1915, PC Records. There
are thousands of other letters expressing this sentiment in the PC
Records. The letters to Governor John M. Slaton are scattered in
three different places: the records of the Georgia Prison Commission, and the John M. Slaton Papers, both in the Georgia
State Archives (Atlanta); and Slaton, Brandeis. See also LM to
Herbert Hass, May 28, 1915; Elmer Murphy to Leo Frank, May 1,
1915, Slaton, Brandeis; Victor Morgan to Leo Frank, April 29,
1915, *ibid.;* Harry Levenson to Louis Brandeis, May 21, 1915, Louis
D. Brandeis papers, file 21891, located in the law offices of Nutter,
McClennen and Fish, Boston; John M. O'Connor to Julius Rosenwald, May 18, 1915, Rosenwald papers; Louisville *Herald,* May
17, 1915, Frank Papers; and AC, May 11, 1915, p. 1; May 16,
1915, p. 1; May 24, 1915, p. 5; May 28, 1915, p. 7; May 29, 1915,
p. 1; May 30, 1915, p. 5; May 31, 1915, p. 5; June 1, 1915, p. 4;
AJ, May 29, 1915, p. 2; *The New York Times,* May 15, 1915,
p. 11; May 18, 1915, p. 6; May 25, 1915, p. 6; May 29, 1915, p.
12; May 30, 1915, II, 14; June 5, 1915, p. 6; Woodward, *Tom
Watson,* p. 436; "Frank's Prophesy of Vindication Comes True
10 Years After Georgia Mob Hangs Him as Slayer," *The Jewish*

Advocate, XLII (October 18, 1923), 20. One of the reasons for Chicago's great concern over Leo Frank may have been because of the influence of Albert Lasker, Julius Rosenwald, and the B'nai B'rith, all of whom lived, or made their main headquarters, in the city.

11. AC, May 27, 1915, p. 1; TAC, September 28, 1915, p. 6.

12. AJ, May 23, 1915, sporting section, p. 4; AG, May 29, 1915, Frank Papers; TAC, June 9, 1915, June 10, 1915, *ibid.*; Brunswick *News*, June 17, 1915, *ibid.*, *The North Georgia Citizen*, May 27, 1915, p. 4.

13. *The Jeffersonian*, June 10, 1915, p. 3.

14. Woodward, *Tom Watson*, p. 442; [a follower] to Tom Watson, June 25, 1915, Slaton, Brandeis.

15. *The Jeffersonian*, June 3, 1915, pp. 3, 4.

16. Estimates of the June 5 crowd varied from 2,000 to 8,000; TAC, June 9, 1915, Frank Papers; *The Jeffersonian*, June 17, 1915, p. 3; July 15, 1915, p. 6; *The New York Times*, June 6, 1915, II, 4. See also *The Dalton Citizen*, June 10, 1915, p. 4; AJ, June 13, 1915, pp. 1, 10; AC, June 4, 1915, p. 1; June 13, 1915, p. 5A; *The New York Times*, June 5, 1915, p. 6; *American Jewish Review*, n.d., clipping, John M. Slaton's "Miscellaneous" Scrapbook, Slaton Papers, Georgia Archives; Franklin Bliss Synder, "Leo Frank and Mary Phagan," *The Journal of American Folklore*, XXXI (1918), 264; see Appendix B.

17. According to Georgia law, the Prison Commission had advisory powers only: the final decision rested with the Governor.

18. The impact of the letter was offset, however, by the fact that in 1913, the same graphologist, Albert Osborn, had informed Hugh Dorsey that the notes might have been written with the assistance of an intelligent person. Albert Osborn to Prison Commissioners, May 17, 1915, May 18, 1915, PC Records. *The New York Times*, May 27, 1915, p. 4.

19. L. S. Roan to Messrs. Rosser and Brandon, and R. R. Arnold, December, 1914 (no specific date), PC Records. AC, June 1, 1915, p. 1.

20. *Ibid.*, pp. 1, 4.

21. AC, June 10, 1915, pp. 1, 2.

22. TAC, June 10, 1915, Frank Papers.

23. *Ibid.*

24. Knight, *A Standard History of Georgia*, II, 1168.

25. Georgia's antiquated county unit system gave dispropor-
tionate power to the rural counties of the state. With 159 counties, each allowed a minimum of one vote, none allowed more
than three votes, a minority of the population could select state-
wide candidates. V. O. Key, Jr., *Southern Politics in State and
Nation* (New York, 1950), p. 119.

26. Knight, *A Standard History of Georgia*, II, 1125, 1126,
1128, 1164; Woodward, *Tom Watson*, pp. 439–40; John Temple
Graves, "The New Governor of Georgia," *Cosmopolitan Magazine*, LV (August, 1913), 335–37.

27. Woodward, *Tom Watson*, p. 443.

28. Memo of conversation held by Samuel Boorstin with John
M. Slaton, October 12, 1953, Anti-Defamation League Files, New
York City. Conley's lawyer had also made this remark publicly;
see pp. 194–95.

29. See Appendix C.

30. The New York *World*, July 4, 1915, editorial section, p. 1.

31. *Ibid.;* Garrett, II, 626; A. L. Henson [Essay—no title], "Leo
Frank Folder," Files of the Anti-Defamation League, New York
City; Powell, p. 292; Knight, *A Standard History of Georgia*, II,
1168.

32. AC, June 21, 1915, extra, p. 1; AC, June 22, 1915, pp. 1,
2, 9.

33. AC, June 21, 1915, extra, p. 1.

34. AJ, June 14, 1915, p. 1. An examination of these letters led
Slaton to observe that Jim Conley seemed more of a pervert than
the man he had accused. No explanation was given for Conley's
sudden decision to admit that he had written the letters. These
letters are deposited in the Georgia State Archives. They are also
in Leonard Dinnerstein's "The Leo Frank Case" (unpublished
Ph.D. dissertation, Columbia University, Department of History,
1966), the Appendix.

35. AJ, June 21, 1915, pp. 1, 3, 4; *The New York Times*, June
22, 1915, p. 6.

36. Quoted in *The Times-Picayune* (New Orleans), June 27,
1915, p. 1.

37. Powell, p. 289. In a letter written in 1961, John M. Slaton,
Jr., Governor Slaton's nephew, observed: "During the last days

of my uncle's, Governor John M. Slaton's, life, he expressed to me the thought that the unfolding of time had established the innocence of Leo Frank." John M. Slaton, Jr., to Harold Marcus, January 5, 1961; copy among the Leo Frank letters, Brandeis University.

38. See Appendix C.

39. The editors of *The Atlanta Constitution* made no editorial comment about either Slaton or the commutation.

40. Slaton kept scrapbooks of the newspaper reaction to the commutation. He had two books, about 15″ X 27″, with newspaper clippings, arranged alphabetically by state, and within each state, by city. One book is marked, "Alabama to North Carolina" and the other "Ohio to Wyoming and Miscellaneous." Then there are other scrapbooks, one marked "Georgia Favorable," one marked "Georgia Critical," and one marked "Miscellaneous" which have additional newspaper clippings. By going through these books one can see that an overwhelming majority of newspapers did support Slaton's action. In Georgia the newspapers that opposed the Governor were primarily rural. There are also letterbooks, which contain letters from all over the country, praising and condemning the commutation. Again, most of the commentary is favorable, and, again, all letters are arranged alphabetically, first by state and then by city within the state. In this collection all states seem to be represented except Arkansas. All scrapbooks and letterbooks are among the Slaton Papers, Georgia State Archives.

41. Quoted in *The American Jewish Review*, IV (July, 1915), 2, Frank Papers.

42. Knight, *A Standard History of Georgia*, II, 1169.

43. SMN, June 22, 1915, p. 1; *The New York Times*, June 22, 1915, p. 6; June 24, 1915, p. 5; *The American* (New Orleans), June 22, 1915, p. 1.

44. Frank Papers; clipping, June 23, 1915, Boston *Herald-Traveler Library*; New Orleans *American*, June 23, 1915, p. 1; *The New York Times*, June 24, 1915, p. 5; *The Jeffersonian*, July 22, 1915, p. 2.

45. *The Jeffersonian*, June 24, 1915, pp. 1, 2, 3.

46. There seems to have been no consensus about the size of the crowds. *The Atlanta Constitution* gave no figures but used

the phrase, "several thousand people," AC, June 22, 1915, p. 1; *The New York Times* and The New Orleans *American* placed the figure at 10,000, both June 22, 1915, p. 1; The New York *Evening Post*, June 21, 1915, p. 1, stated 2,500; and in 1942 Hal Steed used the number, 5,000, Steed, p. 240.

47. *Ibid.* AC, June 22, 1915, pp. 1, 2; June 29, 1915, p. 1; New Orleans *American*, June 22, 1915, p. 1; June 23, 1915, p. 1; *The New York Times*, June 22, 1915, p. 1; Powell, pp. 290–91.

48. Quoted in *The American Israelite*, July 8, 1915, p. 1.

49. AC, June 27, 1915, pp. 1A, 4A, June 29, 1915, p. 6; *The New York Times*, June 27, 1915, p. 1.

50. Clipping, June 28, 1915, Slaton Scrapbook, Georgia Archives. There are many other clippings expressing the identical sentiment throughout the scrapbooks.

51. *The American Israelite*, July 29, 1915, p. 4.

52. Cash, p. 140. For this same view see also, Macdonald, *The Kansas City Star*, January 17, 1915, p. 3C; Ward Greene, pp. 132–33; Steed, p. 238; and Albert Bushnell Hart, *The Southern South* (New York, 1912), p. 70.

53. *The Cherokee Advance*, June 25, 1915, p. 4.

VIII. VIGILANTE JUSTICE

1. *The Marietta Journal and Courier*, June 25, 1915, p. 1; July 9, 1915, p. 2; July 16, 1915, p. 6; AC, July 18, 1915, p. 2A; July 19, 1915, pp. 1, 2; *The New York Times*, July 14, 1915, p. 1; Nathaniel E. Harris, *Autobiography* (Macon, Georgia, 1925), p. 366.

2. *The American Israelite*, July 22, 1915, p. 17.

3. Leo Frank to Mrs. Leo Frank, June 23, 24, 29, July 2, 5, 6, 8, & 9, 1915. Frank Papers, Brandeis University (Waltham, Mass.).

4. Leo Frank to Julius Rosenwald, July 11, 1915, Rosenwald Papers. Leo Frank to Oliver Wendell Holmes, July 10, 1915, a letter that was in the possession of the late Mark de Wolfe Howe. He generously sent me a copy.

5. In his *A Standard History of Georgia and Georgians*, L. L. Knight wrote, "What subtle irony in the choice of such a weapon with which to inflict death upon one of Abraham's seed!" II, 1185.

6. AC, July 18, 1915, pp. 1A, 2A, July 20, 1915, p. 1; July 22,

1915, p. 7; August 2, 1915, p. 1; AJ, July 18, 1915, p. 1; July 19, 1915, p. 1; *The New York Times,* July 18, 1915, p. 1; July 19, 1915, p. 1.

7. Harris, pp. 365–66; AC, July 19, 1915, pp. 1, 2; July 20, 1915, p. 1; AJ, July 24, 1915, p. 1. Harris recorded his observations about Leo Frank in an autobiography, published a decade later. He remembered that when interviewing Frank, the prisoner laughed "a queer sort of laugh." To Harris, this laugh showed, "a hard, careless heart," and the doubt which the Governor had heretofore held about Frank's guilt "was lessened greatly." As he looked back upon the incident, Harris could not recall why he had been so impressed, but he "felt then that the man was undoubtedly a hardened criminal or a reckless prisoner." Harris, p. 367.

8. AC, July 20, 1915, p. 1; *The American Israelite,* July 22, 1915, p. 7; Leo Frank to W. W. Stevens, August 11, 1915, Frank Papers, Brandeis.

9. Pittsburgh *Press,* July 27, 1915, Detroit *Free Press,* July 19, 1915, Frank Papers; TAC, July 19, 1915, p. 4; "Leo Frank," *The New Republic,* III (July 24, 1915), 300.

10. *The New York Times,* August 17, 1915, p. 1; August 23, 1915, p. 5; AC, August 17, 1915, p. 1; August 18, 1915, pp. 1, 2; F. J. Turner to Mrs. Leo Frank, August 17, 1915, Frank Papers, Brandeis.

11. Steed, p. 240; Harry Golden, *A Little Girl Is Dead,* p. 288; Smith interview, April 2, 1964; F. J. Turner to Mrs. Leo Frank, August 17, 1915, Frank Papers, Brandeis; "The End of the Frank Case," *The Outlook,* CXI (September 15, 1915), 115; AC, August 18, 1915, p. 1.

12. *The New York Times* claimed to have received the information that follows "in a manner which seemingly placed its authenticity beyond all question." August 23, 1915, p. 5.

13. Clipping from the newspaper library of the Boston *Herald-Traveler,* September 21, 1915; "Why Was Frank Lynched?" *Forum,* LVI (December, 1916), 688–89.

14. AC, August 17, 1915, p. 1; August 18, 1915, pp. 1, 2; August 21, 1915, p. 1; AJ, August 7, 1915, p. 3; *The New York Times,* August 18, 1915, pp. 1, 3; August 19, 1915, pp. 1, 3; August 23, 1915, p. 5.

The lynching of Leo Frank was in some ways atypical. The

"typical" Southern lynching usually resulted from the spontaneous uprising of a drunken mob of poorly educated adolescent boys and young men, intent upon avenging an alleged violation of a woman, or giving summary punishment to a suspected murderer. Only in a minority of cases did the "best citizens" actually participate in the lynching. Hadley Cantril, *The Psychology of Social Movements* (New York, 1941), pp. 83, 86; Cash, pp. 309–10; Carl Iver Hovland and Robert R. Sears, "Minor Studies of Aggression: VI. Correlation of Lynchings with Economic Indices," *The Journal of Psychology*, IX (1940), 305–7; Arthur F. Raper, *The Tragedy of Lynching* (Chapel Hill, N.C., 1933), pp. 1, 8–12, 20.

15. Taking souvenirs at lynchings may not have been unusual. In 1899 a national periodical reporter noted the following after a Negro had been burned at Palmetto, Georgia: "Before the body was cool, it was cut to pieces, the heart and liver being especially cut up and sold. Small pieces of bone brought 25 cents, and 'a bit of the liver, crisply cooked, sold for 10 cents.' So eager were [*sic*] the crowd to obtain souvenirs that a rush for the stake was made, and those near the body were forced against it had to fight for their escape." T. G. Steward, "The Reign of the Mob," *The Independent*, LI (1899), 1296. John R. Steelman noted that in a high proportion of lynchings souvenirs are taken by the members of the mob and the onlookers. "A Study of Mob Action in the South" (unpublished Ph.D. dissertation, Dept. of Sociology, University of North Carolina, 1928), p. 412.

16. AJ, August 17, 1915, pp. 1, 3; *The New York Times*, August 19, 1915, p. 3; Steed, p. 240.

17. *The Marietta Journal and Courier*, August 20, 1915, p. 1.

18. AC, August 18, 1915, pp. 1, 2; *The New York Times*, August 21, 1915, p. 4.

19. Irving M. Engel to author, February 19, 1964. AC, August 18, 1915, pp. 1, 2; August 22, 1915, II, 11.

20. AC, August 20, 1915, p. 12; August 21, 1915, p. 3; Racine *Times*, August 30, 1915, Frank Papers.

21. Although the newspaper reporters stated that the lynchers were generally known, none of the names of the alleged participants was published at the time.

22. *The Marietta Journal and Courier*, August 20, 1915, p. 6;

The Greensboro *Herald-Journal*, August 27, 1915, p. 1; clipping from Boston *Herald-Traveler Library*, September 8, 1915; Sacramento (California) *Record-Union*, August 25, 1915, Frank Papers; Justine Wise Polier and James Waterman Wise, editors, *The Personal Letters of Stephen Wise* (Boston, 1956), p. 151; AC, August 18, 1915, p. 1; *The New York Times*, August 18, 1915, p. 1; August 19, 1915, pp. 1, 3; August 23, 1915, p. 5; *The North Georgia Citizen*, August 19, 1915, p. 4; *The Pittsburgh Gazette*, August 26, 1915, Frank Papers. New York City's *Evening Post* observed: "The Coroner's 'quest at Marietta deserves to rank with any Dogberry's day for a sense of the bounds of human penetration: it is doubtful if the most shrewdly stupid Elizabethan villager could have seen less of what was unsafe than some of the witnesses called yesterday." August 25, 1915, p. 8.

23. "Mob-Law in Georgia," *Literary Digest*, LI (August 28, 1915), 392; AC, August 18, 1915, p. 6. See also *The Progressive Farmer*, XXX (August 28, 1915), 790.

24. *The Christian Index*, XCV (August 26, 1915), 3, as cited in Carl Dean English, "The Ethical Emphases of the Editors of Baptist Journals Published in the Southeastern Region of the United States, 1865–1915" (unpublished Th.D. dissertation, Southern Baptist Theological Seminary, 1948), p. 159.

25. Knight, *A History of Georgia and Georgians*, II, 1196; AC, August 19, 1915, p. 12; *The Jeffersonian*, August 19, 1915, p. 1.

26. LM to Herbert Haas, May 7, 1915, May 21, 1915, May 28, 1915.

27. Quoted in *The New York Times*, August 19, 1915, p. 3.

IX. AFTERMATH

1. Woodward, *Origins of the New South*, pp. 158–60.

2. John R. Steelman, "A Study of Mob Action in the South" (unpublished Ph.D. dissertation, University of North Carolina, 1928), p. 128.

3. John M. Slaton, "Governor Slaton's OWN Defense in the Frank Case," *The New York World*, editorial section, July 4, 1951, p. 1.

4. Thomas Walker Page, "Lynching and Race Relations in the South," *The North American Review*, CCVI (August, 1917), 243; Edwin McNeill Poteat, Jr., "Religion in the South," in *Cul-*

ture in the South, ed. W. T. Couch (Chapel Hill, N.C., 1935), p. 258; H. C. Brearley, "The Pattern of Violence," in *ibid.*, p. 687; Josephine Pinckney, "Bulwark Against Change," in *ibid.*, p. 46; Cash, pp. 44, 309–10; Benjamin Kendrick, "The Study of the New South," *The North Carolina Historical Review*, III (January, 1926), 10; John Carlisle Kilgo, "An Inquiry Concerning Lynchings," *The South Atlantic Quarterly*, I (January, 1902), 5–9, *passim;* Charles S. Sydnor, "The Southerner and the Laws," *The Journal of Southern History*, VI (February, 1940), 8–14, *passim;* Eaton, *The Mind of the Old South*, p. 241; Virginius Dabney, *Liberalism in the South* (Chapel Hill, 1932), p. 360; *Christian Index*, July 28, 1892, March 23, 1899, as cited in Rufus B. Spain, "Attitudes and Reactions of Southern Baptists to Certain Problems of Society, 1865–1900" (unpublished Ph.D. dissertation, Vanderbilt University, 1961), p. 188.

5. Although the Ku Klux Klan became as strong, if not stronger, in parts of the North and the West, as it was in the South after the first World War, the origins of the new organization were definitely Southern.

6. Charles C. Alexander, *The Ku Klux Klan in the Southwest* (Lexington, Ky., 1965), p. 3; Arnold S. Rice, *The Ku Klux Klan in American Politics* (Washington, D.C., 1962), p. 2.

7. Kenneth Coleman, *Georgia History in Outline* (Athens, 1960), p. 96. Coleman noted that the Klan had such an enormous following in Georgia that "most office seekers considered Klan membership a prerequisite for election." One sociologist noted that "a very high percentage" of the Atlanta police force belonged to the revised Ku Klux Klan. Sutker, unpublished Ph.D. dissertation, p. 17.

8. Golden, *A Little Girl Is Dead*, p. 300. I questioned Golden about the source for this information. He replied that he had heard it said and then had it confirmed in an interview with one of the lynchers and a son of this lyncher. Golden to Leonard Dinnerstein, January 24, 1966. This point is also made in an unpublished essay by A. L. Henson, in the files of the Anti-Defamation League, New York City.

9. Harold W. Sullivan, *Trial By Newspaper* (Hyannis, Mass., 1961), p. 19; Joughin and Morgan, p. 196; John P. Roche, "American Liberty: An Examination of the 'Tradition' of Freedom," in *Aspects of Liberty*, edited by Milton R. Konvitz and Clinton

Rossiter (Ithaca, N.Y., 1958), p. 147; and George Palmer Garrett, "Public Trials," *The American Law Review*, LXII (1924), 8.

10. Alden Todd to Leonard Dinnerstein, January 19, 1964. Mr. Todd wrote that one of the top editors of *The Atlanta Journal* had expressed the opinion that Dorsey had "deliberately set about to stir up the hate-pack in a cynical bid for political notoriety and power."

11. *Moore v. Dempsey*, 261 U.S. 86 (1923).

12. LM to Adolph Ochs, January 14, 1925, Reznikoff (ed.), *Louis Marshall*, II, 847.

13. *Brown v. State of Mississippi*, 297 U.S. 278 (1936).

14. *Chambers v. Florida*, 309 U.S. 227, 239 (1940).

15. *Ashcraft v. Tennessee*, 327 U.S. 274, 276 (1946); see also *Ashcraft v. Tennessee*, 322 U.S. 143 (1944).

16. *Fikes v. Alabama*, 352 U.S. 191 (1957).

17. *Escobedo v. Illinois*, 378 U.S. 478, 488 (1963).

18. *The New York Times*, June 14, 1966, pp. 1, 24; *Miranda v. Arizona*, 384 U.S. 436, 479 (1966).

19. *Shepherd v. State of Florida*, 341 U.S. 50, 51 (1951).

20. *Rideau v. Louisiana*, 373 U.S. 723, 726 (1963).

21. Justice Black dissented but did not write an opinion.

22. *Sheppard v. Maxwell*, 384 U.S. 333, 340, 355–57 (1966); *The New York Times*, June 7, 1966, pp. 1, 43.

23. *Berger v. United States*, 295 U.S. 78, 84 (1935).

24. *Viereck v. United States*, 318 U.S. 236, 248 (1943).

25. *Miller v. Pate*, 87 *Supreme Court Reporter* 785, 788 (1967); 35 *Law Week* 4180; *The New York Times*, March 21, 1967, p. 20.

26. *Mooney v. Holohan*, 294 U.S. 103 (1935).

27. *Heysler v. Florida*, 315 U.S. 411 (1942). See also *Pyle v. Kansas*, 317 U.S. 213 (1942).

28. *Alcorta v. Texas*, 355 U.S. 28, 31 (1957).

29. *Napue v. Illinois*, 360 U.S. 264, 266 (1959).

30. *B'nai B'rith News*, October, 1913, p. 1.

31. Rembert G. Smith, D.C., "Some Lurid Lessons from the Frank Case," *The Public*, XVIII (October 1, 1915), 952.

32. Alden Todd to Leonard Dinnerstein, January 19, 1964. Todd found some information on Frank while doing research for his study of Brandeis's confirmation to the Supreme Court in 1916: *Justice on Trial* (New York, 1964).

33. Asbury, *The American Mercury*, VII, 91.

34. Pierre Van Paassen, *To Number Our Days* (New York, 1964), pp. 237–38.

35. Telephone conversation with Majorie Merlin Cohen, New York City, February 9, 1964. Forty years after the murder, in fact, citizens still became embroiled in bitter arguments when Frank's guilt or innocence was discussed. Ernest Rogers, *Peachtree Parade* (Atlanta, 1956), p. 71. And as late as 1961 the National States Rights Party inaugurated a campaign to revive interest in Mary Phagan's murder. Clipping, an Atlanta newspaper, May 20, 1961, located among the Frank Papers in Brandeis.

36. *The New York Times*, January 18, 1919, p. 2; February 25, 1919, p. 5; AC, February 25, 1919, p. 6; Golden, *A Little Girl Is Dead*, pp. 311–12.

37. Memo of a conversation had by Samuei A. Boorstin in Atlanta, Georgia, with Governor Slaton, October 12, 1953, ADL files in New York City; John M. Slaton, Jr. (Gov. Slaton's nephew) to Harold Marcus, January 15, 1961, Frank Papers, Brandeis; AC, January 12, 1955, p. 1; *Time*, LXV (January 24, 1955), 19; Golden, *A Little Girl Is Dead*, p. 306.

38. E. Merton Coulter, *Georgia: A Short History* (Chapel Hill, 1947), p. 400.

39. Knight, *A History of Georgia*, II, 1208.

40. AC, September 13, 1916, p. 1; Woodward, *Tom Watson*, p. 473; Golden, *A Little Girl Is Dead*, p. 305.

41. Woodward, *Tom Watson*, pp. 448–49, 458, 461, 466–68, 473, 486.

42. Richard S. Rauh, "The First American Martyr," *Jewish Criterion* (Pittsburgh), August 20, 1915, clipping, Slaton Papers, Georgia State Archives, Atlanta.

43. Herbert Asbury, "Hearst Comes to Atlanta," *The American Mercury*, VII (January, 1926), 91.

44. Smith interview.

45. Francis X. Busch, *Guilty or Not Guilty* (Indianapolis, 1952), pp. 73–74.

46. Ross's article is reprinted in Golden, *A Little Girl Is Dead*, pp. 355–58.

47. Woodward, *Tom Watson*, p. 435.

48. Samuels, p. 222; Roche, *The Quest for the Dream*, p. 91; Golden, *A Little Girl Is Dead*, p. xiv.

Selected Bibliography

NO ATTEMPT HAS BEEN MADE to include all sources cited in the footnotes. For a more extensive bibliography, see Leonard Dinnerstein, "The Leo Frank Case" (unpublished Ph.D. Dissertation, Department of History, Columbia University, 1966).

MANUSCRIPT SOURCES

American Jewish Committee. Minutes of the Executive Committee, 1906–1915. American Jewish Committee Archives, New York City.

Boorstin, Samuel A. "Memo of Conversation had by Samuel A. Boorstin in Atlanta, Ga., with Governor Slaton," October 12, 1953. Anti-Defamation League files, New York City.

Louis Brandeis Papers, File 21891. Law offices of Nutter, McClennen & Fish, Boston.

Leo Frank Papers. American Jewish Archives, Cincinnati.

Leo Frank Papers. Brandeis University, Waltham, Massachusetts.

The Leo Frank Folder. Anti-Defamation League, New York City.

The Leo Frank Correspondence Folder. American Jewish Committee Archives, New York City.

Louis Marshall Papers. American Jewish Archives, Cincinnati.

Prison Commission Records. Georgia State Archives, Atlanta.

Julius Rosenwald Papers. Microfilm from the University of Chicago.

Jacob Schiff Papers. American Jewish Archives, Cincinnati.

John M. Slaton Papers. Georgia State Archives, Atlanta.

John M. Slaton Papers. Brandeis University, Waltham, Massachusetts.

Felix Warburg Papers. American Jewish Archives, Cincinnati.

Woodrow Wilson Papers, Series VI, File 3658. Library of Congress, Washington, D.C.

NEWSPAPERS

The American Israelite (Cincinnati). 1913–1915.
The Atlanta Constitution. 1913–1915.
The Atlanta Georgian. 1913.
The Atlanta Journal. 1913–1915.
The Augusta Chronicle. 1913–1915.
The Baltimore Morning *Sun.* 1913–1915.
The Herald-Journal (Greensboro, Georgia). 1913–1915.
The Jeffersonian. 1913–1915.
The Jewish Advocate (Boston). 1923.
The Marietta Journal and Courier (weekly edition). 1913–1915.
The New York Times. 1913–1915.
The New York World. 1915.
The North Georgia Citizen (Dalton, Georgia). 1913–1915.
The Savannah Morning News. 1913–1915.

Newspaper Clippings:
  Boston *Herald-Traveler* Library, Boston.
  Leo Frank Papers, American Jewish Archives, Cincinnati.
  John M. Slaton Papers, Georgia State Archives, Atlanta.

LEGAL SOURCES AND FEDERAL DOCUMENTS

Ashcraft v. *Tennessee,* 327 U.S. 274 (1946); 322 U.S. 143 (1944).
Berger v. *United States,* 295 U.S. 78 (1935).
Brown v. *Mississippi,* 294 U.S. 278 (1936).
Chambers v. *Florida,* 309 U.S. 227 (1940).
Escobedo v. *Illinois,* 378 U.S. 478 (1963).
Fikes v. *Alabama,* 352 U.S. 191 (1957).
Frank v. *Mangum,* 237 U.S. 309 (1915).
Leo M. Frank v. *State of Georgia: Brief of Evidence.**

* The original stenographic transcript of the trial does not seem to be in existence any more. The *Brief of Evidence,* however, was certified by both the prosecution and the defense as being an accurate record of the proceedings of the trial. It does not include any of the questions asked by the

———— *Motion for a New Trial.*

———— *Amended Motion for a New Trial.*

Georgia Reports: 141 *Georgia* 243 (1914); 142 *Georgia* 617 (1914); 142 *Georgia* 741 (1914).

Heysler v. *Florida,* 315 U.S. 411 (1942).

Miller v. *Pate,* 386 U.S. 1 (1967).

Miranda v. *Arizona,* 384 U.S. 436 (1966).

Mooney v. *Holohan,* 294 U.S. 103 (1935).

Pyle v. *Kansas,* 317 U.S. 213 (1942).

Rideau v. *Louisiana,* 373 U.S. 723 (1963).

Shepherd v. *Florida,* 341 U.S. 50 (1951).

Sheppard v. *Maxwell,* 384 U.S. 333 (1966).

United States. Industrial Commission. *Final Report of the Industrial Commission.* 19 vols. Washington: Government Printing Office, 1902.

United States. Senate. *Report on Conditions of Women and Child Wage-Earners in the United States.* 61st Cong., 2nd Sess., 1910, Senate Document #645, Serial 5685.

———— *A Practical Report from the Immigration Commission.* 61st Cong., 2nd Sess., 1909–1910, Senate Document 196, Serial 5662.

BOOKS

Adler, Cyrus. *I Have Considered the Days.* Philadelphia: The Jewish Publication Society of America, 1941.

———— *Jacob H. Schiff: His Life and Letters.* 2 vols. Garden City, New York: Doubleday, Doran & Co., 1929.

Adorno, T. W., Else Frenkel-Brunswick, Daniel J. Levison, and R. Nevitt Sanford. *The Authoritarian Personality.* New York: Harper and Bros., 1950.

Alexander, Charles C. *The Ku Klux Klan in the Southwest.* Lexington: The University of Kentucky Press, 1965.

Alexander, Henry A. *Some Facts about the Murder Notes in the Phagan Case.* Privately published pamphlet, 1914.

Allport, Gordon W., and Leo Postman. *The Psychology of Rumor.* New York: Henry Holt & Co., 1947.

attorneys, nor does it record any of the spontaneous outbursts of the courtroom spectators.

American Jewish Year Book. 1907–1915.

Baker, Henry Givens. *Rich's of Atlanta*. University of Georgia (Atlanta Division), 1953.

Bell, Earl L., and Kenneth C. Crabbe. *The Augusta Chronicle: Indomitable Voice of Dixie, 1785–1960*. Athens: University of Georgia Press, 1960.

Bettelheim, Bruno, and Morris Janowitz. *Social Change and Prejudice*. New York: The Free Press of Glencoe, 1964.

Blau, Joseph L., and Salo W. Baron (eds.). *The Jews of the United States, 1790–1840, A Documentary History*. 3 vols. New York: Columbia University Press, 1963.

Blum, Isidor. *The Jews of Baltimore*. Baltimore: Historical Review Publishing Co., 1910.

Busch, Francis X. *Guilty or Not Guilty*. Indianapolis: The Bobbs-Merrill Co., 1952.

Cahan, Abraham. *Blätter Von Mein Leben*. 5 vols. New York, 1931.

Cantril, Hadley. *The Psychology of Social Movements*. New York: John Wiley and Sons, 1941.

Cash, W. J. *The Mind of the South*. New York: Alfred A. Knopf, 1941.

Chadbourn, James Harmon. *Lynching and the Law*. Chapel Hill: The University of North Carolina Press, 1933.

Connolly, C. P. *The Truth about the Frank Case*. New York: Vail-Ballou Co., 1915.

Cooper, Walter G. *The Story of Georgia*. 4 vols. New York: The American Historical Society, 1938.

Couch, W. T. (ed.). *Culture in the South*. Chapel Hill: The University of North Carolina Press, 1934.

Coulter, E. Merton. *The Confederate States of America*. Baton Rouge: Louisiana State University Press, 1950.

———— *Georgia: A Short History*. Chapel Hill: The University of North Carolina Press, 1947.

———— *The South During Reconstruction, 1865–1877*. Baton Rouge: Louisiana State University Press, 1947.

Cutler, James Elbert. *Lynch-Law*. New York: Longmans, Green and Co., 1905.

Dabbs, James McBride. *Who Speaks for the South?* New York: Funk and Wagnalls, 1964.

Dabney, Virginius. *Liberalism in the South*. Chapel Hill: The University of North Carolina Press, 1932.

De Haas, Jacob. *Louis D. Brandeis*. New York: Bloch Publishing Co., 1929.

Derfler, Leslie (ed.). *The Dreyfus Affair*. Boston: D. C. Heath and Co., 1963.

Dollard, John, Neal E. Miller, Leonard Doob, O. H. Mowrer, and Robert R. Sears. *Frustration and Aggression*. New Haven: Yale University Press, 1939.

Dykeman, Wilma, and James Stokley. *Seeds of Southern Change*. Chicago: University of Chicago Press, 1962.

Eaton, Clement. *Freedom of Thought in the Old South*. New York: Peter Smith, 1951.

———— *A History of the Old South*. New York: The Macmillan Co., 1949.

———— *The Mind of the Old South*. Baton Rouge: Louisiana State University Press, 1964.

Finklestein, Louis. *The Jews*. 2 vols. New York: Harper & Bros., 1960.

The Frank Case: Inside Story of Georgia's Greatest Murder Mystery. Atlanta: Atlanta Publishing Co., 1914.

Fuchs, Lawrence H. *The Political Behavior of American Jews*. Glencoe, Illinois: The Free Press, 1956.

Garrett, Franklin M. *Atlanta and Environs*. 3 vols. New York: Lewis Historical Publishing Co., 1954.

Glanz, Rudolph. *The Jew in the Old American Folklore*. New York: Waldon Press, 1961.

Golden, Harry. *Forgotten Pioneer*. Cleveland: The World Publishing Co., 1963.

———— *A Little Girl Is Dead*. Cleveland: The World Publishing Co., 1965.

Graeber, Isaque, and Stewart Henderson Britt (eds.). *Jews in a Gentile World*. New York: The Macmillan Co., 1942.

Grantham, Dewey W., Jr. *Hoke Smith and the Politics of the New South*. Baton Rouge: Louisiana State University Press, 1958.

Greene, Ward. *Star Reporters and 34 of Their Stories*. New York: Random House, 1948.

Griffith, Louis Turner, and John Erwin Talmadge. *Georgia Jour-*

nalism: 1763–1950. Athens: University of Georgia Press, 1951.

Gunther, John. *Taken at the Flood.* New York: Popular Library, 1961.

Handlin, Oscar. *Adventure in Freedom.* New York: McGraw-Hill Book Co., 1954.

———— and Mary F. Handlin. *Danger in Discord: Origins of Anti-Semitism in the United States.* N.p.: Anti-Defamation League of B'nai B'rith, 1948.

Harris, Nathaniel E. *Autobiography.* Macon, Georgia: The J. W. Burke Co., 1925.

Hart, Albert Bushnell. *The Southern South.* New York: D. Appleton & Co., 1912.

Henson, Allen Lumpkin. *Confessions of a Criminal Lawyer.* New York: Vantage Press, 1959.

Hero, Alfred O., Jr. *The Southerner and World Affairs.* Baton Rouge: Louisiana State University Press, 1965.

Higham, John. *Strangers in the Land.* New Brunswick: Rutgers University Press, 1955.

Hirsh, Selma G. *The Fears Men Live By.* New York: Harper and Bros., 1955.

Hoffer, Eric. *The True Believer.* New York: New American Library, 1958.

Janowsky, Oscar I. (ed.). *The American Jew.* New York: Harper and Bros., 1942.

Kendrick, Benjamin Burks, and Alex Mathews Arnett. *The South Looks at Its Past.* Chapel Hill: The University of North Carolina Press, 1935.

Knight, Lucian Lamar. *Reminiscences of Famous Georgians.* 2 vols. Atlanta: Franklin Turner Co., 1907.

———— *A Standard History of Georgia and Georgians.* 6 vols. Chicago: The Lewis Publishing Co., 1917.

Korn, Bertram Wallace. *American Jewry and the Civil War.* Philadelphia: The Jewish Publication Society of America, 1951.

Lawson, John D. (ed.) *American State Trials.* 10 vols. St. Louis: F. H. Thomas Law Book Co., 1918.

Learsi, Rufus. *The Jews in America.* New York: The World Publishing Co., 1954.

Lynchings and What They Mean: General Findings of the Southern Commission on the Study of Lynching. Atlanta, 1931.

McCulloch, James E. (ed.). *The Call of the New South*. Nashville: Southern Sociological Congress, 1912.

McKinney, John C., and Edgar T. Thompson (editors). *The South in Continuity and Change*. Durham: Duke University Press, 1965.

McWilliams, Carey. *A Mask for Privilege: Anti-Semitism in America*. Boston: Little, Brown and Co., 1948.

Marcus, Jacob Rader. *American Jewry: Documents of the Eighteenth Century*. Cincinnati: The Hebrew Union College Press, 1959.

———— *Early American Jewry: The Jews of Pennsylvania and the South, 1655–1790*. Philadelphia: The Jewish Publication Society of America, 1953.

Miller, William D. *Memphis during the Progressive Era, 1900–1917*. Memphis: The Memphis State University Press, 1957.

Mitchell, Broadus. *The Rise of Cotton Mills in the South*. Baltimore: The Johns Hopkins Press, 1921.

———— and George Sinclair Mitchell. *The Industrial Revolution in the South*. Baltimore: The Johns Hopkins Press, 1930.

Murphy, Edgar Gardner. *Problems of the Present South*. New York: The Macmillan Co., 1904.

Nichols, William H. *Southern Tradition and Regional Progress*. Chapel Hill: The University of North Carolina Press, 1960.

Powell, Arthur G. *I Can Go Home Again*. Chapel Hill: The University of North Carolina Press, 1943.

Pusey, Merlo J. *Charles Evans Hughes*. 2 vols. New York: The Macmillan Co., 1951.

Raby, R. Cornelius. *Fifty Famous Trials*. Washington: Washington Law Book Co., 1937.

Raper, Arthur F. *The Tragedy of Lynching*. Chapel Hill: The University of North Carolina Press, 1933.

Reznikoff, Charles (ed.). *Louis Marshall: Champion of Liberty*. Philadelphia: Jewish Publication Society of America, 1957.

Reznikoff, Charles, and Uriah L. Engelman. *The Jews of Charleston*. Philadelphia: Jewish Publication Society of America, 1950.

Rice, Arnold S. *The Ku Klux Klan in American Politics*. Washington: Public Affairs Press, 1962.

Robertson, William J. *The Changing South*. New York: Boni and Liveright, 1927.

Roche, John P. *The Quest for the Dream*. New York: The Macmillan Co., 1963.

Rosenstock, Morton. *Louis Marshall, Defender of Jewish Rights.* Detroit: Wayne University Press, 1966.

Saenger, Gerhart. *The Social Psychology of Prejudice*. New York: Harper and Bros., 1953.

Samuel, Maurice. *Blood Accusation*. New York: Alfred A. Knopf, 1966.

Samuels, Charles and Louise. *Night Fell on Georgia*. New York: Dell Publishing Co., 1956.

Simmel, Ernst (ed.). *Anti-Semitism: A Social Disease*. New York: International Universities Press, 1946.

Sklare, Marshall. *Conservative Judaism*. Glencoe, Illinois: The Free Press, 1955.

The Southern Israelite. *One Hundred Years Accomplishments of Southern Jewry*. Atlanta: Southern Newspaper Enterprises, 1934.

Steed, Hal. *Georgia: Unfinished State*. New York: Alfred A. Knopf, 1942.

Thirty Years of Lynching in the United States: 1889–1918. New York: National Association for the Advancement of Colored People, 1919.

Thompson, Wytt E. *A Short Review of the Frank Case*. Atlanta: n.n., 1914.

Todd, Alden. *Justice on Trial*. New York: McGraw-Hill Book Co., 1964.

Tumin, Melvin M. *An Inventory and Appraisal of Research on American Anti-Semitism*. New York: Freedom Books, 1961.

Vance, Rupert B., and Nicholas J. Demerath (eds.). *The Urban South*. Chapel Hill: University of North Carolina Press, 1954.

Vance, Zebulon. *The Scattered Nation*. New York: Marcus Schnitzer, 1916.

Van Paassen, Pierre. *To Number Our Days*. New York: Charles Scribner's Sons, 1964.

Werner, M. R. *Julius Rosenwald: The Life of a Practical Humanitarian*. New York: Harper and Bros., 1939.

Wiernik, Peter. *History of the Jews in America*. New York: The Jewish History Publishing Society, 1931.

Woodward, C. Vann. *Origins of the New South, 1877–1913.* Baton Rouge: Louisiana State University Press, 1951.

—— *Tom Watson: Agrarian Rebel.* New York: Rinehart and Co., 1938.

ARTICLES, PERIODICALS, REPORTS,
AND SERMONS

"Accessory After the Fact," *Southern Ruralist,* XX (June 15, 1913), 12–13.

"An Advertising Campaign against Segregated Vice," *The American City,* IX (July, 1913), 3–4.

Alger, George W. "Sensationalism and the Law," *The Atlantic Monthly,* XCI (February, 1903), 145–51.

Allen, Frederick L. "Newspapers and the Truth," *The Atlantic Monthly,* CXXIX (January, 1922), 44–54.

Allport, Gordon W., and Bernard M. Kramer. "Some Roots of Prejudice," *The Journal of Psychology,* XXII (1946), 9–39.

Annual Report to the Atlanta Chamber of Commerce. 1909.

Anon. "The Atlanta Massacre," *The Independent,* LXI (October 4, 1906), 799–800.

Anon. "Jews in America," *Fortune,* XIII (February, 1936), 79–85, 127–41.

"Anti-Semitism and the Frank Case," *The Literary Digest,* L (January 16, 1915), 85–86.

Asbury, Herbert. "Hearst Comes to Atlanta," *The American Mercury,* VII (January, 1926), 87–95.

"The Atlanta Riots: A Southern White Point of View," *The Outlook,* LXXXIV (November 3, 1906), 557–66.

Baker, Ray Stannard. "Following the Color Line," *The American Magazine,* LXIII (April, 1907), 563–79.

—— "What Is a Lynching?" *McClure's Magazine,* XXIV (January, 1905), 299–314.

Bell, Daniel. "The Face of Tomorrow," *Jewish Frontier,* XI (June, 1944), 15–20.

Benson, Berry. "Five Arguments in the Frank Case." n.p., n.d. [*ca.* 1914]. Microfilm from Southern Historical Collection, University of North Carolina.

Bernstein, David and Adele. "Slow Revolution in Richmond, Va.," *Commentary,* VIII (1949), 539–46.

Berthoff, Rowland T. "Southern Attitudes toward Immigration, 1865–1914," *Journal of Southern History*, XVII (August, 1951), 328–60.

Bettelheim, Bruno. "The Dynamics of Anti-Semitism in Gentile and Jews," *The Journal of Abnormal and Social Psychology*, XLII (1947), 153–68.

—— and Morris Janowitz. "Reactions to Fascist Propaganda— a Pilot Study," *Public Opinion Quarterly*, XIV (Spring, 1950), 53–60.

Bricker, L. O. "A Great American Tragedy," *The Shane Quarterly*, IV (April, 1943), 89–95.

Brown, James. "Christian Teaching and Anti-Semitism," *Commentary*, XXIV (December, 1957), 494–501.

Cahnman, Werner J. "Socio-Economic Causes of Antisemitism," *Social Forces*, V (July, 1957), 21–29.

"The Case of Leo M. Frank," *The Outlook*, CX (May 26, 1915), 166–68.

Casson, Herbert N. "The Jew in America," *Munsey's Magazine*, XXXIV (January, 1906), 381–95.

"Classical Anti-Semitism," *The Nation*, LXI (1895), 50–51.

Connolly, C. P. "The Frank Case," *Collier's*, LIV (December 19), 6–7, 22–24; (December 26), 18–20, 23–25.

Cooper, Eunice, and Marie Jahoda. "The Evasion of Propaganda: How Prejudiced People Respond to Anti-prejudice Propaganda," *The Journal of Psychology*, XXIII (1947), 15–25.

Cox, Oliver C. "Race Prejudice and Intolerance—A Distinction," *Social Forces*, XXIV (December, 1945), 216–19.

Coxe, John E. "The New Orleans Mafia Incident," *Louisiana Historical Quarterly*, XX (1937), 1067–1110.

Curran, John W. "The Leo Frank Case Again," *Journal of Criminal Law and Criminology*, XXXIV (March, 1944), 363–64.

de Graffenried, Clare. "The Georgia Cracker in the Cotton Mills," *The Century Magazine*, XLI (February, 1891), 483–98.

"Dixie Conditions Stir Unionists—Description of Actual State of Atlanta Textile Workers Make Delegates Weep," *The Textile Worker*, III (December, 1914), 21.

Drachman, Bernard. "Anti-Jewish Prejudice in America," *The Forum*, LII (July, 1914), 31–40.

"Due Process of Law in the Frank Case," *Harvard Law Review*, XXVIII (1915), 793–95.

Eakin, Frank. "What Christians Teach About Jews," *Christian Century*, LII (September 18, 1935), 1173–76.

Edwards, Lyford P. "Religious Sectarianism and Race Prejudice," *American Journal of Sociology*, XLI (September, 1935), 167–79.

Ellinwood, Rev. F. F. "The Duty of Christendom to the Jews," *The Missionary Review of the World*, III, New Series (November, 1890), 801–07.

Ellis, William T. "Advertising a City Free from Its Vice," *The Continent*, XLIV (April 3, 1913), 461–63.

"The End of the Frank Case," *The Outlook*, CXI (September 15, 1915), 114–15.

"Facts about the Atlanta Murders," *The World's Work*, XIII (November, 1906), 8147–48.

Fenichel, Otto. "Psychoanalysis of Antisemitism," *The American Imago*, I (March, 1940), 24–39.

Few, William Preston. "Southern Public Opinion," *The South Atlantic Quarterly*, IV (January, 1905), 1–12.

Fischkin, E. A. "Jewish Problems in Chicago," *The Reform Advocate*, XXXII (January 26, 1907), 830–37.

Fishberg, Maurice. "White Slave Traffic and Jews," *The American Monthly Jewish Review*, IV (December, 1909), 4, 23.

Fleming, Walter L. "Immigration to the Southern States," *Political Science Quarterly*, XX (June, 1905), 276–97.

Foster, Roger. "Trial by Newspaper," *The North American Review*, XCLIV (May, 1887), 524–27.

"The Frank Case," *The American Hebrew*, XCVI (December 4, 1914), 146.

"The Frank Case," *The Ohio Law Bulletin*, LX (1915), 395–96.

"The Frank Case," *The Outlook*, CVIII (December 16, 1914), 859–60.

"Frank's Prophesy of Vindication Comes True 10 Years After Georgia Mob Hangs Him As Slayer," *The Jewish Advocate* (Boston), XLII (October 18, 1923), 20.

Frenkel-Brunswick, Else, and R. Nevitt Sanford. "Some Personality Factors in Anti-Semitism," *The Journal of Psychology*, XX (1945), 271–91.

Garner, James Wilford. "Lynching and the Criminal Law," *The South Atlantic Quarterly*, V (October, 1906), 333–41.

Golden, Harry L. "Jew and Gentile in the New South: Segregation at Sundown," *Commentary*, XX (November, 1955), 403–12.

Goldenweiser, A. A. "Atlanta Riots and the Origin of Magic," *The New Republic*, III (July 3, 1915), 225.

Gottheill, Gustav. "The Position of the Jews in America," *The North American Review*, CXXVI (1878), 293–308.

Graeber, Isaque. "An Examination of Theories of Race Prejudice," *Social Research*, XX (August, 1953), 267–81.

Graves, John Temple. "The New Governor of Georgia," *Cosmopolitan Magazine*, LV (August, 1913), 335–37.

"A Gross Injustice," *The Jewish Messenger*, LXXVIII (July 12, 1895), 4.

Handlin, Oscar. "American Views of the Jew at the Opening of the Twentieth Century," *Publications of the American Jewish Historical Society*, XL (June, 1951), 323–44.

———— "Prejudice and Capitalist Exploitation," *Commentary*, VI (1948), 79–85.

Hartogensis, B. H. "Religious Intolerance in Maryland," *The Jewish Exponent* (Philadelphia), XLV (April 12, 1907), 8.

Hendrick, Burton J. "The Great Jewish Invasion," *McClure's Magazine*, XXVIII (January, 1907), 307–21.

———— "The Jewish Invasion of America," *McClure's Magazine*, XL (March, 1913), 125–65.

Higham, John. "Anti-Semitism in the Gilded Age: A Reinterpretation," *Mississippi Valley Historical Review*, XLIII (March, 1957), 559–78.

———— "Social Discrimination against Jews in America, 1830–1930," *Publications of the American Jewish Historical Society*, XLVII (1957–1958), 1–33.

———— "American Anti-Semitism Historically Reconsidered," in *Jews in the Mind of America*, edited by Charles Herbert Stember. New York: Basic Books, 1966.

Hourwich, Isaac A. "Is There Anti-Semitism in America?" *The American Hebrew*, XCIII (October 17, 1913), 683–84.

Hovland, Carl Iver, and Robert R. Sears. "Minor Studies of Aggression: VI. Correlation of Lynchings with Economic Indices," *The Journal of Psychology*, IX (1940), 301–10.

"How Atlanta Cleaned Up," *The Literary Digest*, XLVI (May 3, 1913), 1012–13.

Hühner, Leon. "The Jews of Georgia in Colonial Times," *Publications of the American Jewish Historical Society*, X (1902), 65–95.

Hyman, Herbert H., and Paul B. Sheatsley. "Some Reasons Why Information Campaigns Fail," *Public Opinion Quarterly*, XI (1947), 412–23.

Ianniello, Lynne. "Trial by Prejudice," *The ADL Bulletin*, XX (March, 1963), 6–7.

"Is a Dreyfus Case Possible in America?" *The Independent*, LXI (July 19, 1906), 166–68.

"The Jews in the United States," *The World's Work*, XI (January, 1906), 7030–31.

"Jews in the White Slave Traffic," *The Temple*, II (February 25, 1910), 176.

Johnson, Harvey. "Atlanta, the Gate City of the South," *The American City*, V (July, 1911), 3–8.

Joseph, David Herman. "Some More of It, and Why," *The Temple*, I (December 10, 1909), 3, 8–10.

Josephus. "The Jewish Question," *The Century*, XLIII (1891–1892), 395–98.

The Journal of Labor, 1913–1914. (Official Paper of the Atlanta Federation of Trades and the Georgia Federation of Labor.)

"Justice or Conviction," *Southern Ruralist*, XX (November 15, 1913), 16–17.

Kallen, Horace M. "The Ethics of Zionism," *The Maccabean*, XI (August, 1906), 61–71.

———— "The Roots of Anti-Semitism," *The Nation*, CXVI (February 28, 1923), 240–42.

Kaufman, Walter C. "Status, Authoritarianism, and Anti-Semitism," *American Journal of Sociology*, LXII (January, 1957), 379–82.

Keedy, Edwin R. "The 'Third Degree' and Trial by Newspapers," *Journal of the American Institute of Criminal Law and Criminology*, III (November, 1912), 502–05.

Kendrick, Benjamin. "The Study of the New South," *The North Carolina Historical Review*, III (January, 1926), 3–15.

Kilgo, John Carlisle. "An Inquiry Concerning Lynchings," *The South Atlantic Quarterly*, I (January, 1902), 4–13.

Knapp, Robert H. "A Psychology of Rumor," *Public Opinion Quarterly*, VIII (Spring, 1944), 23–37.

Krauskopf, Joseph. "Is the Jew Getting a Square Deal?" *The Ladies Home Journal*, XXVII (November 1, 1910), 12.

Kuh, Edwin J. "The Social Disability of the Jew." *The Atlantic Monthly*, CI (April, 1908), 433–39.

"The Last Legal Stage of the Frank Case," *The Outlook*, CIX (April 28, 1915), 958–59.

"Legislature of Maryland," *Niles' Register*, XV, Supplement (1819), 9–13.

"Leo Frank," *The New Republic*, III (July 24, 1915), 300.

"Leo Frank and Liberty of the Press," *America*, XIII (August 28, 1915), 494.

Lifshutz, E. "Repercussions of the Beilis Trial in the United States," *Zion*, XXVIII (1963), 206–22.

Lipset, Seymour Martin. "Working-Class Authoritarianism," in *Society and Self*, edited by Bartlett H. Stoodley. New York: The Free Press of Glencoe, 1962, pp. 527–57.

Loeb, Rabbi J. T. "Circumstantial Evidence and Capital Punishment," *The American Jewish Review*, III (October, 1913), 3–4.

Loewenstein, Rudolph M. "The Historical and Cultural Roots of Anti-Semitism," *Psychoanalysis and the Social Sciences*, I (1947), 313–56.

Lund, Fredrick Hansen. "The Psychology of Belief," *The Journal of Abnormal and Social Psychology*, XX (1925), 63–81, 174–96.

Lundberg, George A. "The Newspaper and Public Opinion," *Social Forces*, IV (June, 1926), 709–15.

McClure, S. S. "The Tammanyizing of a Civilization," *McClure's Magazine*, XXXIV (November, 1909), 117–28.

McGill, Ralph. "Tom Watson: The People's Man," *The New Republic*, CXIX (August 23, 1948), 16–20.

McKelway, A. J. "Child Labor in the South," *The Annals*, XXXV (January, 1910), 156–64.

McWilliams, Carey. "How Deep Are the Roots?" *Common Ground*, VII (Autumn, 1947), 3–14.

Macdonald, A. B. "Has Georgia Condemned an Innocent Man to Die?" *The Kansas City* (Mo.) *Star*, January 17, 1915, pp. 1C–3C.

Miles, Charles A. " 'White Slaves' of the Cotton Mills," *The Textile Worker*, III (June, 1914), 6–7.

Miller, Robert Moats. "A Note on the Relationship between the Protestant Churches and the Revived Ku Klux Klan," *Journal of Southern History*, XXII (August, 1956), 355–68.

"Mob Law in Georgia," *Literary Digest*, LI (August 28, 1915), 392.

Morais, Nina. "Jewish Ostracism in America," *The North American Review*, CXXXIII (1881), 265–75.

Morse, Nancy C., and Floyd H. Allport. "The Causation of Anti-Semitism: An Investigation of Seven Hypotheses," *The Journal of Psychology*, XXXIV (1952), 197–233.

Moseley, Clement Charlton. "The Case of Leo M. Frank, 1913–1915," *The Georgia Historical Quarterly*, LI (March, 1967), 42–62.

Munson, Gorham. "Anti-Semitism: A Poverty Problem," *Christian Century*, LVI (October 4, 1939), 1199–1201.

Murphy, Elmer R. "A Visit with Leo M. Frank in the Death Cell at Atlanta," *Rhodes' Colossus*, March, 1915, pp. 3–12.

Niebuhr, H. Richard. "Fundamentalism," in the *Encyclopedia of the Social Sciences*. 15 vols. New York: The Macmillan Co., 1931. VI, 526–27.

Oppenheimer, Francis J. "Jewish Criminality," *The Independent*, LXV (September 17, 1908), 640–42.

"An Outlaw State," *The Outlook*, CX (August 25, 1915), 945–47.

Page, Thomas Walker. "Lynching and Race Relations in the South," *The North American Review*, XXVI (August, 1917), 241–50.

"The Passing of Tom Watson," *The Outlook*, CXXXII (October 11, 1922), 228–29.

Petegorsky, David W. "The Strategy of Hatred," *The Antioch Review*, I (September, 1941), 376–88.

Postal, Bernard. "Jews in the Ku Klux Klan," *The Jewish Tribune*, XCIII (September 14, 1928), 24, 60.

"The Prosecution of Leo M. Frank," *Frost's Magazine*, I (August, 1913), 1–4.

"Race Prejudice against Jews," *The Independent*, LXV (December 17, 1908), 1451–56.

"The Real Case," *Southern Ruralist*, XX (January 15, 1914), 20–21.

Riesman, David. "The Politics of Persecution," *Public Opinion Quarterly*, VI (Spring, 1942), 41–56.

Rivkin, Elias. "A Decisive Pattern in American Jewish History," *Essays in American Jewish History*. Cincinnati: The American Jewish Archives, 1958, pp. 23–62.

Robinson, Duane, and Sylvia Rohde. "Two Experiments with an Anti-Semitism Poll," *The Journal of Abnormal and Social Psychology*, XLI (April, 1946), 136–44.

Roche, John P. "American Liberty: An Examination of the 'Tradition' of Freedom," in *Aspects of Liberty*, edited by Milton R. Konvitz and Clinton Rossiter. Ithaca: Cornell University Press, 1958, pp. 129–62.

——— "Civil Liberty in the Age of Enterprise," *The University of Chicago Law Review*, XXXI (Autumn, 1963), 103–35.

——— "The Curbing of the Militant Majority," *The Reporter*, XXIX (July 18, 1963), 34–38.

Rose, Arnold. "Anti-Semitism's Root in City-Hatred," *Commentary*, VI (1948), 374–78.

Ross, Edward Alsworth. "The Hebrews of Eastern Europe in America," *The Century Magazine*, LXXXVIII (September, 1914), 785–92.

Rysan, Josef. "Defamation in Folklore," *Southern Folklore Quarterly*, XIX (September, 1955), 143–49.

Schofield, Harry. "Federal Courts and Mob Domination of State Courts: Leo Frank's Case," *Illinois Law Review*, X (1916), 479–506.

Schwartz, David. "The Leo Frank Case," *Congress Weekly*, X (December 24, 1943), 6–7.

Slaton, John M. "Governor Slaton's OWN Defense in the Frank Case," *The New York World*, editorial section, July 4, 1915, p. 1.

Smith, George Horsley. "Beliefs in Statements Labeled Fact and Rumor," *The Journal of Abnormal and Social Psychology*, XLII (1947), 80–90.

Smith, Rembert G., D.D. "Some Lurid Lessons from the Frank Case," *The Public*, XVIII (October 1, 1915), 952–53.

"The South and Immigration," *Harper's Weekly*, LVII (June 21 and July 12, 1913), 2–3, 5.

"The State of the Fulton Bag and Cotton Mills, Atlanta, Ga.,"
The Textile Worker, III (April, 1915), 5.

Stewart, Senator William M. "The Great Slave Power," *The Arena*, XIX (May, 1898), 577–82.

Sydnor, Charles S. "The Southerner and the Laws," *The Journal of Southern History*, VI (1940), 3–23.

Szajkowski, Zosa. "The Attitude of American Jews to East European Jewish Immigration (1881–1893)," *Publications of the American Jewish Historical Society*, XL (1950–1951), 221–80.

Thomas, W. I. "The Psychology of the Yellow Journal," *American Magazine*, LXV (March, 1908), 491–96.

Thomas, William I. "The Psychology of Race-Prejudice," *The American Journal of Sociology*, IX (March, 1904), 593–61.

Tolman, Albert H. "Some Songs Traditional in the United States," *The Journal of American Folklore*, XXIX (April-June, 1916), 155–97.

"The Trade in White Slaves," *The American Review of Reviews*, XXXIX (March, 1909), 371–72.

Train, Arthur. "Did Leo Frank Get Justice?" *Everybody's*, XXXIII (March, 1915), 314–17.

"Trial by Newspapers," *Journal of the American Institute of Criminal Law and Criminology*, I (March, 1911), 849–51.

Turner, George Kibbe. "The Daughter of the Poor," *McClure's Magazine*, XXXIV (November, 1909), 45–61.

Tuttle, Rev. A. H., D.D. "The Jew," a sermon. Baltimore: Mt. Vernon Place M.E. Church, January 22, 1893.

Twain, Mark. "Concerning the Jews," *Harper's Magazine*, XCIX (1899), 527–35.

"The United States Supreme Court and the Frank Case," *The Central Law Journal*, LXXX (1915), 29–32.

Untermyer, Samuel. "Evils and Remedies in the Administration of the Criminal Law," *The Annals* of the American Academy of Political and Social Science, XXXVI (July, 1910), 145–60.

Yarros, V. S. "The Press and Public Opinion," *The American Journal of Sociology*, V (1900), 372–82.

Ward, Robert De Courcy. "Immigration and the South," *The Atlantic Monthly*, XCVI (November, 1905), 611–17.

Watson, Charles H. "Need of Federal Legislation in Respect to Mob Violence in Cases of Lynching of Aliens," *Yale Law Journal*, XXV (1916), 561–81.

Watson's Magazine. 1914–1915.

Wechsler, Israel S. "The Psychology of Anti-Semitism," *The Menorah Journal*, XI (April, 1925), 159–66.

Weir, Hugh C. "The Menace of the Police," *The World To-Day*, XVIII (1910), 52–59, 171–78, 308–13, 599–606; and XIX (1910), 839–45.

"Why Was Frank Lynched?" *Forum*, LVI (December, 1916), 677–92.

"Will the Jews Ever Lose Their Racial Identity?" *Current Opinion*, L (March, 1911), 292–94.

Wilson, J. G. "The Crossing of the Races," *The Popular Science Monthly*, LXXIX (November, 1911), 486–95.

Wise, Stephen S. "The Case of Leo Frank: A Last Appeal," *Free Synagogue Pulpit*, IV (May, 1915), 79–96.

Wolf, Nathum [*sic*]. "Are the Jews an Inferior Race?" *The North American Review*, CXCV (April, 1912), 492–95.

Woods, Henry, S.J. "The Crime at Marietta," *America*, XIII (September 11, 1915), 535–37.

UNPUBLISHED MATERIAL

Abrams, Arthur J. "The Formation of the American Jewish Committee." Unpublished thesis, Hebrew Union College, 1960. Deposited in the American Jewish Archives, Cincinnati, Box 2270.

Berman, Myron. "The Attitude of American Jewry towards East European Jewish Immigration, 1881–1914." Unpublished Ph.D. dissertation, Columbia University, 1963.

Carargeorge, Ted. "An Evaluation of Hoke Smith and Thomas E. Watson as Georgia Reformers." Unpublished Ph.D. dissertation, University of Georgia, 1963.

Colvin, Mary Richards. "Hoke Smith and Joseph M. Brown, Political Rivals." Unpublished Master's thesis, University of Georgia, 1958.

Dawidowicz, Lucy S. "Louis Marshall's Yiddish Newspaper, *The Jewish World*." Unpublished Master's thesis, Department of History, Columbia University, 1961.

English, Carl Dean. "The Ethical Emphases of the Editors of Baptist Journals Published in the Southeastern Region of the

United States, 1865–1915." Unpublished Th.D. dissertation, Southern Baptist Theological Seminary, 1948.

Evans, Mercer G. "The History of the Organized Labor Movement in Georgia." Unpublished Ph.D. dissertation, Department of Economics, University of Chicago, 1929.

Flower, Edward. "Anti-Semitism in the Free Silver and Populist Movements and the Election of 1896." Unpublished Master's thesis, Department of History, Columbia University, 1952.

Haimowitz, Morris L. "The Development and Change of Ethnic Hostility." Unpublished Ph.D. dissertation, Department of Sociology, University of Chicago, 1951.

Halpern, Rose A. "The American Reaction to the Dreyfus Case." Unpublished Master's thesis, Department of History, Columbia University, 1941.

Herzog, Joseph D. "The Emergence of the Anti-Jewish Stereotype in the United States." Unpublished thesis, Hebrew Union College, 1953.

Jones, Alton DuMar. "Progressivism in Georgia, 1898–1918." Unpublished Ph.D. dissertation, Department of History, Emory University, 1963.

McCall, Bevode C. "Georgia Town and Cracker Culture." Unpublished Ph.D. dissertation, Department of Sociology, University of Chicago, 1954.

Morse, Nancy Carter. "Anti-Semitism: A Study of Its Causal Factors and Other Associated Variables." Unpublished Ph.D. dissertation, Department of Psychology, Syracuse University, 1947.

Moseley, Clement Charlton. "Politics, Prejudice and Perjury: The Case of Leo M. Frank, 1913–1915." Unpublished seminar paper, Department of History, University of Georgia, 1965.

Polloch, Theodore Marvin. "The Solitary Clarinetist: A Critical Biography of Abraham Cahan, 1860–1917." Unpublished Ph.D. dissertation, Columbia University, 1959.

Rainey, Glenn Weddington. "The Race Riot of 1906 in Atlanta." Unpublished Master's thesis, Emory University, 1929.

Roberts, DeWitt. "Anti-Semitism and the Leo M. Frank Case." Unpublished essay in the files of the Anti-Defamation League, New York City.

Roberts, Essie. "A History of Child Labor Legislation in Georgia and Alabama." Unpublished Master's thesis, Columbia University, 1916.

Rogers, William Curran. "A Comparison of the Coverage of the Leo Frank Case by the Hearst-Controlled Atlanta *Georgian* and the Home-Owned Atlanta *Journal*, April 28,1913–August 30, 1913." Unpublished Master's thesis, University of Georgia, 1950.

Shapiro, Yonathan. "Leadership of the American Zionist Organization, 1897–1930." Unpublished Ph.D. dissertation, Columbia University, 1964.

Spain, Rufus B. "Attitudes and Reactions of Southern Baptists to Certain Problems of Society, 1865–1900." Unpublished Ph.D. dissertation, Vanderbilt University, 1961.

Steelman, John R. "A Study of Mob Action in the South." Unpublished Ph.D. dissertation, Department of Sociology, University of North Carolina, 1928.

Sutker, Solomon. "The Jews of Atlanta: Their Social Structure and Leadership Patterns." Unpublished Ph.D. dissertation, Department of Sociology, University of North Carolina, 1950.

Weisberg, Lee Arnold. "Beyond a Reasonable Doubt: A Study of the Leo Frank Case." Unpublished Honors Paper, Department of History, Yale University, 1963.

Yeomans, Manning Jasper. "Some Facts about the Frank Case." Typewritten thesis, Emory University, n.d. [*ca.* 1915].

PERSONAL COMMUNICATIONS

A. Interviews

Alexander Brin, in Boston, August 15, 1964. Mr. Brin covered the Frank case for the Boston *Traveler* in 1915.

Harold Davis, in Atlanta, January 24, 1964. Mr. Davis is an editor of *The Atlanta Journal.*

Alexander Miller, in the offices of the Anti-Defamation League, New York City, September 15, 1964. Mr. Miller was at one time the regional director of the Anti-Defamation League in Atlanta. In 1953 he sponsored a study of the Leo Frank case.

McLellan Smith, in Washington, April 2, 1964. Mr. Smith covered the Frank case as a cub reporter for *The Atlanta Georgian.* He was at the press table during the trial.

B. *Telephone Conversations*

Marjorie Merlin Cohen, February 9, 1964, New York City. Mrs. Cohen was interested in the Frank case as a graduate student in Georgia. She was refused access to the records of the case by Rabbi David Marx.

Franklin Garrett, in Atlanta, January 24, 1964. Mr. Garrett is the author of *Atlanta and Environs*, and one of the best versed people on Atlanta's history.

Wilber Kurtz, January 24, 1964, in Atlanta. Mr. Kurtz has resided in Atlanta since 1913. He is a student of the city's history and extremely well versed in the subject.

Louise Samuels, October 19, 1963. Mrs. Samuels is co-author of *Night Fell on Georgia*.

C. *Letters from:*

Irving M. Engel, February 19, 1964. Mr. Engel is a former President of the American Jewish Committee.

Harry Golden, January 24, 1966. Mr. Golden has written about Frank in his book, *A Little Girl Is Dead*.

Alton DuMar Jones, May 21, 1964. Mr. Jones's Ph.D. dissertation is "Progressivism in Georgia."

Ralph McGill, January 28, 1964. Mr. McGill is publisher of *The Atlanta Constitution*.

DeWitt H. Roberts, February 14 and 19, 1964. Mr. Roberts did a study of the Frank case for the Atlanta office of the Anti-Defamation League in 1953.

McLellan Smith, February 24, 1964. Mr. Smith covered the Frank case as a reporter for *The Atlanta Georgian*.

Alden Todd, January 19, 1964. Mr. Todd has written a book on the confirmation of Louis D. Brandeis to the United States Supreme Court: *Justice on Trial*.

Index

Addams, Jane, 118
Adler, Cyrus, 74
Alexander, Henry, defense lawyer, 87, 101, 108, 109
American (New Orleans), 131
American Hebrew: quoted, 74
American Jewish Committee, 62-63, 74-76, 90 ff., 106; *see also* Marshall, Louis, and individual names
Anti-Defamation League, 157; Atlanta chapter, 59
Anti-Semitism: toward Frank, 1, 18-19, 20, 32-33, 52-53, 60, 63, 74, 75, 106, 120-21, 129; in trial testimony, 52-53, 60; in Georgia, 64, 70-72, 116-17, 130-32, 157-58; in United States, 66-72 *passim*, 74; development in South, 66-71; reasons for, 69; in North, 70, 72; in France and Russia, 72-74; Beiliss case, 73, 74; Dreyfus affair, 73, 74; of jurors, 77; in Atlanta, 116, 130, 158; of Watson, 97-99, 119-20, 132, 134; Anti-Defamation League, 157; *see also* Jews
Arkansas Gazette (Little Rock), 93
Arnold, Reuben R., defense counsel, 37, 45-47, 52, 91, 107; and first appeal, 77, 78; before Georgia Supreme Court, 81
Asbury, Herbert, 157, 161
Atkinson, Justice Samuel C., 81-82
Atlanta: workers and working conditions, 7-8; crime in, 8-9, 16, 71-72; official fear of violence in Phagan case, 15, 25, 54, 59-61, 109,

110, 113, 116, 120, 126; mass meetings, 120-21; reaction to commutation, 132-33; reaction to lynching, 144-45; City Council, 145; *see also* Police, Atlanta
Atlanta Constitution, 11; quoted on murder, 6, 15-16, 19-20; coverage of Phagan murder, 13, 16, 18, 29-31, 34; assumption of Frank's guilt, 31; quoted on trial, 36, 46, 47, 49, 51, 56, 94; trial coverage, 37-56 *passim*, 54; quoted, 64, 93-94, 133, 146, 159, 170; unpublished story of evidence, 158
Atlanta Georgian, 11; quoted on murder, 6, 14, 22, 24, 25, 29, 34-35, 170; coverage of Phagan murder, 13, 14-15, 29-31; quoted on trial, 36, 46, 49-50, 60; trial coverage, 37-60 *passim*; support of Frank, 79-80, 119; and retractions, 85; and commutation, 129-30; article on trial by "Old Police Reporter," 172-77
Atlanta Journal: quoted on murder, 14, 20, 25; coverage of Phagan murder, 14, 29-31; trial coverage, 37-45 *passim*; quoted on trial, 40, 45, 94; and evidence, 84-85; and verdict, 94-95; support of Frank, 94-95, 119; and new trial, 97-98, 115, 119; and commutation, 129-30
Augusta Chronicle, 119, 120, 122, 130, 138; quoted on murder, 6, 15; on trial, 59-60